Pro Tools® 7
Session Secrets

Pro Tools® 7 Session Secrets

Professional Recipes for High-Octane Results

Scott Hirsch

Steve Heithecker

Wiley Publishing, Inc.

Acquisitions and Developmental Editor: MARIANN BARSOLO
Technical Editor: TED LoCASCIO
Production Editors: JONATHAN COPPOLA AND SARAH GROFF-PALERMO
Copy Editor: JUDY FLYNN
Production Manager: TIM TATE
Vice President and Executive Group Publisher: RICHARD SWADLEY
Vice President and Executive Publisher: JOSEPH B. WIKERT
Vice President and Publisher: DAN BRODNITZ
Book Designer: FRANZ BAUMHACKL
Compositor: HAPPENSTANCE TYPE-O-RAMA
Proofreader: CANDACE ENGLISH
Indexer: TED LAUX
Cover Designer: RYAN SNEED
Cover Image: GETTY IMAGES

Dear Reader,

Thank you for choosing *Pro Tools 7 Session Secrets: Professional Recipes for High-Octane Results*. This book is part of a family of premium-quality Sybex graphics books, all written by outstanding authors who combine practical experience with a gift for teaching.

Sybex was founded in 1976. Thirty years later, we're still committed to producing consistently exceptional books. With each of our graphics titles we're working hard to set a new standard for the industry. From the paper we print on to the writers and professional artists we work with, our goal is to bring you the best graphics books available.

I hope you see all that reflected in these pages. I'd be very interested to hear your comments and get your feedback on how we're doing. To let us know what you think about this or any other Sybex book, please send me an email at sybex_publisher@wiley.com. Please also visit us at www.sybex.com to learn more about the rest of our growing graphics line.

Best regards,

DAN BRODNITZ
Vice President and Publisher
Sybex, an Imprint of Wiley

Acknowledgments

Scott Hirsch would like to thank Sarah Spengler, who took the time to introduce me to Pro Tools many years ago; Emily Gorton for graciously putting up with my frustrations as a new writer; James Kim, Michael Taylor, Dan Carr, and Thomas Heyman for musical inspiration; Eileen, Arthur, and Jessica for being the family to lean on; Matt Donner and Greg Gordon for providing a stimulating work environment; Wendy Levy for enthusiasm and support; Chris Forrest for being a mentor, contributor, and all-around hero; Justin Phelps for lending his supreme audio expertise; Hideki Yamashita for technical wizardry; Dan Brodnitz for providing the spark that started this whole thing; and Mariann Barsolo for her expertise and patience.

Steve Heithecker would like to thank Martha Jarvis, my better half, who has put up with and supported and inspired me all these years; Greg Gordon and Matt Donner at Pyramind for their friendship, opportunities for the future, and for the use of some great toys; Mariann Barsolo for her encouragement and belief in us on this project; Dan Brodnitz for seeing this possibility and making it happen; Hideki Yamashita for his pursuit of technical perfection; Greg Jordan for the countless great experiences and all the years of musical and technical excellence; Jerry Johnson for lighting my musical fire many years ago; and final heartfelt thanks to the powers that be for never putting it out.

We would also both like to thank technical editor Ted LoCascio, production editor Jonathan Coppola, and copy editor Judy Flynn.

About the Authors

In the recording studio, Scott Hirsch feels right at home behind the controls or playing the instruments. Whether he is engineering a session at his home studio, sound-designing a film, teaching digital audio classes, or composing his own music, there is always a use for Scott's masterful Pro Tools skills. After graduating from UCSB with a degree in film studies with an emphasis on sound, Scott was introduced to an early version of Pro Tools and never looked back. With a growing number of critically acclaimed records and several feature-length films and documentaries under his belt, Scott teaches audio as a Digidesign Pro Tools and Apple Logic certified instructor at the media hub Bay Area Video Coalition (BAVC) and at Pyramind, the institute for advanced digital audio training in San Francisco. Scott is also a member of The Court & Spark, a San Francisco rock band.

Steve Heithecker is a veteran San Francisco–based producer/engineer, keyboardist, and educator. Steve has written, produced, and recorded music for many albums of many genres, as well as live theater, film, and video. With a passion for keyboards and all things MIDI, he now lives in a world of virtual synths and samplers and may often be heard muttering, "More CPU, more CPU." He was cofounder of Digital Art & Music in San Francisco and now works and teaches out of Pyramind, where he is the Reason Resident as well as one of the valued Pro Tools instructors. Steve is also an accomplished graphic designer with more than 25 albums to his credit.

Contents

Chapter 3   **Editing: Slip, Shuffle, and Spot Your Way Home**   **83**

Chapter 6   After the Bounce, or Life outside of Pro Tools   213

Chapter 7   Postproduction and the World of Surround   231

Introduction

Digital audio workstations are becoming more powerful and less expensive, and a new breed of media producer is emerging—the independent audio engineer. Small independent/home recording studios can now compete on a professional level, thus breaking down the dominance of the big exclusive recording studio. For those of us already working in the field, this is old news. We've already been reaping the benefits of taking production out of the hands of the select few and putting it into the hands of the creative masses. Since so many budding audio enthusiasts can now take advantage of these new powerful tools, the demand for digital audio education is coming faster than books can be written.

There are many "How to use Pro Tools" books on the shelves out there. Rather than repeating what has already been said, we set out to make a guide that goes beyond the conceptual theories of using Pro Tools and concentrates on real-world scenarios for the working engineer, musician, or sound designer. As Pro Tools users with countless hours logged and many lessons learned, we brainstormed all of the things we do beyond the basic operation of Pro Tools that make our recordings special and the artists happy. We placed these tips and techniques in a step-by-step recipe format for quick access and maximum practicality.

Above all, this book's goal is to simplify and reduce the technical demands of working in Pro Tools in order to inspire your artistic vision. We hope that our suggestions unlock the door to an endless flow of inspiration, creativity, and success.

What You Will Learn from This Book

Pro Tools 7 Session Secrets: Professional Recipes for High-Octane Results reaches beyond the scope of a traditional "how to" book by concentrating on Pro Tools working methods in real-world scenarios. The book takes a round trip through all the key stages of a Pro Tools session, including recording, MIDI, editing, mixing, postproduction, and mastering. Through this journey, you'll learn the fastest workflow techniques, professional power user tips, ideas on how to get specific sounds, expert suggestions on how to work more efficiently, and advanced insight into the new features of Pro Tools 7.

The aim of this book is not to be an all-inclusive, comprehensive guide, but rather to broaden your creative horizon by turning your fundamental Pro Tools skills into real-world know-how. For example, we'll show you how to set up a headphone mix properly for a band, record specific instruments and vocals, employ the benefits of other audio programs like Logic and Reason, farm out to external effects properly, prepare your mix for a mastering house, and so on. All of these concepts require Pro Tools know-how but also extend far beyond what you would ever find in a manual.

Who Should Read This Book

This book is for anyone who has a basic understanding of Pro Tools but wishes to take these skills to the next level. Pro Tools users often hit an imaginary wall when learning the program. They get to the point that they theoretically understand how to work in Pro Tools but are not prepared to achieve actual results in a real-world situation. This book breaks down that wall by providing recipes and suggestions on why, how, and when to employ powerful working secrets of Pro Tools.

Pro Tools 7 Session Secrets spans a lot of territory. Any Pro Tools user with an elementary understanding of Pro Tools will find this book essential, ranging from beginner/intermediate-level users to audio professionals trying to break old habits.

How to Use This Book

Pro Tools 7 Session Secrets is presented in the natural progression of a Pro Tools session, beginning with recording and following through to mixing and mastering. However, the book is not necessarily intended for use in a linear fashion. The chapters are presented in a recipe-book style so you can look up any subject at any time. While some of the concepts are cross-referential, the chapters do not build on each other. Each chapter begins with the essentials and then evolves into the step-by-step techniques on how to achieve specific results. Along the way, you'll find sidebars that serve to demystify important aspects of digital audio and Pro Tools. Quick tips are also provided in each chapter as suggestions for a faster and more powerful workflow.

How This Book Is Organized

Chapter 1, "Recording and Microphones," shows you how to prepare your Pro Tools system's I/O setup for maximum efficiency while recording, including headphone mixes for multiple performers. The chapter explores a number of recording essentials like setting up a click track, dealing with phase, and punch techniques. Recipes are given for microphone techniques of common musical instruments.

Chapter 2, "MIDI with Confidence," outlines all of the new powerful MIDI features of Pro Tools 7, including Instrument tracks and Real-Time Properties. Power-user techniques are given to master MIDI in Pro Tools. The chapter also touches on integrating outside programs and machines via MMC and ReWire.

Chapter 3, "Editing: Slip, Shuffle, and Spot Your Way Home," gives in-depth approaches to using and understanding all of Pro Tools's editing tools so you can take full advantage of all the powerful new editing features in version 7. In addition, this chapter will focus on looping recipes, hidden power-user editing commands, and getting the most out of the four different editing modes to enhance productivity and speed.

Chapter 4, "The Way of the Insert: Inserts and FX," describes how you can master inserts in Pro Tools and includes some awesome recipes for plug-ins and hardware-based FX. The chapter includes techniques on using Sound Replacer and Auto-Tune, side-chaining FX, printing FX, and more.

Chapter 5, "Mixing in Pro Tools: Directing Audio Traffic," explains how to use Pro Tools mixing functions to masterfully command your mix. You will learn automation recipes, panning techniques, complex routing options, and EQ and compression recipes.

Chapter 6, "After the Bounce, or Life outside of Pro Tools," expands on the endless possibilities of what to do after you have completed your mix in Pro Tools. The chapter shows you how to properly prepare for a mastering session or master yourself inside Pro Tools. The chapter also demystifies all of the different audio formats out there, as well as shows you how to properly encode MP3s and create podcasts.

Chapter 7, "Postproduction and the World of Surround," provides essential instructions on how to use your Pro Tools system for video and film postproduction and how to use it in a multichannel surround environment. This chapter delineates some working methods and techniques for postproducing with Pro Tools, including how to prep an audio session from a video project, syncing to external video decks, calibrating monitors, working with stems, and using postproduction editing tricks and 5.1 surround setups.

The appendices, "Setting Up Pro Tools" and "Using Control Surfaces with Pro Tools," provide you with hardware, software, and setup information for getting the right system for you in place.

Hardware and Software Considerations

Pro Tools is a hardware-specific program. This means that you must have an attached Digidesign or compatible M-Audio hardware interface for Pro Tools or Pro Tools M-Powered to run the software. This book is written for Pro Tools users with any of the three levels of Pro Tools hardware platforms: M-Powered, LE, or HD. A few of the sections of the book are platform-specific and are labeled as such, but for the most part, we attempted to keep the book valid for all three versions of Pro Tools.

Pro Tools is a cross-platform application, running on Macintosh OS X and Windows XP operating systems. The recommended system compatibility is ever changing. For the most up-to-date information, go to www.digidesign.com/support and click Compatibility for the latest system requirements and recommended configurations.

This book's appendix has some more-specific suggestions on different tiers of Pro Tools systems.

Conventions Used in This Book

You'll find keyboard shortcuts presented throughout the book with the Mac shortcut followed by the Windows shortcut, as in this example:

⌘+Shift+A / Ctrl+Shift+A

If there is something new in Pro Tools version 7, you will see an icon next to the paragraph, as the one in the margin here.

Contact the Authors

You can contact Scott Hirsch at www.scotthirschsound.com.

You can contact Steve Heithecker at Pyramind Studios in San Francisco: steve@pyramind.com.

Recording and Microphones

Digital audio recording is all about 1s and 0s. The binary system is used to encode all the glorious sound fed into the computer so you can tweak, manipulate, process, mix, and edit to your heart's delight.

This chapter will take you beyond elementary recording setups in Pro Tools and focus on real-world techniques both inside and outside the software. The goal is efficiency. The faster you can get a solid sound coming through the monitors, the more time and energy you'll have for that moving performance. We will focus on the basic elements of mic placement for the most common instrumentation of a rock band, but most concepts apply to sound design, broadcast, or any type of recording.

1

■

RECORDING AND MICROPHONES

Chapter Contents

Recording Preparation
The Headphone Mix
The Click Track
Punch Techniques
Recipes for Bass, Drums, and Acoustic
   and Electric Guitar
Voice Recording

I/O Recording Techniques

Using Pro Tools to record a band can be a fun, creative, and rewarding experience for everybody involved. The streamlined virtual nature of the Pro Tools interface coupled with the instantaneous nature of hard disk recording is a godsend for those who want more time to create. And that's what it's all about, isn't it? In the old days of analog recording, we had to wait around for extensive patching, calibration of tape machines, setup of multiple headphone mixes, and so on. With Pro Tools, you can make all this happen in a fraction of the time. The key to all of this is preparation, preparation, preparation. We will illustrate how you can set up and manipulate the Pro Tools I/O, create lightning-fast headphone mixes, and record into your Pro Tools interface so that you have more time for the good stuff: recording the hits.

It's now time to introduce you to an imaginary band we'll use to help illustrate Pro Tools concepts throughout the book: The Condensers, a typical small rock band made up of a drum kit, a bass guitar, an electric guitar, and a vocalist.

Preconfiguring the I/O Setup

You need to be ready for the band before they even walk through the door. Here's how to preconfigure the I/O setup to accommodate the band:

1. Choose I/O from the Setup menu. Click the Default button that appears in the I/O Setup dialog.

2. Click on the Output tab at the top of the dialog to access the Output panel.

3. Double-click the default output names to highlight the field. Name your outputs as shown in Figure 1.1:
   - 1–2 MIX
   - 3–4 PHONES MIX 1
   - 5–6 PHONES MIX 2
   - 7–8 PHONES MIX 3

4. Press Enter to lock in the changes. This will provide you with a "control room" mix and three separate and distinct headphone mixes for the individual performers of The Condensers.

Note: These setup ideas are designed to work with at least an eight-channel Pro Tools interface. Users with a Digi 002, Digi 002 Rack, or any HD interface will be able to configure the I/O to resemble the examples in this chapter. Due to differences in the interfaces, there will be some variation in the dialog texts for different systems.

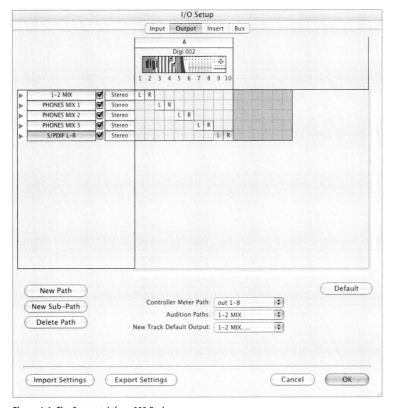

Figure 1.1 The Output tab for a 002 Rack

5. Click on the Input tab (Figure 1.2) to access the Input panel and rename inputs 1–8 to Mic 1–8. If you are tracking a combination of Mic and Line inputs, you can be more specific here by naming the first four inputs Mic/Line and the second four Line, for example. Click the disclosure triangles for each channel to have access to the mono paths.

6. Click on the Bus tab to access the Bus panel and assign names to the busses that follow the instrumentation. For The Condensers, the Bus panel will look like Figure 1.3.

Note: When you are done with the I/O setup, you may save it as a recallable I/O setup file. These are located by default in the Hard Drive > Applications > Digidesign > Pro Tools > IO Settings folder on your computer and may be taken with you to other sessions on your FireWire drive, iPod, or other removable media storage devices. You also have the option to click the Export Settings button. This will allow you to save your I/O settings to a specific location, such as the desktop.

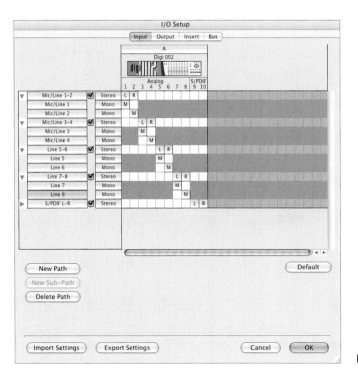

Figure 1.2 The Input tab

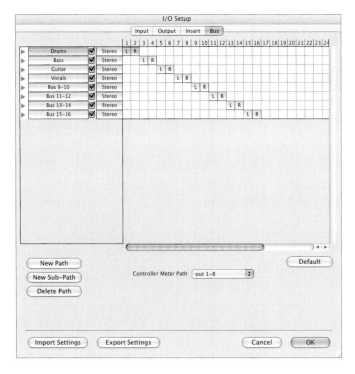

Figure 1.3 By assigning names to these busses, you will be able to bring up correctly labeled submix faders using aux channels.

Setting Up the Mixer

Now that you have the I/O in place, you can set up the mixer with appropriate channels and input and output assignments needed to track the Condensers. Here you can configure the available I/O to be labeled to accommodate the recording configuration you use for The Condensers.

The TDM mixer will look something like Figure 1.4.

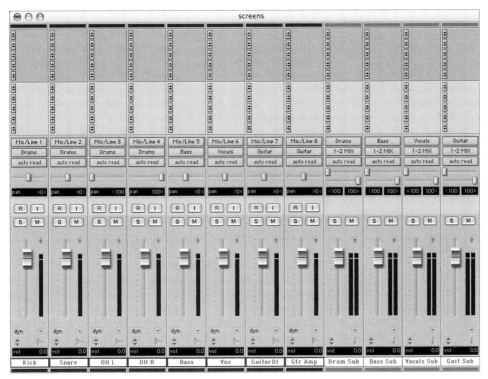

Figure 1.4 Note that the outputs are assigned to the corresponding busses you labeled in the I/O setup; this makes it easy to set up submixes across the auxiliary channels on the right.

Note: This is where the size and type of your Pro Tools hardware interface is crucial to how you proceed. TDM Pro Tools interfaces, such as the trusty old 888s or the newer HD systems, are going to have eight or more available inputs without microphone preamps. We are going to assume here that if you have a TDM system, you also have access to enough available mic pres to fill up at least eight channels of input and output (a single DIGI 96 I/O). For LE users, we will assume the use of a 002 system, using the four onboard Mic pres and the four Line inputs. The LE mixer will look like Figure 1.5.

Since the LE example uses only the four onboard mic pres shown in Figure 1.5, the stereo drum overhead was made into a mono channel, which opened up a mic pre for the vocal. If you can't part with the stereo overheads, it is possible to keep them with the use of an additional mic pre for the vocal, plugged into channel 8. Another option is to track the band sans vocals and overdub them later.

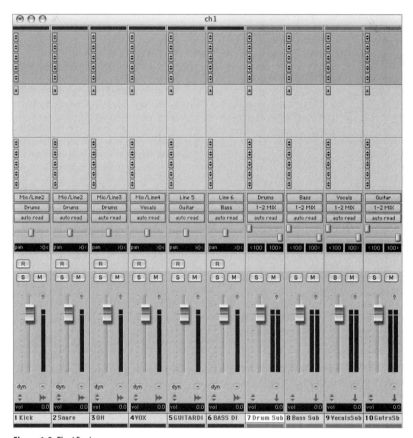

Figure 1.5 The LE mixer

Note: Remember also that this mixer and its I/O setup will be saved into the session. You may make this session a stationary pad (Mac) or a template (Windows). For Mac users, save the session, get info (⌘+I) on the session file, and check the Stationary Pad box. This will force you into a Save As when you open the file, making sure that you do not overwrite it. You may also lock the file here to prevent it from being erased. Windows users may right-click on the saved session file, choose Properties from the context menu, and check the Read Only box. This will ensure that the session will not be written over.

The Headphone Mix

There's nothing a band likes more than to have a good headphone mix. A lot of engineers say that the headphone monitoring is the number-one thing to get ready in a recording situation because no matter how good the sounds being recorded are, if the band isn't comfortable, the performances will suffer.

Since you labeled three separate outputs as CUE MIX in your I/O setup, you can now use sends on each submix track to give three mixes to the band and still have your own control room "main mix" coming from the 1-2 outputs. To take full advantage of the separate headphone mixes, you are going to need either three headphone distribution amps like the ROLLS HA43 Headphone Amp or a headphone matrix amp like the Mackie HMX 56 Six-Channel Headphone Matrix Mixer and the corresponding cables.

You now have the option of putting the three headphone sends on each individual audio track for the most flexibility (see Figure 1.6).

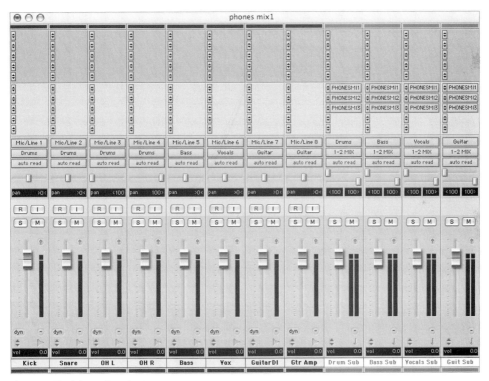

Figure 1.6 Headphone mix option 1

Or, you can put the headphone sends on the auxiliary submix channels (see Figure 1.7).

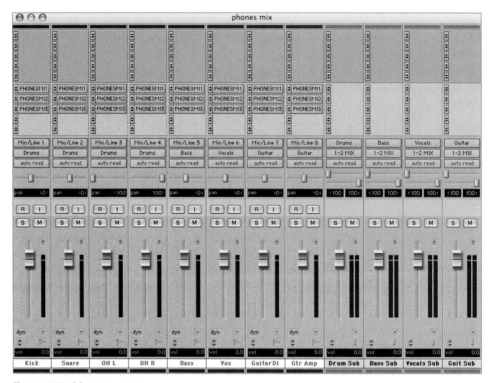

Figure 1.7 Headphone mix option 2

The outputs 3-4, 5-6, and 7-8 on the Pro Tools interface will now feed those headphone mixes. Typically, in this situation the drummer and vocalist prefer to each have their own mix, while the guitarist and bassist can agree on a third mix together.

Note: To assign and manage multiple track outputs quickly, select the tracks you wish to assign by (⌘+ clicking / Ctrl+clicking) on each additional track name you want to select. Option+Shift+click / Alt+Shift+click on the output assignment and choose the bus or output you wish to send the tracks through. This will assign only the selected tracks to that bus. The same quick key works for send assignments, as in the headphone mixes in this chapter. Be careful not to only press Option/Alt here, because all tracks will be assigned regardless of selection. This is not undoable!

The Click

One of the first considerations in recording is tempo. When we think tempo, we think click track. When we think click track, we should think, "No problem, bring it on." Tempo changes and even meter changes are a piece of cake. We need the click track not only for music's sake but in order to put us on the grid to edit with the most flexibility and efficiency. Pro Tools is very clever in dealing with tempo, tempo changes, and tempo mapping. So if we have a bumpin' little dance piece or some tasty electronic track, we know it will probably be a constant tempo throughout the track. Most electronic and hip-hop music in general stays with one tempo, so setting up a click for that is very simple. But in the case of multiple tempos and even meter, Pro Tools has the ability to map out these changes with musical precision.

The click track in Pro Tools has a number of different built-in sounds available to choose from (see Figure 1.8).

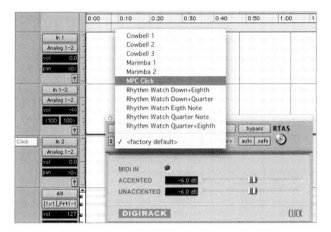

Figure 1.8 Click sounds

Better yet, perhaps, is the ability to choose from any other MIDI devices you might have, such as a nice old JV2080 or even NI's Battery for the perfect sample of a stick click.

And now for the nuts and bolts: After selecting Grid mode (F4), the first choice to make is which tempo mode works better for the song, Manual or Conductor? If the track is geared to one tempo for the entire song, then you can use Manual Tempo mode. If the track has multiple tempo changes, you must use the Conductor mode and make tempo changes in the Tempo Ruler track. It's easy to set up a basic click, so there can be no excuses. Create a mono aux track for the click because using an aux track saves a voice. Make sure the Inserts view is showing in the Edit or Mix window and insert an instance of the click plug-in (see Figure 1.9).

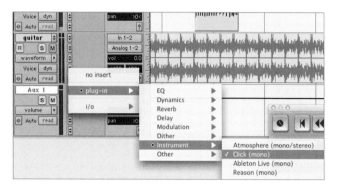

Figure 1.9 Inserting a click from the Edit window

Show the transport bar by pressing ⌘+Keypad1 / Ctrl+Keypad1

Note: To quickly change views in the transport bar, click the green maximize button in the upper-left corner of the transport bar. Option+click / Alt+click or ⌘+click / Ctrl+click to get the rest of the views in the transport bar without going to the pull-down menu.

Pro Tools defaults to Conductor mode (Tempo Ruler enabled at 120 Beats Per Minute, or BPM). To change to Manual Tempo mode, click the Tempo Ruler Enable button (the button that looks like Arthur Fiedler) and deselect it (see Figure 1.10).

Figure 1.10 Manual Tempo mode in the fully expanded transport bar

Now you are in Manual mode. At this point you can manually enter the BPM into the counter window if you know the tempo. Manual Tempo mode also acts as a track mute so the tempo track ignores any tempo changes you have created. In the BPM window on the transport bar, click and select the current tempo, and you can either mouse up and down, type in the tempo, or move the slider bar horizontally to increase or decrease the BPM.

If you need to use Tap Tempo to find the BPM, make sure you are in Manual Tempo mode and click in to the BPM window. You can use your computer keyboard to tap tempo. Use the T key on your keyboard and tap in up to eight taps. Pro Tools averages the taps and calculates the tempo. If you would rather use a MIDI keyboard to tap in the tempo, then choose Setups > Preferences > MIDI > General and make sure the Use MIDI to Tap Tempo preference is checked. On your MIDI keyboard, tap the tempo on any key up to eight times to get your tempo. Having the singer or guitarist play for you to get the tempo is a age-old rock and roll tradition.

If there are multiple tempos in the session, then highlight the Tempo Ruler Enable button on the transport bar (see Figure 1.11).

Figure 1.11 Conductor mode

Take your cursor to the Tempo ruler at the top of the Edit window. In order to insert tempo changes, you need to bring up the Tempo Change prompt box and tell it what to do. Click the Add Tempo Change button in the upper-left portion of the Edit window, which is the + symbol next to the word *Tempo*.

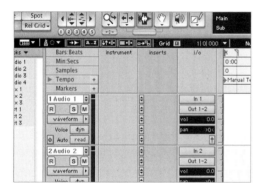

You can also press Control+click / Start+click in the Tempo ruler to bring up the Tempo Change box (see Figure 1.12).

Figure 1.12 Tempo Change box

In the Tempo Change prompt box, you can enter the new tempo and give it a location on the timeline. The old what and where. Very easy. Every time a different tempo is needed, call up the Tempo Change box and tell it the new BPM and location; Pro Tools's grid and click will follow right along. With the click sound selected and the tempo mapped out, you then need to turn on the click by enabling the Metronome Click button on the transport bar.

Note: With everything set up, it's easy to toggle the click on and off by pressing 7 on the numeric keypad.

Now that you have some pointers for setting up Pro Tools, let's move to the studio and get things set up to record.

Note: Microphone manufacturers chosen in the following section are by no means a comprehensive list. We chose them because they are some of the more commonly found microphones in home and commercial recording studios.

Recording Drums: Less Is More and More Is Less

You can approach recording drums in two ways: the natural open room sound, which we like to think exists on the Led Zeppelin end of the spectrum, and the tight closed and controlled sound, which belongs on the Fleetwood Mac side of the spectrum. Everything else falls somewhere in between. The following sections outline each of these methods and how it is possible to capture those wild transient sound waves that drums produce with accuracy and confidence.

Drums require at the very minimum two microphones and at the maximum up to eight or nine microphones of all different types, so it is necessary to beg, borrow, or steal to have all those well-matched preamps and microphones ready to go and patched into your available Pro Tools inputs. Go back to the section "Preconfiguring the I/O Setup" at the beginning of this chapter for some ideas on preproduction.

The next point is not to be taken lightly. More important than any recording technique or microphone choice is the instruments you are starting with. If you have a poorly tuned, junky-sounding drum kit, there is absolutely no way you are going to get it to translate well into a recording and you'll probably end up hating yourself and losing friends along the way if you try to make it work. In addition, the player's technique is something to take into account. Drumming for the recording studio requires a whole different skill set than playing drums live at a show. All the intricacies in feel, dynamics, and technique are going to show up indiscriminately when you hit Record, so be prepared to deal with them.

The Roomy Drum Sound

Now let's get down to brass tacks. The big room sound always starts with the overhead microphones. If you can get the whole kit to sound balanced in the overheads, most of your work is done and you can blend in other more closely mic-ed sources like salt and pepper to taste. Use your best cardioid condenser microphone here, but if you are going with a two-microphone stereo overhead setup, make sure you have a pair of the same type microphone. Small-diaphragm condensers like Neumann KM 184s, Schoepps 221s, or AKG 451s do the trick here, but you could get a huge sound out of a pair of Neumann U67s, AKG 414s, or even some Audio Technica 4050s. Phase correlation is everything here, so you may try them in an XY correlation, with the capsules pointed 90° at each other on a boom stand about a foot above the drummer's head. Make sure the drummer doesn't harm your precious microphone with his sticks though! A spaced pair works well here, with the two microphones facing downward and several feet apart from one another. In this case, it helps to monitor both microphones in mono, with their tracks panned center to check for phase anomalies. Keep the 3:1 rule in mind (see the sidebar "Phase"). If you are getting too much cymbal, you can try putting the microphone lower, about 3 or 4 feet in front of or behind the drum set.

Once the balance is perfect and the drums are sounding good, you can microphone up the kick and snare. The most popular microphone for the snare is the Shure SM57. Its ability to handle the fast transients and high sound pressure levels are unrivaled, so most people don't stray from it. But hey, no one is stopping you from a little experimentation—definitely see how other dynamic microphones sound. The biggest sound variation will come from placement of the snare microphone, so start with the microphone over the rim of the drum angled 45 to 60° downward pointing at the center of the drum. All snares are different, and each player hits differently, so you may need to experiment with the angle of the microphone to get the optimum sound.

Mic-ing the kick drum can be tough. The low frequencies take distance to fully develop, so at close range they are sometimes hard to grab ahold of. Start with a dynamic microphone that can handle high sound pressure levels, like an AKG D-112, Sennheiser 421, Beyerdynamic TGX150, or Shure Beta 52. If the kick drum has a hole cut in it (this is recommended), place the microphone halfway in the hole pointed directly at the beater on the front head. The distance is crucial and variable, so experiment a bit until you get the optimum mix of attack and low end. The brighter attack will come from the beater hitting the front head and the low-end sounds will develop inside the drum.

That's it for the minimal style. This setup will yield the biggest, roomiest sounding results. Speaking of big and roomy, don't forget the room microphone! In addition to this setup, it is always nice to find a spot in the room where you can put a satellite condenser microphone. It is tricky to find this spot because if you are too close, it will not add much, but if you are too far, it may sound too reverby. This microphone should be recorded onto a separate track and can be later crushed to smithereens by a compressor to get that huge Bonham sound!

The Tighter, More-Controlled Drum Sound

Ahem, tighter please.... If it is control you are after, you've come to the right place. After all, Pro Tools offers us many options with editing, Sound Replacer, looping, Strip Silence, Beat Detective, and so on. (See Chapter 3, "Editing: Slip, Shuffle, and Spot Your Way Home," for more editing ideas.) Almost all of these tools require the drum recordings to be clean and the sounds to have good isolation from each other.

To get a tighter sound by close mic-ing, you can start with the basic setup for the big roomy sound we mentioned earlier but add more microphones to the mix.

The snare can sometimes benefit from a microphone underneath as well. This can pick up the metal snares for more bright character. Just about any microphone will work for this, and the phase will usually have to be inverted 180 degrees with a plug-in inserted on this microphone track (see Figure 1.13).

Figure 1.13 The phase flip symbol on Pro Tools plug-ins

The toms can be mic-ed 2 or 3 inches from the top heads near the rim, pointed toward the center with a dynamic microphone. Sennheiser 421s are popular choices here, as are SM57s. Make sure the capsule is angled in a way to cancel out cymbal noise here since you are going for isolation.

If the hi-hat isn't cutting through the way you want it, you can mic it angled away from the snare using a small-diaphragm condenser microphone like the AKG 451 or Neumann KM 184. It may be a good idea to filter out lower frequencies with an equalizer, or EQ either during or after tracking for this microphone.

Since you are tracking digitally and hard drive space is so cheap, if you've got the microphone and inputs, there can be no harm in tracking drums with this more-complex setup. As you will see in the Chapter 3, there is no limit to what is possible with isolated drum sounds in Pro Tools. After all, it is much easier to remove unnecessary tracks than to wish nonexistent tracks into being!

Dealing with Phase

If you are recording with microphones, it isn't long before you have to deal with the concept of phase. This is critical with drums, but it applies for all recording. Although it seems intimidating, it is actually a simple concept and with the right methods and some tricks in Pro Tools, easy to deal with.

Phase Technique 1: The 3:1 Rule

The 3:1 rule is a handy guideline that can help with phase relationships. To use the rule, the distance between two mics should be at least three times the distance between each mic and the sound source. This will help with keeping phase cancellations to a minimum, making sure that the sounds hit each microphone at the same part of their cycles.

In practice, you've got each mic 7 inches from an acoustic guitar. To use the 3:1 rule, you would spread the two mics at least 21 inches apart from each other.

Note: It is not a bad idea for an engineer to keep a tape measure handy when tracking live instruments.

Phase Technique 2: Listen While Placing Mics

Trust your ears. A good technique when mic-ing something with multiple mics is to listen through Pro Tools as you or your assistant moves the mics around. If you are listening to to the mics mixed together, you will hear the difference when one of the mics is moved. Remember, the mics share a relationship with each other and the sound should be judged as a better or worse situation. You are looking for a best-possible relationship, one in which the mics all sound right together. With a little practice, you will know when you have hit the sweet spot and you will learn what it sounds like when mics are not sharing a good phase relationship. In a bad phase relationship, the sound has a weird EQed sound, or it's thin or filtered.

Phase Technique 3: Invert

If your waveforms are near 180° out of phase, you may select a region and invert by using the Audio Suite plug-in named Invert. This will effectively flip the phase on the entire region and invert the waveform (see Figure 1.14).

Figure 1.14 Invert Audio Suite plug-in

Phase Technique 4: Waveform Alignment

Once the information is already recorded, take a look at the waveforms in detail in Pro Tools. It is possible to nudge the waveform forward or backward slightly to put one source in better phase with another. You can change your nudge values by opening the green nudge pull-down menu.

A good choice here is 1 millisecond since we are planning to move the region very subtly. With the region selected, use the plus and minus keys on the numeric keypad to nudge the region forward until its waveform is inline with the other region (see Figure 1.15).

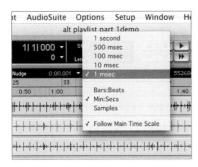

Figure 1.15 The nudge pull-down menu

Figure 1.16 shows two kick drum tracks a little out of phase due to the difference in their waveforms.

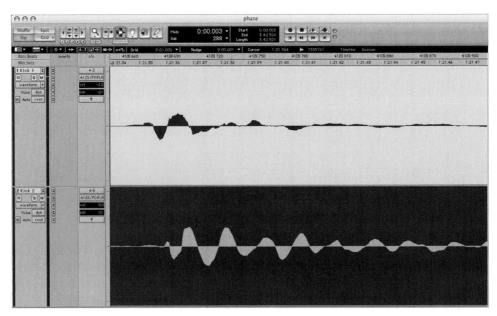

Figure 1.16 Out-of-phase kicks

Figure 1.17 shows the kick drum sounds after being nudged into a better phase relationship.

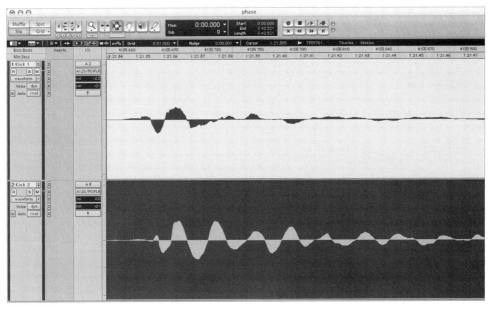

Figure 1.17 In-phase kicks

Phase

What does it mean to be "in phase" or "out of phase" when recording? Simply, when a single source is being recorded by more than one microphone, the sound hits the microphones at different times. Because sound travels through the air in repetitive cycles, the microphones are receiving the signal at different points in the cycles of the sound waves. When you mix the two signals together in playback, the two sounds may add or subtract from each other, causing certain aspects of the original sound to be either missing or emphasized.

Take the example of the drummer's kick drum from our favorite band, The Condensers. When the beater is struck, air molecules are pushed into vibrations, which you measure in sound waves. These sound waves always travel at a constant speed, about 761 MPH, or the speed of sound. Although all sound travels at this speed, the number of times sound waves repeat their cycles is what gives different sounds their unique pitch. In the case of the kick drum, a lot of the sound being produced will have a lower pitch. You can measure the pitch of the sound made by how many times the vibrations complete their cycles in a second. This unit of measurement is called *frequency* (how frequently the waves repeat). In the audio world, you measure frequency as cycles

Continues

Phase *(Continued)*

per second, or Hz. So the frequency of the sound waves determines the pitch of the sound. When you graph this out, or look at it very zoomed in on a Pro Tools track, you can see this waveform in detail.

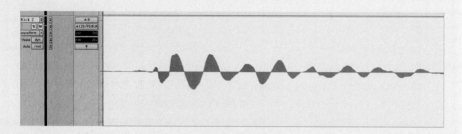

Pro Tools's graphic waveform draws are extremely accurate and very useful when dealing with phase!

The waveform in the region called Microphone B is a graphical picture of the sound waves coming from a kick drum. When the sound hits microphone B, which happens to be inside the kick drum itself, microphone B records this waveform into the timeline.

When the same sound from the kick drum hits microphone A, which is an overhead microphone, it's actually slightly later because the microphone is farther away from the actual drum and it took longer for the sound to reach it.

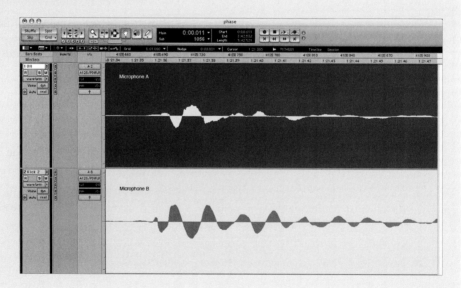

Continues

Phase *(Continued)*

The phase issue occurs when you play both tracks together. Notice how microphone B's peak occurs at the same time as the valley of microphone A's waveform? These two conflicting signals will partially cancel each other out, resulting in a very un-phat kick drum sound. Not usually the goal!

So with this example, you can see that every time you use more than one mic to record, there will always be a phase *relationship* between all the mics in the room. Mics are rarely completely or 180° out of phase or in phase but rather slightly more in or out from each other. Don't let this scare you! There are some tried-and-true techniques to help you deal with this. Some engineers do not view phase as a problem but rather a bounty. It is our approach in this book to embrace phase relationships and use them to our sonic advantage. Keep in mind that Pro Tools always offers the advantage to slightly nudge one waveform forward or backward in time to help with the phase relationships. See the section "Dealing with Phase" for more on this.

Recording the Electric Guitar

In comparison to some other instruments, recording the electric guitar is a relatively simple, fulfilling, and zesty enterprise. In terms of different guitar tones, the guitar player, the effects pedals, and the amp settings are going to be as important as microphone placement and technique. But there are a few tricks of the trade to get that ungodly crunch or the wistfully expressive chime of the electric guitar.

The first myth to dispel with amp recording is that the size and loudness of the amp has anything to do with how it will translate when recorded. It's not the size that matters; it's how you use it. In fact, if anything, the bigger, louder amps will sound smaller in comparison to the smaller ones. Jimmy Page used a tiny 8-inch speaker, 12-watt Fender Champ to record some of his most raunchy guitar solos. That said, if it is overdrive you are going for, the amp gain has to be at a certain level for the amp to start achieving that lovely natural overdrive.

Start simple, with one cardioid microphone placed as close to the grill of the amp as possible, pointed directly at the outer portion of the best-sounding speaker in the cabinet (if there is more than one). The more you angle the microphone toward the center of the cone, the brighter the tone will get. Favorite microphones for this are the Shure SM57, Audio Technica 3035, Sennheiser 421, and Beyerdynamic TGX50 (yes, it is a kick drum microphone, but try it; you'll be pleasantly surprised).

If you want a more complex sound, add a room microphone about 5 to 8 feet in front of the amp. This technique works well in good-sounding rooms or even wood hallways. Condenser microphones work well for this, but be mindful of phase issues that will arise. Move the room microphone while listening to both microphones and also abide by the 3:1 rule and you should do fine.

Condenser, Dynamic, and Ribbon, Oh My ...

One of the most frequently asked questions we hear is, What is the difference between a condenser and a dynamic mic? And then, What is a ribbon mic? And then, of course, What does 48v mean and what is this phantom power stuff? All good questions indeed. Remember, each category of microphone (condenser, dynamic, ribbon, piezoelectric, etc.) refers to the physical method in which it converts sound waves into electrical current or voltage. Let's get to it and look at the three most common mic types.

Condenser

Condenser mics are the standard for most studio applications that require maximum clarity, subtlety, and detail in the recording—vocals, acoustic instruments, string sections, ambient room sound, and stereo overheads on a drum kit just to name a very few. Here's why we like them: They have a flatter frequency response than dynamics, and they are more sensitive and can pick up the subtle nuances of a performance more effectively, and because they are powered, they have a higher output than dynamic mics. And come on; with the proximity effect, every singer can at least try to sound like Bryan Ferry! Be careful though; these mics are easily overloaded. Monitor your preamps or board carefully to avoid clipping and distortion.

Here's the breakdown: Condensers need to be powered to operate. To power a condenser microphone, you can use an internal power source such as a battery or you can use externally supplied phantom power (see below). Physically, the condenser mic is a capacitor, converting acoustical energy to electrical energy using two plates containing voltage between them. The thinner outer plate acts as the diaphragm. The diaphragm vibrates when it is struck by sound waves, and as it moves back and forth it changes capacitance. This is then routed to the microphone wires as AC voltage and then out of the microphone via a three-pin XLR cable. It should be noted that the market for condenser mics has changed considerably in the past five years. One of the downsides of condensers in the past might have been the high asking price, but in this new millennium you can find condenser quality for a dynamic price. There have never been as many quality microphones available for such an inexpensive entry point. Competition is good. Some of the more popular condenser microphones include the Neumann U87, the TLM 103, the AKG 414, and the Audio Technica 4050.

Phantom Power

Phantom power is a method of carrying a DC current through audio cables to power condenser microphones as well as other gear. Condenser mics, being capacitors, need to be powered to operate. In the beginning, condensers had their own power supply and were bulky and cumbersome. Phantom power freed condensers from needing to supply their own juice. Condenser mics can get their power from an internal battery as well. Many people see the old 48v on the side of a

Continues

mixing board and never really know what it all means—one of the great mysteries of recording. The wiring for the audio traveling through a microphone is AC current, but to operate the microphone needs DC current too. Phantom power lets you feed both with one cable.

Dynamic

The venerable old dynamic microphone is the workhorse of the industry. More people have SM57s than Neumann M49s; that's for sure. Dynamics are valued for their price, durability, and ability to handle very LOUD music. Many types of dynamic microphones are unidirectional, allowing the microphone to focus in a certain area and reject any sounds from behind. On stage, the dynamics are more useful than condensers or ribbons because they don't distort or feed back as easily and require no power. Dynamics are more durable than condensers in general; toss an SM57 against a wall and you get a dented but functioning SM57. Toss a Telefunken U47 against the wall and you get a very broken, very expensive microphone and then probably lynched by every engineer and singer that has ever used one. Dynamic mics work on the principle of having sound waves move a diaphragm that is connected to a coil (moving coil). As the diaphragm moves, the coil connected to it moves across a magnet, creating a current in the coil, which is carried away from the microphone along the internal wires to the cable. Some of the more common uses are toms, snare, kick, guitar amps, and horns. Some of the more tried and tested dynamics are Shure SM57 and SM58, Sennheiser 421, and AKG D-112.

Ribbon

Well, if you know about ribbon mics, then you can wipe up the drool from the page now. How about the RCA 77A, one of the most famous microphones of all time? Developed in the late '20s, ribbon microphones need no external power supply and deliver some of the most sought-after sound ever recorded. You find fewer and fewer of the vintage ribbons these days for a number of reasons, but newly manufactured ribbons are on the rebound. The color of sound they can capture is almost an opiate to some engineers. Talk about them and their eyes glaze over. They are very fragile microphones and can be ruined in an instant if mishandled. This is how they work: A metallic ribbon is placed in a magnetic field, and as sound waves vibrate the ribbon, it creates a very small electric current. Because of this, the microphone has a very low output and needs a clean and powerful preamp to crank it up to suitable levels. Most ribbon microphones are very sensitive at the front and back (0° and 180°) but dead on the sides (90° and 270°) and can be as warm and lush as an afternoon on a tropical beach. Now if we can just get a gig recording wave sounds (sound waves) all day, we're good! Some vintage examples of ribbon microphones include the Coles 4038 and the Shure SM33 as well as the RCA dynasty of ribbon microphones that inspired a generation of broadcasting and recording. The newer class of ribbon microphones includes Royer Labs R-121 and Beyerdynamic M-160.

A word about ribbons: Because of their mellow high end, ribbon microphones work especially well in capturing a classic, warm, vintage tone on clean guitars. There's nothing like a Fender amp with some tremolo and spring reverb going into a Coles ribbon microphone. Sweetness.

Capturing the Acoustic Guitar

How could something as innocent and pure as a simple wooden acoustic guitar cause so much strife when you try to record it? The acoustic guitar can be a very elusive instrument to capture. The reasons are many. For such a simple device, it produces quite a complex sound, one full of rich overtones, dynamic transients, and a full frequency range of full low end and brittle treble. Getting the acoustic guitar to translate in a recording exactly how it sounds in the room it is being played in pushes recording tools and technology to the limit of their capabilities. There is a method to the madness, however, and the following techniques will get you closer to achieving that captivating acoustic guitar recording into your Pro Tools session.

Line 'em up! When you know you are going to track an acoustic guitar, the first thing to do is gather as many of them as you can. Even though DJ turntables outsell guitars to young American teens, you know you have a few friends who have one lying around. You will be surprised at how a certain unlikely cheap guitar will sound more appropriate than a very expensive Martin for the song you are recording. Another surprising fact is that often the large-bodied D-28-style instruments will actually sound tiny in comparison to the little parlor-style acoustic half its size, which sounds huge when mic-ed up.

Be aware of the room you are recording in. The sound of the acoustic guitar has a lot of live energy that will react to the surface of the room, so the same guitar will sound much different in a small deadened room than it will in a large live wood one.

The next thing to ask yourself is, What role is the acoustic going to play? Is it the intimate central element of a sensitive folk song, or is it playing a strummed support role along with electric guitars, keyboards, drums, and bass?

For that intimate sound, start simple. Place one cardioid condenser microphone 6 to 10 inches in front of the sound hole pointed directly at the 12th fret or where the body meets the neck. The Neumann KM 184 and the Schoepps 221 are good small-diaphragm microphones to try, while it is possible also to get outstanding results with large-diaphragm condensers like the Audio Technica 4040, the Neumann U87, and the AKG 414. The slightest movement here will mean a lot, so if you angle the microphone more toward the sound hole, you'll get more bass, and if you angle it more toward the fingerboard, you'll get more string and fret noise. Listen carefully to the performer playing the part they intend to record as you angle the microphone. It also helps to get on your knees and use your ear to locate the sweet spots around that general area.

For a wider, bigger sound, you have two options. The first option is to add another "over the shoulder" microphone. This microphone should be similar in type to the ones mentioned previously. It can be placed about 1 foot above the right shoulder of the (right-handed) performer, and the capsule should be angled downward at the body of the guitar. Be careful not to point the capsule directly at the sound hole or the sound may get too boomy. This microphone should be able to pick up the guitar's body, while the other microphone can play a part in capturing more intricacies in the picking. Since you are using two microphones, heed the laws and rules of proper phase correlation as outlined in the sidebar on phase. Once the part is recorded, panning the two tracks a little apart from each other opens up the sound of the guitar in the mix (see Figure 1.18).

Figure 1.18 Two acoustic tracks

The other option for getting a sound more appropriate for strummed support tracks is to go stereo. This requires two identical small-diaphragm microphones. AKG 451s or Neumann KM 184s do the trick well. The capsules of the microphones should be angled 90° from each other, and the point where their angles converge and should be pointed at the 12th fret about 7 to 12 inches away.

Getting That Bass Guitar

Big bottoms anyone? The idea here is to capture the low end in a way that has a deep bass response but still retains its definition in the mix. Surprisingly, the upper mid frequencies are almost as important as the lower fundamentals in making this happen.

Many engineers are split about whether it is preferable to record electric bass through a direct insert box, or DI, directly or to mic the bass amplifier's cabinet. We say if you have the channels, do both. Both sounds have characteristics all their own that can be mixed together at a later time to get the perfect sound. Pro Tools's accurate waveform editing makes it easy to align both signals in phase, and hard drive space is cheap as ever, so go ahead and record both signals!

Polar Patterns

We're switching polar patterns, and we're not talking global warming!

The polar pattern on a microphone describes the physical area that is sensitive to approaching sound waves. So even though sound waves may surround the entire microphone, by selecting different patterns, you can determine which areas of the microphone will be sensitive to the waves. This allows an engineer to either focus a microphone's sensitivity or not, depending on the situation.

Unidirectional

When you need to isolate the microphone on the old Marshall stack as much as possible, a unidirectional microphone pattern is used to get the most of the amp and the least of the sound around it. Its typical polar pattern (cardioid) allows sound to enter from the front and, to a lesser extent, from the sides but offers maximum rejection to sound from the rear. The unidirectional microphone is also subject to the proximity effect. The proximity effect exaggerates the lower frequencies when a sound source is less than a foot away from the sensitive area of the microphone. This can be a cool trick to bring out bass response, but be careful how close you get! There are two other types of cardioids: supercardioid and hypercardioid. Both are similar to the cardioid's pattern but offer further refinements. Supercardioid has a more narrow focus than cardioid (115°), which helps in isolating a recording but has a bit of pickup in the rear. hypercardioid, with the tightest focus (105°), has the best side rejection from a unidirectional mic so it can really eliminate bleed, feedback, and background noise but opens up to more rear pickup. Hypercardioid is the typical microphone type built into a video camera because of these qualities.

Omnidirectional

Now say perhaps you want to record a cello in a church and the church sounds like Abbey Road Studios; then you might choose an omnidirectional microphone so you get the instrument and the room sound as well. An omnidirectional microphone records in a 360° field and has no proximity effect.

Bidirectional or Figure 8

If you need to record an interview with two people and have one microphone, then a bidirectional mic is the ideal choice since it records from the front and back (0° and 180°) equally well but rejects sounds from the sides (90° and 270°).

With a basic knowledge of these patterns, you can be much more effective getting the right sound by design, not by accident!

A good bass tone always starts with the player, the gear, and the bass. Nothing stands in the way of a well-intonated instrument, a dynamically consistent player, and a solid-sounding amp. However, if you've got those things at your disposal, you are going to want to capture them correctly.

When mic-ing the cabinet, it is best to use a large-diaphragm cardioid polar pattern microphone, either dynamic or condenser. This type of microphone will react best to the characteristics of the bass, and it is possible to take advantage of the coveted low-end response by utilizing the proximity effect that occurs in this polar pattern. Good dynamic microphone choices are the Sennheiser 421, Electro Voice RE-20, and Beyerdynamic TGX50. Suitable condenser mics are the Audio Technica 4060 or 4050, AKG 414, or for unlimited budgets, a FET or tube Neumann U47.

Place the microphone 6 to 10 inches from the best-sounding speaker cone in the cabinet. Experiment with the mic placement relative to the cone. The closer the capsule is to the center of the speaker cone, the more bright the sound will be, while moving it to face the outer edges of the cone will make for a warmer, darker sound.

A DI is a box that converts the line output of the bass, which is a high impedance signal into the low impedance signal that your Pro Tools interface likes to see (or hear). Like mic pres, all DIs are not created equal and will have a large impact on the sound you get. Popular DIs on the market are the Sans Amp, Countryman, and Yamaha. It is important to note here that many amplifiers have extensive tone controls and a built-in line-ready output. This can be a good way of getting a direct signal too.

Going for the Lead Vocal

Think about your favorite songs. Put yourself in that time and place. What is it you remember the most? That special voice, the incredible harmony, and the chorus you can't get out of your head? Robert Plant at the end of "Stairway to Heaven"? Vocals are a main part of the story in modern music, but tracking a good-sounding vocal is and always has been a challenge.

It's common to use a large-diaphragm condenser mic with a cardioid pattern to track most vocals when the dynamic range is not excessive. This can get a great sound but you can overload the mic if the singer is really pushing it.

Take the mic and find the spot in the room with the least amount of sonic debris (listen). Place the singer's mouth about an open hand's length away from the mic, about 8 to 12 inches, and position the mic above the mouth slightly. This is a good starting point for something with some dynamics in it. Not full on screaming, but good old rock and roll. If you want to get a more intimate breathy sound, position the mic about 3 to 6 inches away from the singer's mouth and about an inch or two above the mouth to keep out unwanted pops and such. The cardioid mic suffers from the proximity effect, so be sure to utilize this to the fullest.

Let's say you have some LOUD vocals to record. Time for plan B. You can back off the mic to about 1 to 3 feet away from the singer's mouth and about 8 to 10 inches above the mouth. Or you can go with plan C, which is the trusty SM57 or Sennheiser 421. These mics will deal with your problem. It's a different tone to be sure, but who says it's not a good one? Remember to get close to the microphone and watch where you point it because it is very directional.

Now the preamp comes into play. Preamps are cool. Use a tube preamp on the front end of a digital system to give your sound that analog color. Use a solid-state pre-amp for more clarity and detail (see the sidebar "Preamplifiers"). A good preamp by itself will not save a bad recording, but it will make a good recording sound better. It is a vital part of the recording chain. Monitor these levels carefully and don't overload the signal. The preamp feeds the compressor.

Depending on who's singing or rapping, you can bring in some compression to the chain. A little compression on the way in goes a long way, but often it is necessary. A good starting point is a 2:1 ratio on your compressor. This means for every db going in above the threshold, there is 1/2 db coming out. A ratio up to 5:1 is typical for vocals, and a ratio above 10:1 becomes noticeable as an effect. The higher ratios act as limiters. Less is more is the rule of thumb. If you overcompress as you record, you can't fix it later; besides, the cool compressors in Pro Tools are half of the fun! The compressor feeds Pro Tools.

When audio comes into a Pro Tools system, you need to control the level from the devices in your mic chain. Be sure to monitor all of your devices and watch for overloads. If you overload your mic chain anywhere, the distortion will pass through everything after that. Think of these things when you record:

- Mic choice
- Placement
- Preamp
- Compression
- EQ
- Levels

Other Vocal-Recording Considerations

Every recording technique involves some background knowledge in order to fully utilize the concepts. Here is a handful of things to consider when planning your vocal recordings.

Preamplifiers

Why is a preamp necessary? Microphones are analog devices. When you record with them into the digital world that is Pro Tools, you take this analog information and convert it into a digital signal. One of the things your Pro Tools hardware interface does is this analog-to-digital (or A-to-D) conversion. The analog information microphones provide comes in the form of electrical AC current (see the sidebar "Condenser, Dynamic, and Ribbon, Oh My . . ."). When this current comes down the cable of the microphone, its signal isn't optimized for the converter. In essence, it is too low. This is where the mic pre comes in: The preamp amplifies the signal to the optimum level for the A-to-D converter. To make a long story short, the mic pre comes between the microphone and the Pro Tools A-to-D converter, and we use the gain control on the mic pre to set the level coming in to Pro Tools.

Are all preamps created equal? No. If you've snooped around the audio marketplace at all, you will be aware of hundreds of different preamps out there, all shapes and sizes, all different colors and flavors. Remember, unless it is built into the interface, like on the 002 or Mbox, higher-end Pro Tools systems require an external preamp. Of course, this doesn't mean that you have to use the built-in preamps, either.

So what makes them better or worse? For starters, different types of preamps actually sound different. In addition, some preamps may actually work better or worse with different microphones. Many engineers are constantly on the hunt for that elusive "match made in heaven"—the perfect combination of mic and preamp.

So what makes them different? For one, you get what you pay for. The price is going to have everything to do with the quality and ultimately the sound of the preamp. Generally, the more expensive preamps are made to more consistent specifications and with higher-quality components. Within these guidelines, however, there are differences, the two main ones being tube or solid state.

Tube preamps are often held in a mythical light because they were all that was available in the "golden age" of recording. Certainly there is something to that classic tube preamp sound. This is due mainly to the fact that when tubes respond to fast transient information, they tend to "round off" the edges of sudden sharp sounds, like drums and other percussive sounds. In addition, the "color" of the tube preamp that many describe as "saturated" or "warm" is actually due to the tube circuit's natural distortion. Many modern manufacturers are putting tubes back in their products to emulate this classic sound. One of the more famous examples of a vintage tube preamp is Bill Putnam's 610, while a popular modern tube preamp is the Avalon VT-737SP.

Solid state preamps can react much more quickly to transient information and ultimately can be more objective in their sound. A vintage example of a solid state preamp is the API 512, while a popular modern one found in studios is the Focusrite Red series preamp.

The Mic

Well, this is a loaded topic. Who do you infuriate first? Just kidding, but really people do have strong opinions about microphones. Every microphone has its day, but where and when it does is the question. Since we are talking about recording vocals, we will start with condenser microphones.

Condenser microphones are the most common microphones used to track lead vocals in a studio setting. On stage, you would use a less sensitive dynamic mic, but in the studio where everything can be controlled, fragile microphones can be treated like royalty. Condenser microphones offer more detail and clarity than dynamic microphones, so when you want to record the most accurate vocal performance, a condenser is a good choice.

The ribbon microphone is highly sought after for broadcast and vocal work. It has a classic sound that recorded a generation of artists. Although vintage ribbons are expensive, rare, and delicate, there is a growing trend to manufacture ribbon microphones again. A number of companies are putting out a quality product.

While it's not the party line, we like using dynamic microphones to track vocals if we need a unique sound or something sounding a little vintage. These mics can take a real load before they break up, so think screamer! All it takes is one punk experience to teach you about protecting your condenser and ribbon diaphragms from Sid "wannabe" Vicious.

The Room

Before we talk gear, we need to talk room. Try to treat the room with some nonreflective material, and at the very least, deaden the area behind the singer a bit. Try not to be too close to a wall and not in the center of the room because of the standing waves. Off of the middle a bit is a good start. Always remember to be interactive with the microphone. Move it around and listen to what the room sounds like. Test, probe, and question at all times!

The Mood

The last thought on vocal recording would be the environment. As a producer, it is very important to do what it takes to put your artist in a position to succeed. You need to be part baby–sitter, part therapist, part mind reader, and part bad cop to get the job done. Candles, incense, insults, jokes—you do it all to set the mood.

Overdubbing and Punching without Fear

One of the most difficult and dangerous (yet exhilarating) aspects of analog recording was the old punch-in. Punch out too soon and you don't get the entire take. Punch out too late and, oh boy, you've got problems. Maybe you just erased part of the only good vocal take your singer had in him. Worse than that, maybe you just ruined a client's track and now the free studio time starts. No undo! We have all done this, but it still hurts. You will never ruin a track with automated overdubbing in Pro Tools! So if you have a vocalist who just gave a great vocal performance except for one phrase, no problem. To start with, you have to configure Pro Tools's monitoring system to best fit your vocalist's needs.

Selection-Based Punching

There are two modes in Pro Tools for record monitoring: Auto Input Monitoring, which is the default mode, and Input Only Monitoring. You can toggle between the two from the Track pull-down menu or by using Option+K / Alt+K (see Figure 1.19).

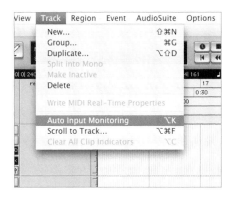

Figure 1.19 Here is where to change your input monitoring mode on LE systems

Auto Input Monitoring mode is the most common mode used when overdubbing. Auto Input Monitoring mode configures Pro Tools to play back the audio on the track up until the punch-in point and then switches to monitor the input source. After punching out, Pro Tools switches back to monitor the audio already on the track. So you hear the track, then you hear the microphone, and then you hear the track again. This entire process is selection-based, as are most things on a computer. Select the audio you need to replace and a little extra in the beginning and end of your selection. Performers are notorious for changing their phrasing and the extra selection will help accommodate for this. Don't be afraid to come out of grid mode to slip mode (F2) to make your selection. (See "The Many Modes of Pro Tools" in Chapter 3 for more on Pro Tools modes.) This method is foolproof, and even in the worst-case scenario, there is always everyone's best friend, Mr. Undo.

Since it is difficult for even a seasoned musician to punch in with no lead-in, you need to set up the pre-roll. Pre-roll can be enabled on the transport bar or by pressing ⌘+K / Ctrl+K (see Figure 1.20).

Figure 1.20 Pre-roll enabled

Once pre-roll is turned on, you need to give it a count. How much time does your vocalist need to feel comfortable with the vibe of the track before coming in? Everyone is different in this, so try 1 bar and go from there. To enter the countoff, click in the Pre-Roll Amount window in the transport bar and type in the desired amount.

Note: Always press Return or Enter to lock in changes when you manually enter numeric data in Pro Tools.

The Main Counter Selection determines the kind of counting for the pre- and post-roll. This can be Bars and Beats, Minutes and Seconds, and Samples in LE and Timecode and Feet & Frames in TDM. At this point, you are ready to go. Press 3 on your numeric keypad to record, and let it rip. Automatic, every time.

Note: Use Input Only Monitoring mode when it is not desirable for the performer to hear playback of their previous takes. This is good for those situations in which the performer focuses on the previous takes instead of concentrating on the take at hand. This allows you to make your punch selection without informing the performer exactly what is being punched.

QuickPunch Mode

At first glance, QuickPunch mode seems like a throwback to the analog style of punching in and out. It is enabled from the Options menu, or by Control+clicking / Start+clicking the record button in the transport window until a little *P* appears inside the red button (see Figure 1.21).

Figure 1.21 QuickPunch mode

With QuickPunch enabled, you get to manually click the record button or press F12 when you want to record onto a record-enabled track. This happens in real time during playback just as on a tape deck. This is handy, but there are a couple of hidden features lurking in QuickPunch mode that are incredibly valuable to your recording chops:

- QuickPunch is the only way you can punch in and out of a track more than once without stopping playback. So if you have three words interspersed throughout a singing verse that need to be replaced, you can let the track play and grab those three spots without having to stop and locate each one separately.

- During QuickPunch, Pro Tools is secretly recording the whole time when the track is playing back, regardless of when you manually punch in and out. This means that if you missed the in or out point, you can trim the handles of the regions and have access to all of the performance—a real lifesaver!

> **Note:** Use QuickPunch mode when you are doing an ordinary selection-based punch-in with a pre-roll and post-roll enabled. This way, if your performer or voice-over talent jumps the gun or holds out a note longer than your punch-in selection, you will have access to the material that would have been chopped off in a normal selection-based punch.

Loop Record Techniques

If you're the type of Pro Tools user that wears multiple hats in the studio (engineer, musician, producer), you'll find the Loop Record feature very useful. Sometimes when recording yourself, it is easy to get frustrated with having to simultaneously start and stop recording, reset the playback cursor, and set up for an additional take. With Pro Tools's Loop Record, you can set up a loop record selection that will record again and again without having to stop after each take. Loop Record is also especially useful for helping musicians, voice-over talent, and foley artists nail difficult passages by repeating them over and over without any downtime. As if that wasn't cool enough, after loop recording, you can make a composite of all of these different performances that may have never been possible to achieve in one take. Because Pro Tools keeps accurate track of all the subsequent takes, it is easy to audition and recall each take and edit them together.

Making a Selection

On the record-enabled target track, make a selection for the appropriate amount of time. This could be the length of a verse, or in the case of Figure 1.22, it is an eight-bar guitar solo. It is important here to make a selection a bit longer than the passage because any pre-roll setting will be active only on the first pass. To make sure the performer knows where they are relative to the song, it is sometimes necessary to include some extra space before the first note of the intended recording start time. In this example, the selection ended up being 10 bars total to give 2 bars pre-roll at the beginning of each looped take.

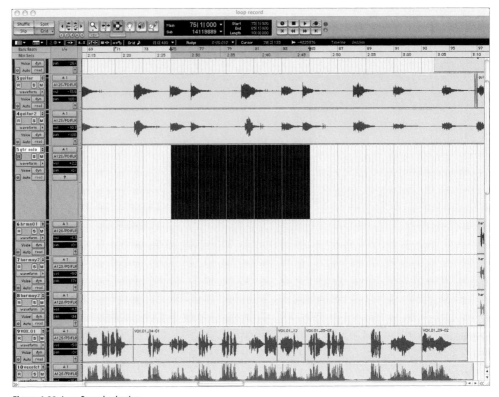

Figure 1.22 Loop Record selection

Enabling Loop Record

You can turn on Loop Record in the Options menu, by Control+clicking / Start+clicking on the record button in either the dedicated transport panel in the Edit window or the floating pop-up transport bar two times so that the red record button has a loop around it.

Record

To begin recording, press ⌘+spacebar / Ctrl+ spacebar, Keypad3, or F12. Note that if you are recording yourself, you can always let this first pass go to get situated behind your instrument or microphone. When the recording gets to the end of the selection, it will start over at the beginning again and repeat infinitely until you hit stop.

Edit

Once you have recorded multiple takes you will notice a new *whole file* named after your track in boldface type in the Regions list (right column in the Edit window). This whole file is actually all of the takes you just recorded combined in one long file. Below this you will see a list of takes with numbered suffixes after each take. These are separate versions of all the takes you just recorded! In other words, these are *region definitions* that point to each take separately in the larger whole file. (All of these files are highlighted in Figure 1.23.)

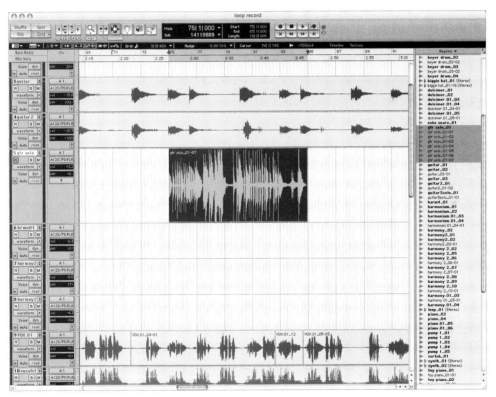

Figure 1.23 The guitar solo was looped seven times, as indicated by the regions numbered 01 through 07 after the name **gtr solo_01**. The **gtr solo_01** in boldface type is all of the takes combined into a single whole file.

After you finish loop recording, the last take (region named gtr solo_01-07) remains in the track's playlist in the Edit window. Now go to the Pro Tools > Preferences > Edit tab to set a preference that will allow you to listen to and compare all of the takes quickly and efficiently on the same track without having to move anything around (see Figure 1.24).

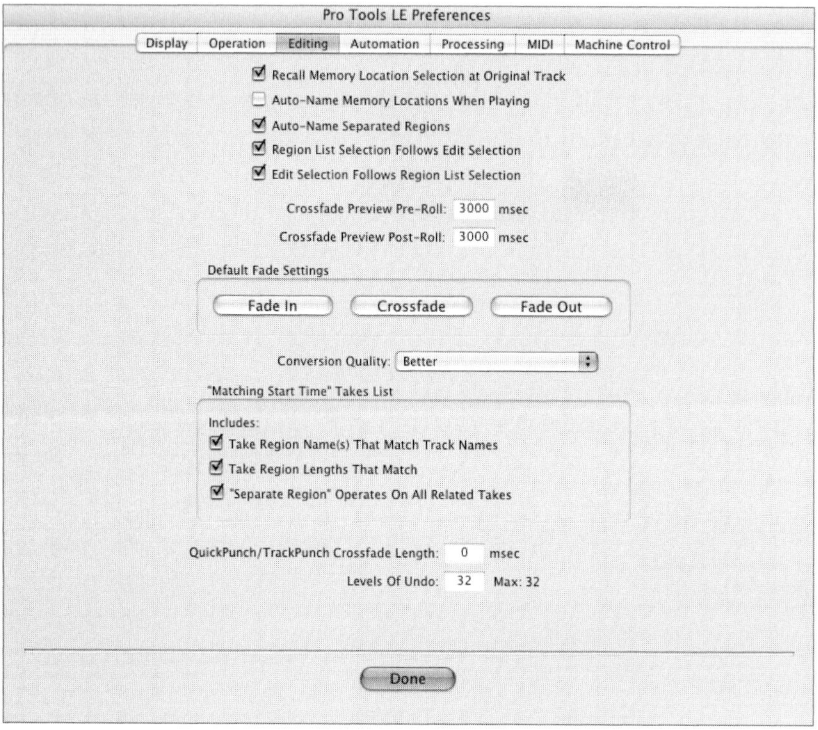

Figure 1.24 "Matching Start Time" Takes List preferences

Because all of the loop-recorded takes share the same track name and are subsequently the same length, checking the "Matching Start Time" Takes List options titled Take Region Names(s) That Match Track Names and Take Region Lengths That Match will make Pro Tools think of them as all belonging together.

Select the region of the last take (gtr solo_01-07 in Figure 1.26) by double-clicking on the region with the Selector tool. ⌘+Click / Ctrl+click on the region with the Selector tool and you will get a pull-down menu showing all related takes. This is a list of all of the loop-recorded takes right in the Edit window. You can select and listen to all of the looped performances right from here. Make sure you use the Selector tool and the entire region is selected for this to work (see Figure 1.25).

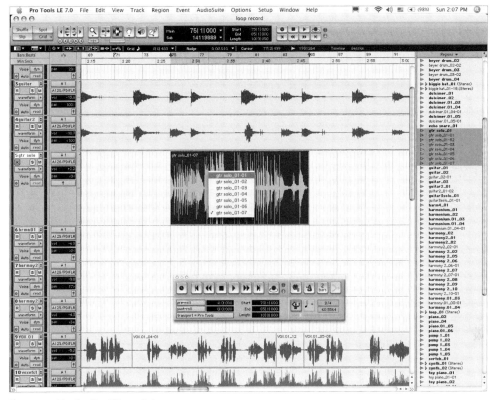

Figure 1.25 The Matching Takes pull-down menu

Each take you select in this pull-down menu will replace the selected region in the Edit window so you can audition all the different takes you recorded and choose the best one, as shown in Figure 1.25.

Comp It

Now wouldn't it be cool to take the best parts of different takes and put them together to make a composite? There is a third preference in the "Matching Start Time" Takes List that makes this extremely easy. It is called "Separate Region" Operates On All Related Takes. Check this box in the Preferences > Edit tab (see Figure 1.24). This makes it so that you can separate the region showing and the splice will cut through all the other related takes at exactly the same point. You can visualize this by imagining that all the loop-recorded takes are like layers of a cake and you are cutting through all the layers at once in the same spot. ⌘+E / Ctrl+E will separate the region where your selector cursor is (see Figure 1.26).

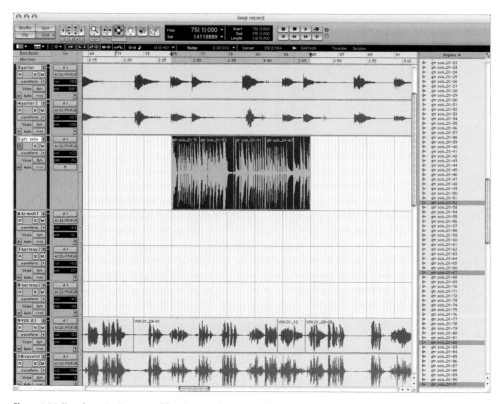

Figure 1.26 Here the region is separated four times, with sections of four different takes used.

Once the layers are cut, you can mix and match different parts of the take to arrive at a final composite. This could be something that is not even physically possible to play in one take. Is this cheating? Ask producer/musician Brian Eno, who did this back in 1972 on *Another Green World* by splicing tapes of many different guitar performances. This type of composite editing is common in the history of multitrack recording, but with Pro Tools it just takes a whole lot less time!

Clean Up

You will notice that this kind of editing makes many different numbered versions of regions in your Regions list. It may be useful here to select all of your final composite in the Edit window, choose Edit > Consolidate, and make a new whole file out of your comped performance. Once this is done, you may want to select Unused Audio Except Whole Files from the Regions list pop-up menu and get rid of all the unused regions you created while making your composite. You can read more about this type of cleanup process in Chapter 3.

Alternate Playlist Recording Techniques

Using alternate playlists is one of the most powerful and versatile techniques in Pro Tools. While the concept of recording multiple takes of an instrument or vocal performance and then "comping" or combining the takes into one cohesive performance has been around for decades in the recording world, never has it been so fast, painless, and easy as it is with Pro Tools's alternate playlists. The audio regions and the placement and order of those audio regions on a track in Pro Tools is deemed that track's playlist. Pro Tools lets you store and save an infinite number of these playlists within a track as alternate playlists. This means that every track can contain additional recording takes or other arrangements, ready to be called up instantaneously and edited from. This technique can help save valuable screen real estate, time, and energy while recording. It's all about efficiency here, so you have more time to be creative.

It's the moment you've been waiting for: time to record the lead vocal. Depending on the singer, vocals recording can be tricky. Some singers (even very popular ones) require many takes to get their part correct. Others need a few takes to warm up. Using alternate playlists, there is no reason why you shouldn't be recording all of the takes. Singers sometimes hit their best performances right away, while other times they hit a peak halfway through the session and everything goes downhill from there. A lot of the time it is hard to judge these performance nuances in the midst of a tracking session. By using alternate playlists, you can go back to previous takes and compare and contrast. You also have the option of selecting the best parts of each take and combining them right then and there during the tracking session.

Record with Alternate Playlists

The Alternate Playlists menu is in the small pull-down menu identified with an up/down arrow to the right of the track name. If it is the first time you open this in a session, you will see New, Duplicate, and the name of the track you are in (see Figure 1.27).

Figure 1.27 The alternate playlists menu

After the first take has been recorded, you can choose New from this list and Pro Tools will prompt you to use your track name_01 or allow you to rename the new playlist you are creating. You may find it useful to use the names Pro Tools gives you since they are created numerically, but you can rename it if you wish. When you click

OK, the track will appear empty with your new track name. Don't worry. Your previous take is not gone; it is still available from the same pull-down menu, but you now have a new, clean playlist to record an additional take. You may do this as many times as you wish, and although each track will contain more media on your hard drive, all the different takes are contained neatly within the one track in the Edit window. There is also no additional strain on system resources to have as many of these as you want hiding inside your track.

Edit on the Fly with Alternate Playlists

Once you have a few playlists in the track, your Alternate Playlist menu will look like the one in Figure 1.28.

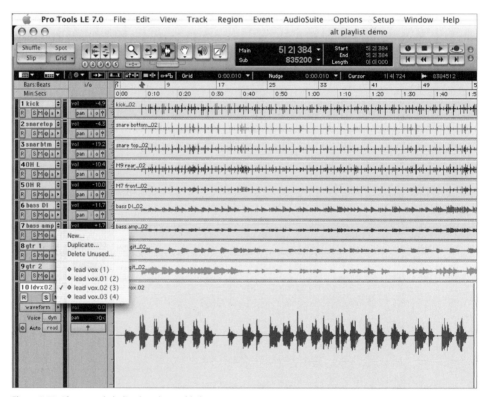

Figure 1.28 After several playlists have been added

You can now pick and choose between all of these performances instantly by calling up each take and listening one by one, or you can make a master take or a comped track (see the sidebar "Comping"). A good technique here is to make a new playlist titled comp or master and put the most solid performance in the track. Then, using simple copy (⌘+C / Ctrl+C) and paste (⌘+V / Ctrl+V) editing, you can assemble a track with all the good parts. Pro Tools makes this easy because it keeps your selection in the same spot while you call up different playlists. Here's how:

1. Find your best performance; in this case it is titled lead vox.02-01.
2. Open the Alternate Playlist menu and choose Duplicate.
3. Name the new track Vocal Master.
4. Select a part of a phrase from another take that you want to use; in this example, it is the last two words of a verse in the lead vox.03-01 track (see Figure 1.29).

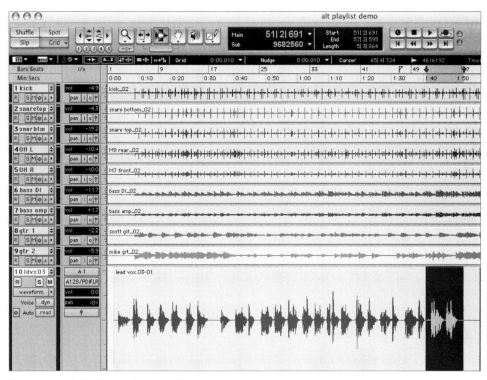

Figure 1.29 A selection from an alternate playlist

5. Copy to the Clipboard.
6. Move to your comp or master playlist track. Notice how the selection stays in exactly the same spot between playlists.
7. Paste your selection (see Figure 1.30).
8. Repeat as many times as necessary to make a solid track.
9. When you're finished, it is a good idea to check all of the transitions, cross-fade them together, and consolidate the selection. You'll learn more about this in Chapter 3.

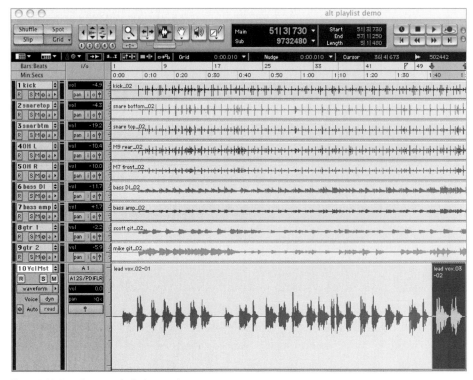

Figure 1.30 Paste from one playlist into another

Comping

Comp is short for *composite*. The term is used often in recording to refer to tracks that are assembled from a slew of performances of an instrument or vocalist recorded in different takes and then put together to form a final track. This technique has been around since the beginning of multi-track recording. In the tape-based analog world, comping required the use of many tracks, which then had to be bounced and mixed through the mixer onto a final comped track. This was a tedious, time-consuming process that ultimately resulted in a final comped track that was always one generation away from the original recording, thus increasing noise floor and tape hiss. In the digital world, you can comp tracks together quickly and easily without any generation loss.

Wait for Note and the Lonely Guitarist

Just about every piece of music software since the mid '80s has a function called Wait for Note. It's a MIDI function, but we are liberating this technique to use in an audio application. You need something that will trigger MIDI to do this. A keyboard is the obvious choice, but there are many other options today. A MIDI controller is incredibly valuable in a modern studio because of its ability to work as a control surface as well as a keyboard. So you need to track a guitar part but everyone else has gone home. The guitar rig and the computer live in different parts of the room. Hmmm… This is a fairly typical situation in a home studio as well, where people often work alone (and late at night).

Set up a MIDI keyboard as close as you can to the spot where you will track the guitar. If you have a sustain pedal, this works best, but anything that will trigger MIDI will work. Now, back in Pro Tools, record-enable your audio track, no MIDI track required, and then if it's not visible, show the transport bar (⌘+ Keypad1 / Ctrl+Keypad1), enable the wait for note button (the pause symbol over a MIDI cable) and start recording (see Figure 1.31).

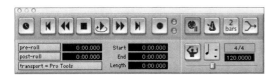

Figure 1.31 Wait for Note enabled

At this point the computer is ready to record as soon as you trigger the keyboard. It will wait for as long as you need to get comfortable and ready to play. Step on your sustain pedal or just press any key on your MIDI controller, and red lights for everybody.

Dealing with Latency while Recording

Latency is the dirty word of digital audio. Note that the first four letters of the word spell *late*. This is what latency is all about. When you experience latency, you hear things later in time than you are supposed to. Although there are many advantages of digital audio over analog, latency is an example of a new set of problems and challenges that didn't exist in the analog world. Everything essentially moves at the speed of electricity in the analog world, which is fast enough not to cause any problems. In digital audio, especially the host-based systems like Pro Tools LE, in which all of the audio processing is handled by your internal CPU, the number-crunching required to run plug-ins, combine streams of audio in the mixer, and record in real time actually takes a few milliseconds to process. For LE systems, the length of the time lag will differ depending on the speed of your processor and the amount of RAM you have. Ever wondered why the higher-end Pro Tools TDM systems cost so much more than LE systems? This is one of the reasons. *TDM* stands for *Time Division Multiplexing*, a technology used by Digidesign that solves many of the problems of latency and lands audio perfectly on time, even with a lot of plug-in processing and many streams of audio happening at once. But do not fret; there are a few ways to deal with latency to make it a non-issue. As long as you identify and acknowledge the problem of latency, you can get around it to make seamless and professional-sounding recordings even in the LE world.

Listen to Your Host: Adjusting Host-Based Settings in Pro Tools LE

Pro Tools LE is a host-based system, which means it is the only system that has the internal CPU handling all plug-in processing. The first thing to look at when dealing with latency on an LE system is the playback engine preferences in the Setup menu (see Figure 1.32).

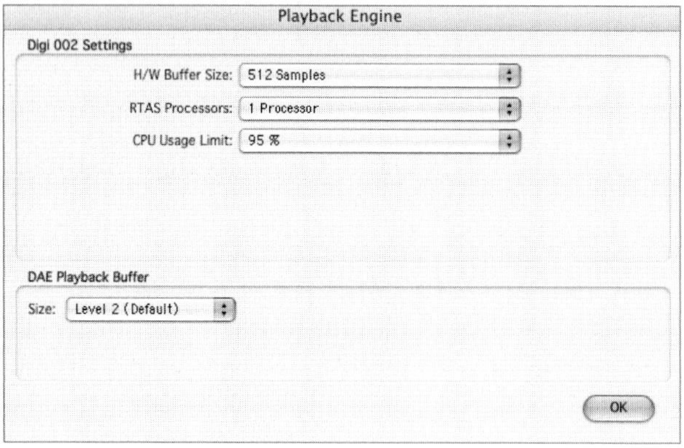

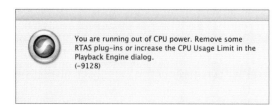

Figure 1.32 Host-based performance settings

In here you will find H/W Buffer Size settings, which are the keys you will need to unlock the latency issues. The lower you can get these numbers, the lower the latency will be. In other words, you'll be playing that killer software synth plug-in via your MIDI controller and you won't experience that crappy time lag that can occur with a high latency. The trade-off is performance. The lower the H/W Buffer Size setting is, the harder it is for your computer to keep up with all the processes it is running. The key here is that you can change these settings anytime, even with a session open. So when you are recording and having no latency is really crucial, you can lower the numbers. Then, when it is time to mix and you need all the plug-ins you can shake a stick at, and latency is not an issue, you will want to set those numbers to the maximum amount. If your computer buckles and you get an error message like the one in Figure 1.33 while playing back audio, then you have hit rock bottom and won't be able to continue at this buffer setting.

> You are running out of CPU power. Remove some RTAS plug-ins or increase the CPU Usage Limit in the Playback Engine dialog. (–9128)

Figure 1.33 You get this dialog box when CPU usage is too high for the playback engine settings.

MIDI with Confidence

2

MIDI, an acronym for musical instrument digital interface, is like a primitive Internet for instruments to communicate with each other. Although it was developed in the early '80s, it is still the preferred protocol for synthesizers, samplers, and keyboards used in the digital audio world of today. In fact, Pro Tools 7 now has more MIDI features than any previous version. Following modern trends of digital audio, Digidesign is banking more than ever on Pro Tools as a compositional tool working in the tick-based realm of MIDI. For we users, this means that we now have more powerful and creative tools to make our music with. This chapter will explore some of the inspirational and creative new tools that have been handed to us in Pro Tools 7.

Chapter Contents

The Nuts and Bolts of MIDI

MIDI: the little computer code that changed it all. Developed in the early '80s with the guidance of Dave Smith from Sequential Circuits, MIDI allows devices from a multitude of manufacturers to trigger, play, sync, and generally get along well with others.

The best way to visualize how MIDI works is to think of the old-timey player piano. In these primitive machines, a scroll of paper with punch holes rolls around a drum tells the piano what notes to play and when to play them. MIDI is like the scroll of paper (the data) and the piano is like the virtual instrument, sampler, or keyboard module, awaiting instructions to know how and when to play.

Modern synths, samplers, drum machines, and sequencers all are powered by the magic of MIDI, which now runs through traditional eight-pin MIDI cables or via USB. In addition to notes and note values, MIDI data holds a slew of other functions. You have the ability to quantize, transpose, layer, edit individual notes, and revoice at any time because MIDI is only the instructions, not the actual sampled audio.

Here are some key MIDI points:

- MIDI is 8-bit data; every parameter has a range of 0 to 127.
- MIDI is never sound.
- MIDI has the ability to capture every part of a musical performance, including velocity, duration, and continuous controller events such as pitch bending.

The Tao of MIDI: A MIDI Haiku

8-Bit Language, slow

Cutoff, Resonance, Sustain

Never Audio

MIDI is a unique beast in the world of music. Musicians and engineers all enjoy somewhat of a love/hate relationship with MIDI. MIDI is flexible, controllable, and dynamic, but it is also temperamental, fragile, and somewhat mysterious. Here are some guidelines to help avoid MIDI meltdowns.

Incommunicado

If you lose MIDI communication during a session (it is known to happen often), troubleshooting should be done in a logical and systematic order:

1. Save and close your Pro Tools session.

Continues

The Tao of MIDI: A MIDI Haiku *(Continued)*

2. Check all physical connections, including power to all devices and cables to and from interfaces and your computer.

3. In AMS (Mac) or your Windows MIDI manager program, make sure the computer can see your MIDI devices. In AMS, this means clicking the Test Setup button and seeing if the blue arrow on the MIDI device icon lights up when you play any MIDI note on your MIDI device.

4. If there is MIDI communication, proceed directly to step 5. If not, power down MIDI devices and restart your computer (a simple restart and power cycle often works wonders for MIDI).

5. Back in Pro Tools, reexamine all of your internal patching. Often it is just a mismatched output or input assignment that is the root of the problem.

Patch Incompatibility

The ability to change a zither sound to an electric bongo is great but not when the electric bongo sound gets altered in the keyboard where it lives and the song sounds horribly wrong the next time you play it. Many a record was recorded with certain keyboards only to have said keyboards crash, burn, or be repossessed. No keyboard, no sounds; no sounds, no record. Having to revoice a song or album is a royal pain. To avoid these kinds of problems, make sure you notate and label the keyboard patches and sounds. The comments field of an Instrument track in Pro Tools is great place to do this.

Drivers

Make sure you have all of the updated drivers for your various MIDI devices. Often a system OS upgrade results in a driver not working properly anymore. Usually a device's website has updated drivers available for download.

AMS for Macs

Audio MIDI Setup (AMS) is native system software used by Mac OS X to control audio and MIDI coming in and going out of the computer. Anyone who might remember Mac OS 9 and Open Music System, or OMS, will feel warm and fuzzy when using AMS. Though you can and perhaps should use other software to control audio, no other MIDI software is needed to interface external keyboards with your computer. You can set up your entire studio of controllers and synth racks as easily as pulling and connecting virtual cables.

The AMS utility lives in the Applications > Utilities folder and is included with every OS X install. Press Shift+⌘+U to quickly open the utilities folder from the Finder level. If you have a dedicated external MIDI patch bay, install the patch bay driver and the patch bay will show up in the AMS MIDI window. When you see the MIDI interface, you can then create your hardware instrument instances, which will reflect your external hardware (see Figure 2.1).

If you are using a keyboard/controller/interface combo such as the M-Audio Oxygen, Radium, or Ozonic, then the MIDI interface is built into the keyboard. Install the software that comes with the keyboard and you will see the device appear in the MIDI window in AMS as a controller rather than a keyboard and you are good to go. To test if the AMS is receiving/transmitting MIDI, click the Test Setup tab on the upper right of the AMS window and the cursor will turn into an eighth note icon. Hit some keys/pads/knobs on the devices/controllers to see if you're getting MIDI (chime and blue arrow means good). To test if you are sending MIDI, click the device in AMS. If the MIDI LED lights up on your hardware device, you are in business. If the arrow tabs, which are used to connect devices, are pointed down, it means the device is an interface. If the arrow tabs point up, it means the device is an instrument.

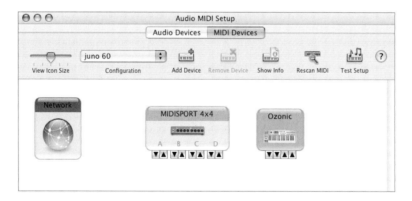

If you have an old-school hardware MIDI keyboard, you will need to add a device in AMS, configure it, and then cable it to your virtual MIDI interface device. To configure your device, double-click on the generic icon to open up the Properties prompt box. The Properties window contains a database of manufacturers and instruments. If you see your device, then you are set. A list of properties is associated with the device because of the database. If you do not see your keyboard, don't worry. You can type in the name and everything will still work. You will need to click the Advanced tab if you

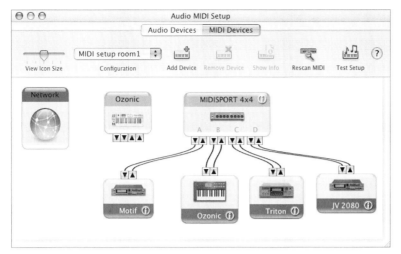

Figure 2.1 The AMS is showing hardware instruments and a MIDI controller all connected to the MIDISPORT interface.

need to tell the computer your keyboard has special capabilities or properties. When you are finished connecting and naming all of your devices, save the setup. Name the setup by date or by keyboard name or whatever makes sense to your studio. This is great for any studio that works with different clients on a regular basis because you can save as many different profiles and configurations as needed. For safety, it is good practice to save a setup for troubleshooting, as well. You could save it as Last Working Config and revert to it when any new configurations are failing.

Note: Hardware MIDI interfaces are notorious for crashing. When in doubt, reboot.

Dealing with MIDI Latency

Latency, the much despised digital processing anomaly that causes lateness in timing, can affect audio and MIDI; no one is safe. MIDI latency rears its ugly head as the time lag between the keyboard press and the keyboard sound. Even though hardware keyboards can experience timing issues with MIDI because of the inherent slow speed (31.5kbps), you have to put a lot of data into the MIDI stream to clog it up. These days, using a computer to generate sound, you will encounter latency of some sort. If you know how to address this problem, you can work around it. To deal with this computer-based anathema, choose Setup > Playback Engine (see Figure 2.2).

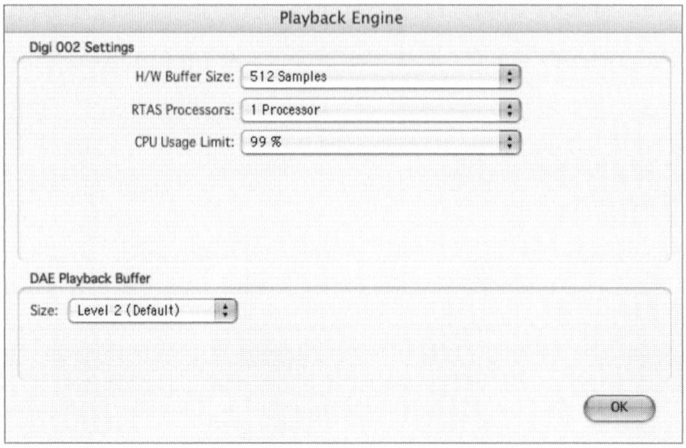

Figure 2.2 The playback engine is the central hub of latency control.

Most every digital audio program has an H/W buffer and an H/W buffer setting. A buffer is a temporary storage area for data as it waits to be told where to go. (We're thinking of Tron right now; anyone else?) A small buffer is like a sports car—fast but not very powerful. A large buffer is like a dump truck—slow but powerful. When you need juice to play back a piece with lots of track, you crank up the buffer size. When you are recording and composing, latency is the bane of modern music, so set the buffer smaller, and the notes will sound as you hit the keys. Don't set the buffer too small, or the computer won't have enough power to play the track. If the audio skips or distorts, that is a sign that your buffer is set too low. Buffers come in all sizes, from around 64 to 8060, with 512 being right down the middle and a good place to start. Know your H/W buffer! Being able to change size easily and quickly depending on the track helps your workflow and keeps it creative.

ReWire under the Hood

ReWire is a protocol for exchanging real-time audio and MIDI data between two computer programs. Developed in 1998 by the boys in the white coats at Propellerhead, ReWire works in the background like an invisible cable. ReWire is an interactive connection, so you can continue to edit and revoice your MIDI tracks with both programs open.

The original ReWire specification allowed 64 channels of audio, while ReWire 2 provides as many as 256 channels of audio and 4,080 channels of MIDI between programs. ReWire 2 offers very accurate and automatic synchronization between host and slave applications. Either Transport bar will start, stop, and control the other application and always stay in perfect sync. At last count, over 25 programs support ReWire. ReWire is free, installs itself, and comes with most of your favorite music software. ReWire is included in every version of Pro Tools 7.

Since latency is a timing issue, you should know about the other area of Pro Tools that addresses MIDI timing. It is called MIDI Track Offsets and it is found in the Event menu. MIDI Track Offsets allows you to compensate for any inherent latency created by your MIDI instruments. By manually changing values by samples for each instrument, you can compensate for this latency. Track offset can be either track-specific or global (see Figure 2.3).

Figure 2.3 The Track Offsets window

MIDI Beat Clock and MIDI Time Code

Did you know that your Pro Tools system is always generating a MIDI pulse in time with the tempo of your song? The pulse is called the MIDI Beat Clock and it can help keep your MIDI devices in sync with Pro Tools. Officially, the pulse is dubbed MTC, which stands for MIDI Time Code, and you can take advantage of it via MIDI Beat Clock to sync up low-frequency oscillators (LFOs), arpeggiators, delays, and rhythmic filter envelopes in your synths, samplers, or drum machines. Because Pro Tools LE systems do not support Society of Motion Picture and Television Engineers (SMPTE) time code, MTC can also be used to sync up Pro Tools LE to other digital audio workstations running Pro Tools TDM, Digital Performer, or Logic. You can even use MTC as a poor man's SMPTE to sync Pro Tools up to another deck, such as an ADAT. This is called MIDI Machine Control (MMC).

MIDI Beat Clock for External Devices

Getting MIDI Beat Clock to send MTC to your attached MIDI devices is a simple process. In Pro Tools 7, the dialog box is located by choosing Setup > MIDI > MIDI Beat Clock.

Pro Tools
7

In this dialog box you see the names of all of your hardware listed in AMS (see "AMS for Macs" earlier in the chapter) plus all of the software synthesizers you have opened in your session. Check the boxes of the devices you want to send the Pro Tools Beat Clock to. The devices you check can take advantage of the tempo generated by your Pro Tools session—even if the tempo changes drastically during your arrangement.

If you ever wanted to get a visual reference of the MIDI Beat Clock pulse that Pro Tools sends, just take a look at the Click plug-in. As shown in Figure 2.4, the plug-in has a green light labeled MIDI IN that pulses in time with your tempo. This is MIDI Beat Clock at work! The Click plug-in uses the MTC signal to sync perfectly in time with your song's tempo.

Figure 2.4 The MIDI Beat Clock at work as shown by the green MIDI IN LED on the Click plug-in

Sync Other Devices to Pro Tools with MIDI Machine Control

Have you ever wanted to control playback of an ADAT deck, another digital audio workstation, or a video deck from Pro Tools? Pro Tools TDM users with a Sync I/O hardware interface typically use SMPTE time code for this (see Chapter 7, "Post-Production and the World of Surround"), but even Pro Tools LE users can take advantage of MIDI Time Code to control outside devices. As long as the device is attached with a MIDI cable and supports MIDI Machine Control, you can control the transport of these devices from your Pro Tools LE session via MTC. Here's how:

1. Select Setup > Peripherals. Choose the Machine Control tab.

2. Click Enable and choose the device you want to control from the Send To pull-down menu as shown in Figure 2.5. Any devices preconfigured in AMS as well as your software synthesizers will show up here.

3. The ID is set to 127 by default, which is a special ID that broadcasts to all MMC IDs. If you know you want to send MMC to a specific ID on your device, you can configure it here.

4. Use the Pro Tools transport window to control playback of your external devices.

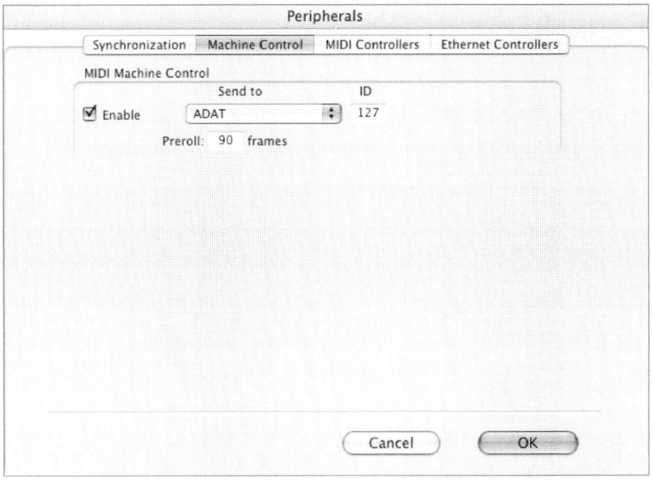

Figure 2.5 Machine controlling an ADAT

You can change some additional settings for MMC playback in the Pro Tools Preferences panel under the Machine Control tab. The Machine Chases Memory Location check box shown in Figure 2.6 will make the machine-controlled device fast-forward or rewind to any designated point in the timeline you put your cursor to. The Machine Follows Edit Insertion/Scrub check box in Figure 2.6 will make the device scrub with your scrub/shuttle tool as you drag it in the Pro Tools Edit window.

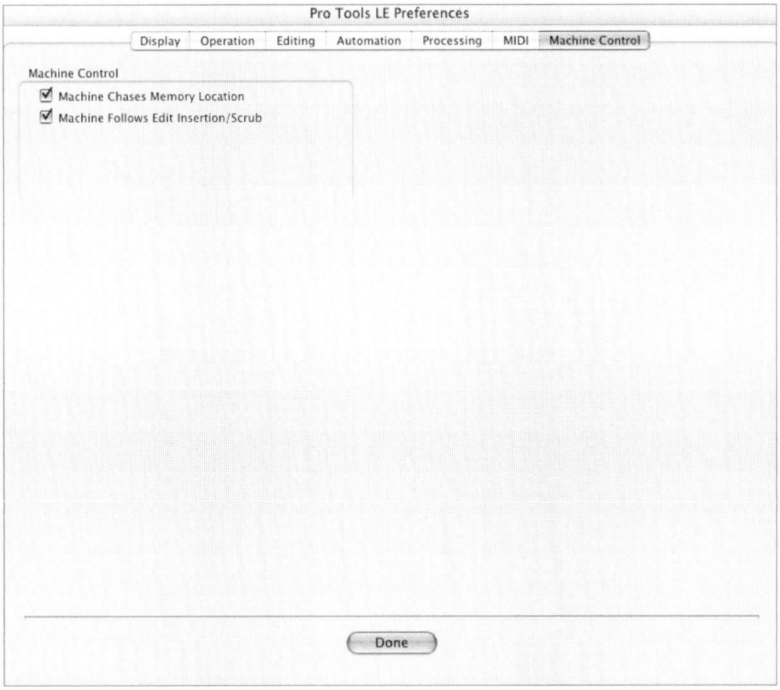

Figure 2.6 Machine Control preferences

Use MIDI Machine Control to Slave Pro Tools to Other Devices

With the same setup for MMC, you can make Pro Tools slave to the playback of other digital audio systems, ADAT decks, or video decks:

1. As you did for the previous exercise, select Setup > Peripherals. Choose the Machine Control tab, click Enable, and choose your device.

2. In the transport window, open the pull-down menu that says Transport=Pro Tools.

3. As shown in Figure 2.7, select MMC in the pull-down menu. Pro Tools will now follow the transport of the configured external device.

Figure 2.7 MIDI Machine Control is enabled here for external control..

CHAPTER 2: MIDI WITH CONFIDENCE ■

4. To take a device offline, open the same pull-down menu in the Transport window, but go to the Online submenu and uncheck the device (Machine or MIDI) you want to take offline (see Figure 2.8).

Figure 2.8 About to uncheck the MIDI device and take it offline

Real-Time Properties

The new MIDI Real-Time Properties in Pro Tools 7 is a quantum leap forward in MIDI production. This function stands out in an upgrade laden with solid improvements. In the past, you had to apply a MIDI Operation as a destructive edit—how '90s! With Real-Time Properties, you can work with functions like Quantize and Duration as if they were real-time plug-ins. You have the ability to change parameters at any time.

For example, if you enable the Qua button in the Real-Time Properties column of the Edit window and choose a quantize setting for your hi-hats track to an $\frac{1}{8}$ note only to realize the setting should be a $\frac{1}{16}$ note, you can nondestructively change the value by clicking and holding the note icon and selecting $\frac{1}{16}$ instead. When it sounds right, you can choose to apply the quantize setting destructively from Track Menu > Write Real-Time Properties. To enable Real-Time Properties from the Edit window view selector (under the edit modes), check Real-Time Properties or choose View > Edit Window > Real-Time Properties.

To launch the Real-Time Properties floating window, select Event > MIDI Real-Time Properties. The floating window offers everything that the track-based Real-Time Properties offers, plus the ability to write Real-Time Properties and to apply Real-Time Properties to more than one selected region in addition to entire tracks.

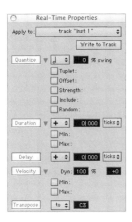

To apply the Real-Time Properties, simply press any of the five property names, and the settings for that particular command will open and the property will take control of the selected regions or track if no regions are selected.

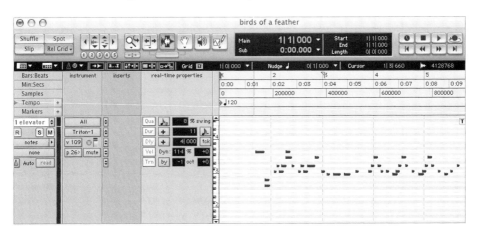

Creative workflow can be more fluid and spontaneous working in a nondestructive environment. You can try any of the different properties on the fly to fine-tune your track during playback. Velocity and Transpose also work as real-time inputs. Turn them on and play your keyboard, and the real-time settings override what you play on the keyboard. Turn them off, and the track returns to what you played. When you apply Real-Time Properties to an entire track, a *T* appears in the upper-right corner of regions. When you do the same to a selected region, an *R* appears in the same spot.

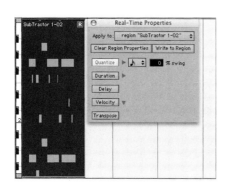

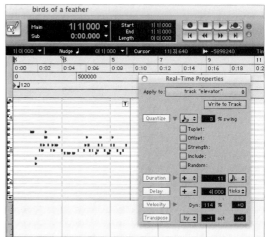

You can have different settings for each region or track, offering incredible flexibility in editing and mixing.

Using Instrument Tracks

One of the most exciting and significant new features in Pro Tools 7 is the instrument track, which calls for a much different workflow technique for routing MIDI in a session. The end result is efficiency and advanced creative control. You can think of an instrument track as a *hybrid* of an aux track and a traditional MIDI track. An instrument track contains only MIDI information in its playlist, but it has the ability to play a hardware or software instrument and send the audio directly to its output so you can hear it. This is a huge improvement over the old way (Pro Tools 6.9 and earlier), when two tracks were required for MIDI to work. MIDI information had to be routed out of a MIDI track to another separate audio or aux track: a royal pain! In addition to providing a more streamlined workflow, Instrument tracks let you do the following:

- Insert RTAS instruments such as Reason, Virus, FM-7, and so on directly on the instrument tracks as plug-ins.

- Play hardware MIDI instruments by assigning them to the Instrument track's MIDI output selector.

- Record, sequence, edit, and automate all MIDI data in the Instrument track's playlist.

- Use the same MIDI data to combine sounds from external hardware synths and samplers with plug-in-based MIDI instruments all in one Instrument track to create layered sounds (see Figures 2.9 and 2.10).

- Use any of the 10 sends available on Instrument tracks for additional effects signal routing, such as a reverb or delay send and return.

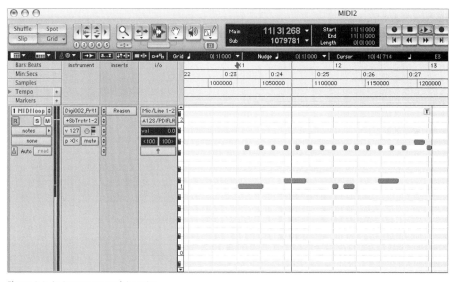

Figure 2.9 An instrument track in action

Note: Notice that the output menu shows two instruments checked in Figure 2.10. This means that this instrument track is controlling more than one instrument in Reason. To do this, hold down Control/Start as you open the MIDI output selector and choose additional instruments. This method allows you to control as many different sounds as you want from the same MIDI sequence.

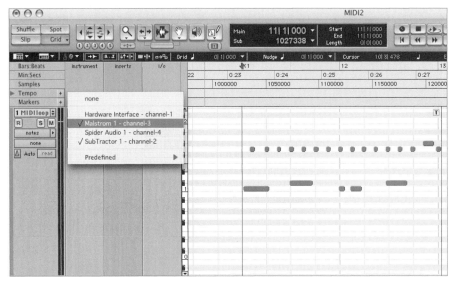

Figure 2.10 Multiple outputs can be chosen by holding Control/Start in the MIDI output selector of the instrument track.

Ticks vs. Samples, Part I

Pro Tools has two distinctly different time-based selection modes: ticks and samples.

MIDI and audio information in Pro Tools is always one or the other. Audio tracks in Pro Tools default as sample-based. Every audio region placed into a track in Pro Tools has a sample location based on the sample rate and where it is on the timeline. MIDI tracks default as ticks-based, referring to the resolution of Pro Tools MIDI, which is 960 ticks per quarter note. When you record or edit MIDI in Pro Tools and you are tick-based, you are working with bars and beats–based information. Bars and beats information is relative data in Pro Tools. Instead of being locked to a sample location on the absolute timeline, bars and beats information can move relative to the absolute timeline if the tempo changes. If four bars of 4/4 at 60 BPM take 16 seconds, then four bars of 4/4 at 120 BPM would take 8 seconds.

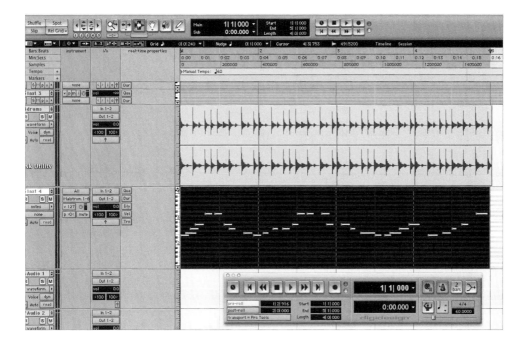

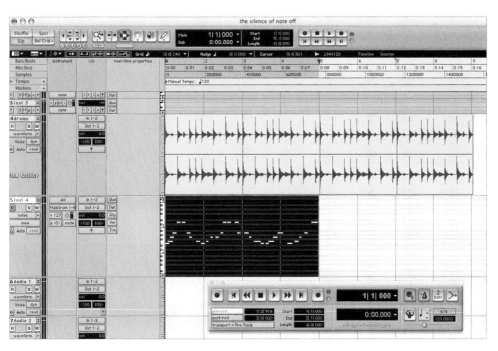

The same track as a sample-based audio track would see 8 seconds as 768,000 samples and 16 seconds as 1,536,000 samples at 96Khz. MIDI and audio tracks can be changed from tick to sample or sample to tick, and you can change this as you create a new track or in the time-based selector of the track in the Edit window, located to the left of the automation mode selector. If you change your MIDI tracks to sample-based time, your data will not move relative to the timeline. Conversely, if you change an audio track to tick-based time, the audio data will change relative to tempo and follow your MIDI (see "Ticks vs. Samples, Part II" in Chapter 3 for more details).

Don't Hate the Player, Hate the Game and Use Input Quantize

If you can think of a cool part but can't play it, don't worry; there are a couple of ways in Pro Tools to play a track into the computer without having the best chops. One method, step record, has been around since MIDI day 1 and is a great choice for entering in difficult passages with just a little music theory knowledge. Another, less-technical method of getting notes into the computer is Input Quantize. Using Input Quantize, you set the note value before you enter it into the sequencer. When you play, the note is placed on the closest selected beat that reflects your note value in the Input Quantize box.

Note: When you are using Input Quantize, Pro Tools will not record your performance the way you are playing it in real time. If you want the feel of your real performance, don't use Input Quantize. To avoid this and still quantize, use Real-Time Properties in an instrument track or go old school in the MIDI operations box and apply your quantization changes.

In Pro Tools, enable Input Quantize (see Figure 2.11) and check out your options. Think about your parts and what rhythms you need to play them. For example, if you want to record a drum part with this method, you need to set up your note values before you play. The production style of kick and hi-hats in electronic music or hip-hop makes this technique a natural. Under the Quantize Grid pull-down, grab a ¼ note and record-enable your MIDI or instrument track. Play at least as fast as ¼ notes and your notes will be put on the grid at ¼-note locations. Play as fast as you can and still your performance will land right on the ¼ note. The hi-hats are the most natural instruments to take advantage of this technique. Go to a ¹⁄₁₆ or even a ¹⁄₃₂ note in the quantize grid and play your heart out. Test different drum sounds to see what works. Some sounds need much more rhythmic flexibility than you can get with this style, so experiment and see. With melodic instruments, ⅛- or ¹⁄₁₆-note bass lines or lead synth lines are a snap to get into Pro Tools. The style of modern electronic music lends itself to this sound.

Additionally, Pro Tools 7 supports real-time groove quantizing, which is a specialized quantize grid from legendary drum machines and programs or even user-definable grooves. In the bigger picture, a *mixture* of Input Quantize and Real-Time Properties quantizing (see the section "Real-Time Properties" earlier in this chapter) allows you to maintain feel in a track while having complete control over every note.

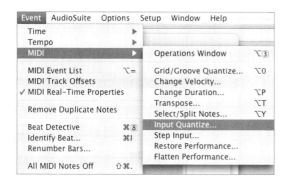

Figure 2.11 Opening Input Quantize

Note: In Pro Tools, enable MIDI Merge in the Transport window to overdub. (See the section "MIDI Loop Recording and MIDI Merge.")

MIDI Loop Recording and MIDI Merge

Loop recording with MIDI is a great way to repeatedly perform a selected passage in a MIDI or instrument track. It works exactly like loop recording on an audio track, as we covered in Chapter 1, "Recording and Microphones." Afterward, you can then compare the takes you recorded and make a comp. But loop recording with MIDI doesn't stop there. Using MIDI Merge mode, you can actually *combine* each pass of your selection. This technique is extremely handy in building complex chords, adding counter melodies, and especially recording a drum sequence drum-machine style.

Loop Recording and Comping MIDI

Loop recording with MIDI provides the same benefits as loop recording audio. You can record as many takes of a selected area on your instrument or MIDI track as you want without stopping playback and then comp the takes together:

1.	Select the area you wish to record on your target instrument or MIDI track. In Figure 2.12, an eight-bar section is chosen.

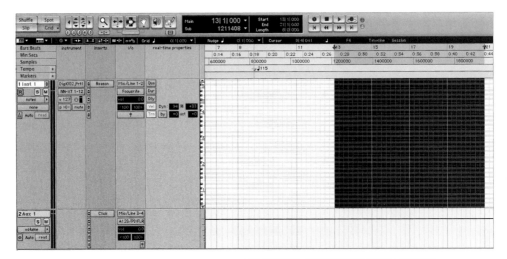

Figure 2.12 An eight-bar selection is made before loop recording.

2. Control+click / Start+click the record button twice to enable Loop Record in the transport window.

3. Record-enable your MIDI track or instrument track as in Figure 2.12. Start recording. When the recording gets to the end of the selection, it will start over at the beginning again and repeat infinitely until you hit stop.

 Note: If you are loop recording yourself, you can always let the first pass go to get situated behind your MIDI instrument.

Once you have recorded multiple takes, you will notice new MIDI regions named after your track in the Regions list. These MIDI regions are actually all of the takes you just recorded with numbered suffixes after each take.

 Note: In Pro Tools 7, all MIDI and audio regions live together in the Regions list on the right column of the Edit window.

If you look ahead to Figure 2.14, you'll see that there were six takes made.

Now you can make a composite out of all of your takes. Remember, for this to work, you must select all three preferences in the "Matching Start Time" Takes List. This is located by choosing Pro Tools > Preferences and selecting the Editing tab (see Figure 2.13).

Figure 2.13 Take Region Name(s) That Match Track Names, Take Region Lengths That Match, and "Separate Region" Operates On All Related Takes are checked here for comping of your looped MIDI recording.

4. Change from Notes view to Region view in your MIDI or instrument track view selector, located underneath the record, solo, and mute buttons in your Edit window track display.

5. Select the entire region last recorded and ⌘+click / Ctrl+click on the MIDI region with the selector tool. You will see a list of all the previous takes (see Figure 2.14). Using this method, all five of the takes can be called up one at a time in the track to compare and contrast.

6. Use ⌘+E / Ctrl+E to separate the region at various locations and create a final comped MIDI region out of all of the takes.

Because you chose "Separate Region" Operates On All Related Takes in the preferences, every splice you make cuts through all of the regions. This makes it easy to pick and choose the best parts of all the takes and comp them together.

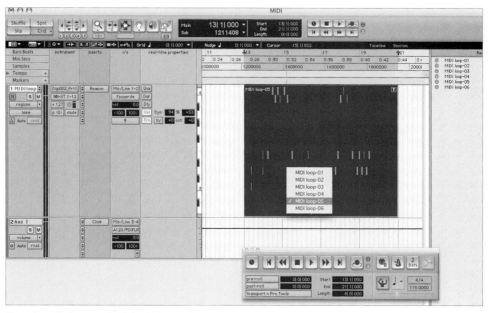

Figure 2.14 The loop-recorded Related Takes are shown here in the pull-down menu.

Loop Recording MIDI and Merging Takes Drum-Machine Style

By using the MIDI Merge mode while loop recording, you can record multiple passes and combine all of your performances into one MIDI region. Beat makers familiar with old-school drum machines love this mode because this is how many sequencing drum machines operate. The key to making this work is to actually *turn off* Loop Record in the transport window.

Note: Merging MIDI data will not work if Loop Record is enabled.

Here's how to use MIDI Merge mode while loop recording:

1. Enable Loop Playback by using the keyboard combination Shift+⌘+L / Shift+Ctrl+L.
2. Turn on MIDI Merge in the Transport window (numeric keypad 9), as in Figure 2.15.
3. Make a selection of how many bars you want to record in the target instrument or MIDI track.
4. Every time the selection loops, you can add notes to your performance. Figures 2.16 through 2.18 show the step-by-step building of a drum track using MIDI Merge. All three parts are done here while playback is looped and the MIDI data is merged one part at a time.

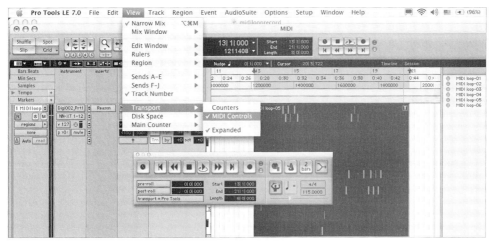

Figure 2.15 MIDI Merge mode is enabled in the transport window. To show these MIDI controls in your Transport, enable them from the View menu.

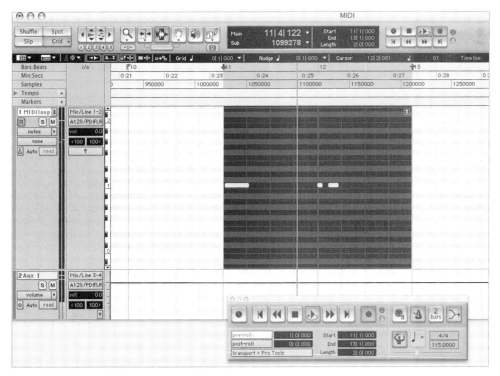

Figure 2.16 A kick drum MIDI sequence is recorded in the first pass.

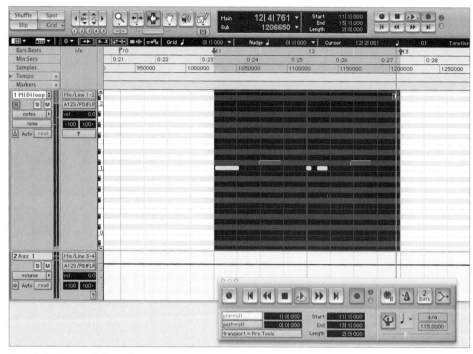

Figure 2.17 The snare is dropped in on pass two.

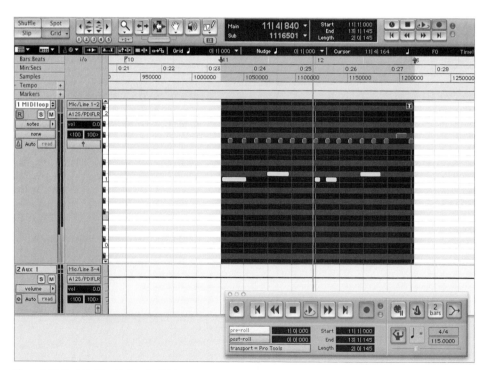

Figure 2.18 The hi-hat is added on the third pass.

The Many Reasons for Reason

The year is 1995. Look into any commercial MIDI studio and what do you see? Rack after rack of samplers, drums machines, keyboards, and controllers. Great fun but very expensive, difficult to maintain, and subject to the whims of MIDI. A large selection of keyboards and sounds keeps a studio in business. Hardware keyboards are still around and will be for quite awhile, but in the past few years software keyboards have come a long way. So have computers. Without the advancement in computing power, we would never hear the kind of sound a Reason Combinator can produce. In the span of a decade, computers and software programs changed the music industry. Large keyboard collections are being replaced with NASA-like computers, huge hard drives, and big sample libraries. A small home studio might have more sounds than Keith Emerson and Pink Floyd combined! Reason is ground zero for this movement, from its beginnings as Rebirth to version 3x, Reason has changed the way many people make music. Reason opened the door for the masses to have more sounds than you can shake a stick at and the ability to record, edit, automate, and tweak to your heart's delight. Reason has an extensive and bountiful rack of virtual synths, samplers, drum machines, effects, and loop players. Reason and Reason Adapted (bundled with some versions of Pro Tools) give you a practically unlimited supply of MIDI-controllable sounds that can be streamed directly and controlled globally from your Pro Tools session, all for a fraction of the cost of one real-world hardware sampler or sound module.

Recipes for Combining Reason and Pro Tools

Depending on what your workflow and ultimate goal is, there are different ways you can integrate Reason and Pro Tools via ReWire to expand your sonic horizons and take your music into the stratosphere:

- Record audio to your Reason song
- Sequence in Reason, mix in Pro Tools
- Use Reason strictly for its virtual instruments

Record Audio to Your Reason Song

One limitation of Reason is that it cannot record audio. The following method shows how easy it is to ReWire your complete Reason mix into Pro Tools so you can enjoy the benefits of Pro Tools's recording features and combine them with your (or a collaborator's) already well-produced Reason song:

1. In Reason, use the 14-channel mixer called ReMix to mix your song.
2. As shown in Figure 2.19, the output of ReMix is cabled directly into the Reason Hardware Interface, channels 1 and 2 by default.

Figure 2.19 The back of Reason's rack showing a stereo mix cable scheme

 Note: The input channel numbers 1 and 2 on the Reason interface are called Reason Mix-L and Mix-R by the ReWire plug-in window in Pro Tools. Don't let this confuse you; just remember that 1–2 is synonymous with L-R in the world of ReWire.

3. In Pro Tools, on a stereo aux input (named REASON IN in Figure 2.20), choose Reason by way of Multi-Channel Plug-in > Instrument from the aux's inserts in the Inserts view of the Edit window (see Figure 2.20).

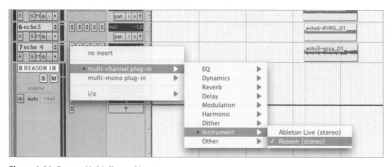

Figure 2.20 Reason Multi-Channel insert

4.   The multi-channel plug-in called ReWire will open and will automatically be routed to Reason Mix-L, Mix-R. This is what you want since you routed the mixed output to the 1–2 channel pair in Reason's hardware interface.

> **Note:** It is a good idea to memorize or write down your Reason song's tempo prior to using ReWire. When ReWired, Reason goes into slave mode and your song will automatically change to whatever tempo is set in Pro Tools. The upside of using Pro Tools to control playback is that you can now make tempo changes during your Reason song, which isn't possible in a stand-alone Reason song.

5.   Your Reason song is now controlled by Pro Tools's playback engine and the audio will stream into Pro Tools via the aux input with the Reason plug-in. You may now add audio tracks to your ReWired Pro Tools session and record away.

Once you are ready to commit to your Reason mix, you will want to record it as audio into your Pro Tools session. This is referred to as "printing your Reason tracks."

6.   Set the output of the REASON IN aux to an available stereo bus (Bus 5–6 in Figure 2.21).

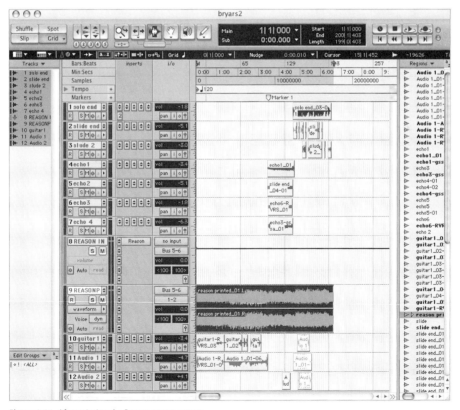

Figure 2.21 After printing the Reason stereo output

7.   Make a new stereo audio track, set its input to the same bus, and record for the length of the Reason song. Figure 2.21 shows the routing and result after recording the stereo Reason mix onto an audio track called Reason Printed.

Note: ReWiring Reason into Pro Tools causes a huge strain on the processing load of your computer. Making tracks inactive is an effective solution.

8.   When you are done printing, disable the aux track by selecting the track and choosing Make Inactive from the Track menu. This breaks the ReWire link and lightens up the processing strain that ReWire is causing. It will also allow you to go back to the Reason song if you ever want to make changes and reprint.

Note: When ReWiring to Reason, always save your Reason song in your Pro Tools session folder. This makes it easy to locate each time you load up your Pro Tools session or reactivate your Reason aux input.

Sequence in Reason, Mix in Pro Tools

Often you compose a piece in Reason and then need to add audio in Pro Tools. With your editing and arranging already done in the Reason sequencer, it's easy to Rewire individual devices into Pro Tools and employ its powerful 48-bit mix engine.

Note: Pro Tools mix engine offers a larger dynamic range and higher fader resolution than Reason's mixer.

Here's how to sequence in Reason and mix in Pro Tools:

1.   When you start your Reason song, do not make a ReMix mixer at the top of your rack. Or, if you have already composed in Reason, remove the ReMix.

2.   Cable the outputs of each instrument individually into the hardware interface at the top of the rack. Be aware that some instruments are mono and others are stereo. Channel 4 is skipped in Figure 2.22 to accommodate for the mono Subtractor and to leave room for other stereo pairs.

3.   In Pro Tools, make enough aux inputs for the channels you have in Reason. In the example in Figure 2.22, there are two stereo and one mono.

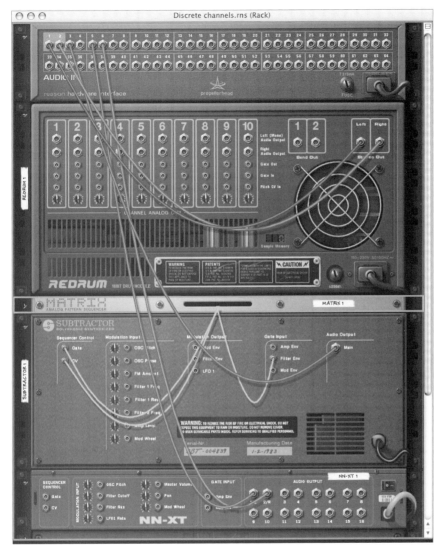

Figure 2.22 Instruments are routed discretely.

Note: If you are married to the effect sends from your ReMix, they will be lost in this transfer. To get around this, you can use a spider in Reason and split the signal from the device to the Reason Hardware Interface (dry) and to the mixer with the effect send (wet). You could then have the effected signal from the ReMix come in to Pro Tools on a return aux track.

4. Open a Reason plug-in on the mono track and multichannel Reason plug-ins on the stereo tracks. As a shortcut, you may select both stereo tracks and hold Option+Shift / Alt+Shift as you instantiate the plug-ins. This will put the multi-channel plug-ins on both selected tracks at once.

5. Label your Aux Input tracks according to the instrument you plan to connect them to.

6. Open the ReWire plug-in windows by clicking on them in the insert panel. You may open more than one at a time by turning off the red target button in the upper-left corner of the plug-ins (see Figure 2.23).

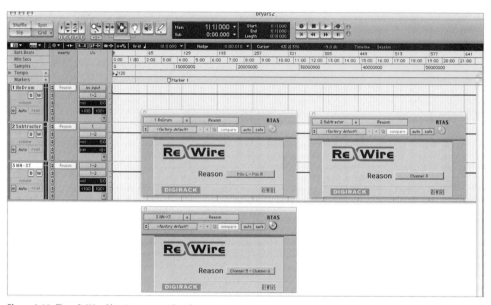

Figure 2.23 Three ReWire Plug-ins connected to three aux inputs

7. As shown in Figure 2.23, the Reason output menus of all three plug-ins have been routed to the appropriate output channels.

Your Reason instrument audio will now stream into Pro Tools. Just as in the method in the section "Record Audio to Your Reason Song," you will eventually want to print these tracks for more efficient use of system resources while mixing. Figure 2.24 shows the end result of routing the aux ReWire tracks to Pro Tools audio tracks and printing them. After this is done, it is always smart to make the aux tracks inactive to alleviate system resources. Making them inactive is better than deleting them in case you need to go back to the original Reason song to change something.

Note: One of the most useful key commands to remember while ReWiring is ⌘ +Tab / Alt+Tab. This will allow you to quickly move between Pro Tools and your ReWired application.

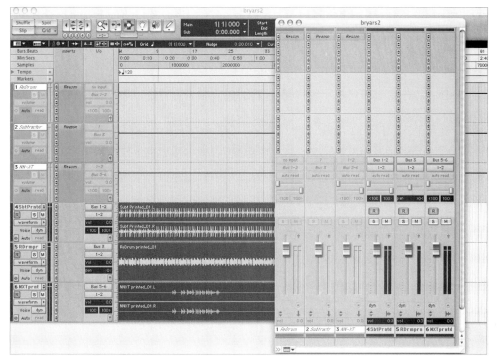

Figure 2.24 After printing individual tracks

Use Reason Strictly for Its Virtual Instruments

If you love Reason's sounds but are more familiar with Pro Tool's MIDI sequencing and mixing features, this method is for you. It provides complete control of every aspect of your production with Pro Tools and uses Reason purely as a glorified virtual rack of instruments.

1. Use the same routing in Reason from the second method (all instruments are connected discretely to the hardware interface).

2. Make three new instrument tracks. This example uses the same Reason song used in the preceding section, so you will make one mono and two stereo instrument tracks to accommodate the ReDrum, Subtractor, and NN-XT instruments in Reason. For more about instrument tracks, see the section "Using Instrument Tracks" earlier in this chapter.

3. Open a Reason plug-in on the mono Instrument track and multichannel Reason plug-ins on the stereo Instrument tracks. As a shortcut, you may select both stereo tracks and hold Option+Shift / Alt+Shift as you instantiate the plug-ins. This will put the multichannel plug-ins on both selected tracks at once.

4. Label your instrument tracks according to the instrument you plan to connect them to.

5. Open the ReWire plug-in windows by clicking on them in the Inserts view of the Edit window. You may open more than one at a time by turning off the red target button in the upper-left corner of the plug-ins (see Figure 2.25).

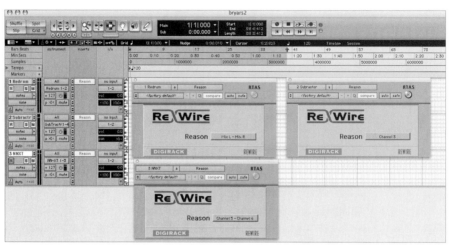

Figure 2.25 Open plug-in windows routed to their respective ReWire channels

6. Pull down the Reason output menu in each of the plug-ins and select the appropriate output channels (see Figure 2.25).

7. Make sure that the Instruments view is showing in either the Mix or Edit window. If not, choose it by selecting View > Edit Window > Instruments View or View > Mix Window > Instruments View.

8. Use the MIDI output selector to send and receive MIDI on the appropriate ReWired device. You will get a list here of all the instruments in your Reason song. Be aware that you will see all devices in the rack (see Figure 2.26).

Figure 2.26 The MIDI output selector showing Reason instruments

If the MIDI input selector of the instrument tracks are connected to an available attached MIDI input device (like a MIDI keyboard), you will now be able to play and record MIDI into the instrument track in Pro Tools and use the sounds from Reason's virtual rack.

To get full MIDI control of Reason devices from Pro Tools, it is necessary to turn off all MIDI input in Reason's sequencer's In column. See Figure 2.27 for more info.

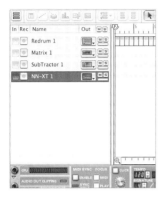

Figure 2.27 Make sure all of the MIDI inputs in Reason are turned off for full Pro Tools MIDI control of Reason instruments.

In the end, it is best to print these sounds to Pro Tools audio tracks for mixing. To do this, bus the output of your instrument tracks to the input of separate audio tracks and record. Figure 2.28 shows a session after the instruments tracks have been routed and printed to audio tracks. Don't forget to make the instrument tracks inactive after this is done to alleviate system resources.

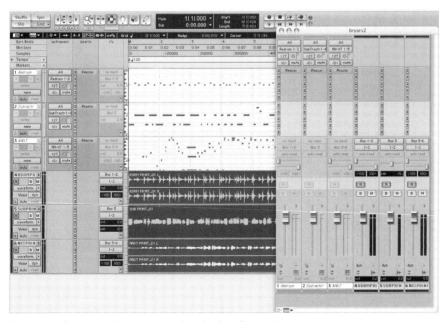

Figure 2.28 After printing the instrument tracks and making them inactive

Note: Sometimes it is creative and groovy to use Reason's ReDrum via ReWire as a more interesting time-keeper than the Pro Tools click. In the end, you may even keep the ReDrum part as a rhythmic element in your final mix, so print it to a track and don't look back!

Farming Out to Other Programs

Unfortunately, you cannot ReWire host applications to each other, such as Logic to Pro Tools or Pro Tools to Digital Performer. There may come a time when you have an awesome piece of music composed in Pro Tools but the allure of a certain sound from another program is very tempting. This is not a problem. With a few simple workaround steps, it is easy to get all the best sounds from your favorite audio applications into your Pro Tools session. The following steps will show how to farm out to Apple's Logic Pro, but the same approach may be used for Digital Performer, Cubase, Acid, and so on:

1. If your song doesn't start at the beginning of the timeline, place your edit cursor at the beginning of the first region and press Enter on the numeric keypad to make a marker called START at the exact beginning of your song (see Figure 2.29).

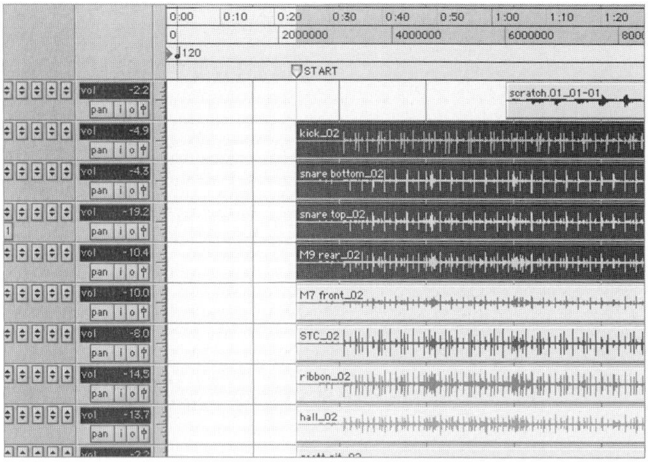

Figure 2.29 This marker will help identify the start point of the song.

2. Select your entire song starting exactly from the designated START marker.

3. Use File > Bounce to Disc to make a temporary mix of your song. You will use this as a reference to play to in Logic, so make sure all the instruments you need to hear are included in the mix.

4. Save and quit Pro Tools and launch Logic.

5. Make sure that the new song file in Logic is set up with the same sample rate and audio file type and tempo as your Pro Tools session.

6. Import the bounced file to the beginning of the timeline (bar 1) in Logic. (Logic supports drag and drop from the browser.)

7. Record the instrument of your liking in Logic to the mix. Figure 2.30 shows how an EVP88 keyboard sound was played via MIDI to add a vintage Rhodes electric piano sound to the song.

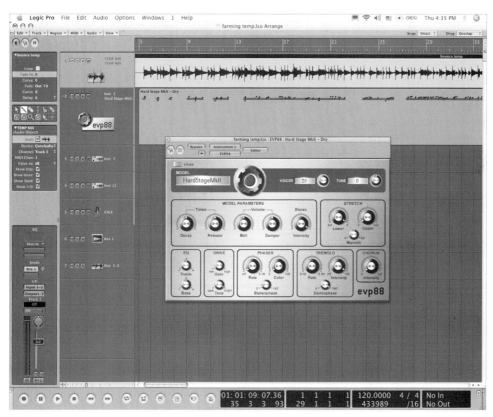

Figure 2.30 Logic's EVP88

8. After recording, solo only the track or tracks you recorded in Logic and bounce them to disc, keeping the same sample rate and bit depth you used in your original Pro Tools session.

9. Make sure you trim the MIDI region in Logic all the way back to match the exact start point of the imported temp mix region (in this case, bar 1). This will ensure that you will be able to sync it up when you go back into Pro Tools.

 Note: If your MIDI region doesn't start at the beginning of the song, the bounce will not sync up properly, so make sure you edit it to start at exactly the same start point as the bounced file.

10. Use File > Import > Audio to Track or drag and drop the new bounced file into an available audio track in your Pro Tools song. Spot the region exactly to the point you designated with the START marker.

 Note: Use Spot mode in Pro Tools to manually place the imported region at an exact numeric location in the timeline.

Everything should be perfectly in sync and the new essential sounds are added to your masterpiece!

Import and Export MIDI between Applications

The pattern-based sequencers in Reason can generate the pulsating, driving, and mesmerizing rhythms distinctive to electronic music.

They are a great resource for producing MIDI data for drums, bass, and leads. The ReDrum and Matrix pattern sequencers are capable of holding 32 different patterns, so you have lots of room to create. Matrix and ReDrum data cannot be exported until the data is taken to a track. It is then fair game to export and start the fun:

1. In the ReDrum, create at least two patterns and copy the patterns to track. If you know the arrangement of your song, use the left and right locators in the Reason sequencer to determine where the data goes. You can assemble your song very easily this way after you have created the patterns.

2. Create a Combinator and attach a Matrix. Load a bass patch into the Combinator and sequence at least two patterns that match your drum patterns. Copy the pattern to track with the same method as the ReDrum and label the tracks.

3. Create another Combinator and attach another Matrix. Load a lead synth patch into the Combinator and sequence at least two patterns that work with the drums and bass. Follow the same method you used in step 2 and copy the patterns to track.

4. Select File > Export MIDI File. Label your file and save it to an easily located destination.

There are two ways to bring MIDI into Pro Tools: You can import MIDI to a track or MIDI to the Regions list.

Importing MIDI to a track places the data on a MIDI track with an inactive output assignment. Anytime you see the output assignment in italics, you know the track is inactive.

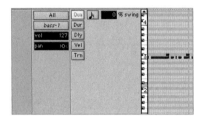

Importing MIDI to the Regions list places your data into the Regions list but not into a track. This allows you to choose what kind of a track will run the show. Create the appropriate track type and drag the data right on in.

Once the data is in the track, select your keyboard from the MIDI output selector and choose the keyboard you wish to revoice the data to. If you have data from the ReDrum, a choice drum synth to voice it to is Stylus RMX from Spectrosonics. Unbelievable sounds and endless possibilities! Let's not overlook our hardware friends either. Revoice a ReDrum pattern to an MPC, an 808, or an E6400 and live a little. If the data is from the Matrix, how about using Trilogy from Spectrosonics? Or an Access virus? Or NI's FM7? Reason can work with other keyboards on its own but in a much more limited way. This is a step beyond ReWiring as well, because you are working with the raw MIDI data and can do with it as you please, whereas in ReWire mode, you bring in the audio channel and can process the audio stream, but not MIDI.

When you are importing ReDrum data into Pro Tools, remember that the ReDrum has only 10 channels, so if you revoice the data to an instrument with more than 10 channels, you may have to remap the sounds in the new instruments to get what you want. Sometimes you get lucky and sometimes accidents in music are a good thing.

 Note: ⌘+click / Ctrl+click on the keys in the track height selector to preview sounds in a MIDI track.

However you revoice the data, there is one more layer to consider. If you ReWire Reason into the session, you can combine the original tracks and the new tracks from the other keyboards together and create numerous possibilities when editing and mixing. This is a great way to mix different soft synths together to get more contrasting texture. Too much from one keyboard can sound a little thin and recognizable.

Cut Off That Frequency!

One of the foremost powers of MIDI is its real-time control over the parameters of a synth. Breathe some life into your sounds with some MIDI manipulation. In the MIDI code, controller 74 is cutoff or frequency, and 71 is resonance. You can access and modulate these controllers in Pro Tools 7:

1. Create an instrument track.

2. In the track view selector (under the record, solo, and mute buttons), in the track choose Controllers > Add/Remove Controller.

3. In the Automated MIDI Controllers prompt box, enable Controllers (64–101). This allows you to address the MIDI functions programmed between 64 and 101 in the MIDI code.

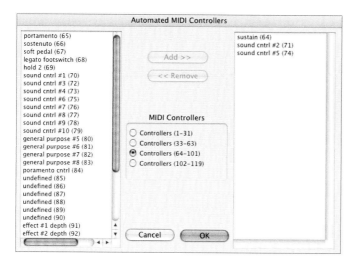

4. Double-click 71 and 74 in the left column and click OK.

    Now you need sound, and since Reason is a great program and comes with some Pro Tools versions, it's a natural choice.

5. Open Reason and create a Subtractor. (See the section "The Many Reasons for Reason" earlier in this chapter for information on how to open Reason into Pro Tools.)

6. In your Pro Tools MIDI track, choose your Reason device from the MIDI output selector, and then go back to the track view selector and select controllers again. Now you should see the new controllers listed as targets (see Figure 2.31).

These two controllers are the rice and beans of the electronic and hip-hop worlds. Can you say filter sweep? On the front of Subtractor there are two filter faders labeled Freq. and Res. Through the magic of MIDI, these are controllers 71 and 74. Old school... You don't have to set up anything on the Subtractor or in Reason for this to work; it's just MIDI. Automating filters is what it's all about. The ability to automate your tracks is paramount in modern music production, whether it's volume or pitch bend or cutoff or mute.

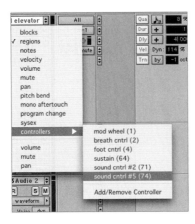

Figure 2.31 The controller pull-down menu now includes controllers 71 and 74.

7. In Grid mode, choose a grid value and use the Pencil tool to draw in your filter sweep. Choose between the seven different modes (see Figure 2.32) and use what makes sense in your track.

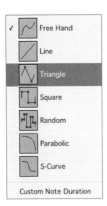

Figure 2.32 The expanded Pencil tool's pop-up window

A long sweep is best with the Line tool for an even sweep. Volume tricks with the square wave give the gated effect, and the triangle wave is great for panning whatever you throw at it. Try a couple of different note values for each action to get your feet wet.

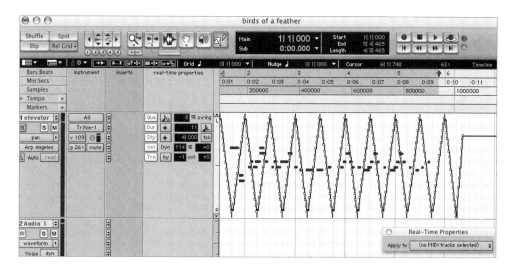

With cutoff and res, you know a couple members of the MIDI code, but what if you want to know more? Most keyboards publish a MIDI implementation chart that documents how the sound maker interprets the MIDI code. Reason is no exception to this rule, and in the main level of the software folder there lays the MIDI chart. This chart tells which MIDI number controls what Reason device function. For example, undefined controller 23 controls Osc 1 Fine Tune in Subtractor. The MIDI chart connects the dots from code to device function and allows you to automate almost anything in Reason from Pro Tools.

Note: Components of MIDI tracks such as volume or pan that can be automated later as printed audio tracks in Pro Tools will have a much higher resolution. MIDI has a range of 128 while at 24 bits; sampled audio has a range of 16,777,216. However, if you are automating any purely MIDI function such as modulation, pitch bend, or a filter sweep, you must do that as MIDI.

Advanced Instrument Research: Digidesign Virtual Keyboards

In 2005, Digidesign took its first steps toward becoming a player in the software-based synth game by acquiring the German virtual keyboard maker Wizoo and creating a new division called Advanced Instrument Research, or A.I.R. Digidesign has released two keyboards to start, hopefully with more to come. If the first two are any indication, good things are ahead. The first release is the free virtual keyboard Xpand! For a first release, this four-part analog/digital-style synth delivers great sound quality, programmability, and a huge library of presets. The second release from A.I.R. is Hybrid. Hybrid is a fully programmable and wicked-sounding analog-style two-part synth offering three oscillators, tons of modulation, step sequencing, multiple effects, and the ability to thoroughly explore the electronic domain. The routing options for the modulation section alone make this synth worth the price.

Xpand! beyond the Presets

Xpand! is a rich-sounding four-part multi-synthesis-style virtual keyboard.

You can combine both the analog-style waveforms with the digital wavetables as you load sounds into the four parts, creating complex sounds with little effort. From wavetable to FM synthesis and from virtual analog synthesis to sample playback, you can mix and match. Xpand! is capable of delivering sounds ranging from natural-sounding acoustic instruments to the wildest-sounding electronica. Each part has separate filtering, arpeggiation, modulation, level, pan, and two FX sends. Most every parameter on the Xpand! can be easily assigned to knobs or faders on a control surface or MIDI controller, and most every parameter on the face of the synth can be automated on a MIDI or Instrument track. The interface of this keyboard is both elegant and simple, making it a breeze and a joy to use.

Xpand! is broken into three basic sections. The top part of the keyboard holds the rotary knobs Xpand! calls Smart knobs and the Smart Knob Assignment Lists. When you choose a part in the Smart Knob Assignment Lists, Xpand! opens that part to edit. The Smart knobs are configured for each part and control parameters native to the style of synthesis selected. If your part is a sample, the knobs control parameters like sample Start Time, Cutoff, and a basic envelope. If you are using an analog-style part, your parameters will include OSC volume, Cutoff Resonance, and a basic envelope.

The middle of the synth holds the selection tabs for the four Edit pages and the Smart window, which contains information about whatever you have selected or are working on. There are Edit pages for the Mixer, Modulation, Arpeggiator, and FX.

The bottom part of the synth holds the programming windows for the Edit pages and the four slots to load parts.

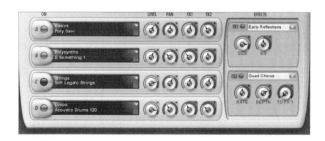

This is where you will set volume, pan, and send FX levels in the MIX tab, set program modulation with the MOD tab, set up arpeggiators in the ARP tab, and load and edit FX with the FX tab. As you change Edit tabs, the Part Selector, On/Off button, and Name field stay the same and the different edit functions change on the right side of the keyboard.

Assigning Xpand!

Here's how to assign Xpand! Smart knobs and all other parameters to MIDI control:

1. Right-click on the desired function. If the function supports Learn mode, you will see it in the pull-down list. Choose Learn and move your controller knob, fader, or wheel. The fader, knob, or wheel will now control the parameter and

you can record the movement as automation. This is a good first step when automating from a control surface or MIDI controller.

2.   To reset a parameter to no controller, right-click the parameter and choose Forget.

Automating Xpand!

To automate Xpand! controls in Pro Tools, follow these steps:

1.   Choose your parameters to automate by opening the Plug-In automation enable prompt box at the top of the plug-in window and choosing the parameters you want to automate. Neither Xpand! nor Hybrid allows you to enable automation with the three-finger salute on the face of the keyboard.

2.   Choose an automation mode and start the track. Any moves you make with your input device will be recorded. Your automation playlists are located in the Track View selector window in the Edit window. You will have one playlist per controller.

Creating Your Own Sounds and Modifying Presets

To create your own patches from scratch, start by loading parts into the parts window. Xpand! is so easy to use and program that you can focus on *making* the sounds more than *how* to make the sounds. It may not be as deep as Hybrid or some other high-end soft synths, but it has a great warm sound, and with its built-in arpeggiators and effects, a mild form of electronic nirvana is easy to achieve. You can have up to four different parts play at once on a single MIDI channel. After you have loaded your parts, you can mix, pan, and more to fine-tune your sound by choosing the MIX tab. Here are some other things you can do:

Move your mix. The MIX tab opens the mixer functions of the keyboard and gives you control for each part over volume, pan, FX 1 and 2 send levels, and the MIDI input control for transpose, fine-tuning and setting up key ranges for each part. A basic part of sound design is control over all of the elements. Choose the part to work on by clicking the letter next to the On/Off button in the load window or by clicking the Smart Knob Assignment List at the top left of the keyboard.

Modulate your music. The MOD tab opens the modulation matrix where you can set up the effects for the modulation wheel with both rate and depth and assign a destination for aftertouch modulation. You can assign the aftertouch to wave, pitch, volume, or filter.

Arrange your arpeggiators. The ARP tab opens the arpeggiator window where you assign a style and rate for each part. You can have up to 4 different arpeggiations at once. You get 27 different modes of arpeggiation and all get assignable rates.

Fix your FX. The FX tab opens the FX page and shows the two FX destinations. FX1 and FX2 have access to the same effect bank, but FX2 has the ability to send the FX back into FX1 for more processing. The effects section isn't the best part of Xpand!, but it does the job well enough. The programmability of the effects is very limited, with only a few parameters per effect.

Hybrid

Digidesign's second release, Hybrid, is an amazing analog-style and deeply programmable synth that has features that can match most any soft synth on the market today.

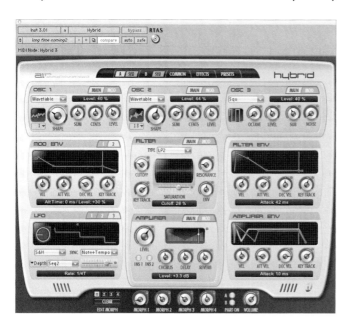

Hybrid may not quite top the incredible sound of Reaktor from Native Instruments, but it makes up for it in ease of use. The basic sound engine is a mix of analog-type waveforms and digital wavetables. The mixture of the two styles creates a sound that is hard to get from a single keyboard.

Hybrid is a two-part synth with two oscillators per voice and a third for sub generation. The oscillators have a wave-shaping function that lets you continue to alter the sound even after you have chosen your wavetable or waveform. This is a great feature for sound design and is just plain fun. The oscillator section has basic tuning with semi tones and cents and a level adjustment. To get to the oscillators choose the Show Part A or B Page tab next to the SEQ tab at the top of the synth. In addition to the oscillators, the Part Pages hold the editing controls for most of the synth programming parameters.

Three assignable modulation sources and destinations are available for all three oscillators, the filter, and the amplifier section. The modulation possibilities are many and easy to program. There are also two modulation envelopes and three LFOs (low frequency oscillators) per part, giving endless possibilities. The modulation and routing so deeply ingrained in the basic structure of the synth give the opportunity to create sound that is as deep, complex, and unusual as you dare. Turn some knobs, move the faders, assign some destinations, and make some cool sound.

The filtering block is set up a little differently than most soft synths and offers some interesting and easy programming choices. Once you get sound to the filter section, with embedded modulation and several different filter types you have many options. The Filter Saturation slider is very cool and delivers variations of sound beyond what most filter sections can achieve. Map the Filter Saturation slider to a Morph knob and sit back and have some fun.

The effects are very usable, but as with Xpand! they are not really the best feature of the keyboard. A total of four effects can be run at once on the two parts and there are three global effects to use over the entire sound.

Instead of an arpeggiator, both parts have step sequencers that can run separately or be linked together. The step sequencer is powerful, intuitive, and fast, allowing you to draw in both notes and velocity like in Reason and also giving you two selectable controller windows to further modulate the sequence. The step sequencer rules in this synth.

Many controls in Hybrid can be mapped to a function called Morph. Morph is a feature that lets you assign different controls, such as waveshapes, filters, and envelopes, to a set of four Smart knobs, modulating anything assigned to them. If you map eight different controls to one knob and turn it, interesting things can happen!

The preset page is much more interesting than a normal bank of presets would be. You get the ability to modulate and manipulate right there on the Preset Page. Adjust A and B controls the OSC, Filter, and AMP sections of Parts A and B. The functions are more basic than if you are in a Part Page but serve well enough in this mode.

The Common page hold some cool Unison features and Morph assignments along with more modulation and pitch control. There is also a master FX section for pitch and controllers.

The routing and automation possibilities for the synth, including automating envelope ADSR, is downright scary and exciting at the same time. Hybrid is sample-accurate so there is no slipping in the timing of the oscillators to blur the sound. Xpand! limits your editing at the waveform level but Hybrid is all about that. The interface is easy to understand and at least somewhat intuitive. The power of this synth is not hidden too deeply beneath the surface. The presets are good as presets go, but under the hood is where the fun lies.

Assigning Controls to Hybrid

Follow these steps to assign automation and MIDI controls to Hybrid:

1. The same method as with Xpand! works to map knobs to knobs from a MIDI device or a control surface. Right-click on the parameter and choose Learn from the pull-down menu.

2. Turn the knob or move the fader you want to use to control that function. Hybrid will now match that controller to that function. In the same pull-down menu, you can find the continuous controller number for that parameter and you can assign the function to a morph Smart knob.

As with Xpand!, most everything in Hybrid can be automated with a mouse, control surface, or MIDI controller and can then be edited with great precision in the automation playlist.

Automating Hybrid Controls

Here's how to automate Hybrid controls in Pro Tools:

1. Choose your parameters to automate by opening the plug-in automation enable prompt box at the top of the plug-in window and picking the parameters you want to automate. Neither Xpand! nor Hybrid allows you to enable automation with the three-finger salute on the face of the keyboard.

2. Choose an automation mode and start the track. Any moves you make with your input device will be recorded. Your automation playlists are located in the Track View selector window in the Edit window. You will have one playlist per controller.

Assigning Morph Controls

To assign Morph controls, follow these steps:

1. Right-click on any usable parameter and choose any of the four Morph controls.

2. This will assign all the parameters you wish to control to this knob. The Morph control knobs are on the bottom strip of the keyboard. Turning the Morph control knob will change all associated parameters. This is a very cool feature and can of course be automated as well to really dial in your changes.

3. If you want to clear the assigned controls, you can click the Clear button above the Edit Morph label. If you want to mute the Morph controls on either part, click off the light next to the right of the Morph section.

Programming the Step Sequencer

Follow these steps to program the Step Sequencer:

1. Choose the SEQ tab of the part you wish to sequence to open the Step Sequencer page.

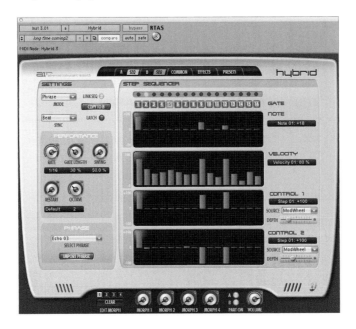

2. Choose the mode to input your sequence. If you choose Step Sequence, you will hear exactly what you enter in the Step Sequencer when you play a note. This is a basic pattern-based sequencer and is easy to use. There are nine modes to input data, including a Phrase mode that lets you load preexisting phrases and even import standard MIDI files as input. Playing notes through the different input modes is a good way to get a feel for what they all offer.

3. If you want to hold the note after you let go of the key, enable Latch. This a good way to run the sequence and tweak the settings since the note will play endlessly.

4. To have both parts play the same sequence, enable the Link SEQ button.

5. Choose your sync mode. You can choose Beat, First Note, or Each Note. Try all three to hear the difference.

6. In the Performance window, choose the rate at which you want the sequence to play. You can also adjust the gate and give the sequence some swing. The gate time can be automated and will drastically alter your sound. This is a great technique for adding dynamics and motion to your sequence. Using the restart knob, you can dictate the number of steps before the sequence starts over.

7. If you choose Phrase mode as input, you can load a preset from the Phrase menu or a standard MIDI file from the Import Phrase button. Load a phrase and generate a sequence from your selection.

8. Draw in your notes in the Note window. If you want to turn off a note, click the number to mute it. If you don't do this, all notes will play.

9. Draw in your velocity in the Velocity window. This is a very Reason-like use of velocity and a breeze to use. Hold the Shift key to draw in a line.

10. Control 1 and Control 2 offer pattern-based modulation with selectable sources and adjustable depth. This gives even more flexibility to programming the sequencer and can help keep your patterns from sounding too stiff by pulsing and modulating with different sources to keep your sound changing over time.

11. Add FX to your sequences by choosing the Effects tab and loading and programming up to two inserts per part. The effects section can turn the basic step sequence into a more complex rhythm and add overall dynamics.

Saving Patches

Here's how to save your own patches to use in any session. This is a synth that begs to be taken well beyond the presets into custom tweaker heaven.

1. When you are happy with your sound, open the Settings menu next to the Librarian menu.

2. If you are saving something that started as a preset, choose Save As to save a copy. If the sound is from scratch, then choose Save. If you save it into the Root Setting folder, you can use it in any session. If you want to use it outside of your own system, change the save plug-ins settings to Session and the sound will be placed in your session folder.

> **Note:** Continuous controllers are MIDI messages with a value from 0-127. These values can dynamically change over time, allowing real-time control over MIDI functions like modulation, pitch bend, and cutoff. Too many continuous controllers can clog the MIDI data stream and affect the timing of your MIDI performance. To prevent this you can thin the MIDI data in Pro Tools or delete unnecessary controllers in the MIDI Event List.

Editing: Slip, Shuffle, and Spot Your Way Home

3

When it comes to audio editing, Pro Tools lets its true colors fly and leaves other audio applications in the dust. Big-time Pro Tools users relish the ability to accurately view and edit audio regions down to the sample level nondestructively. Peering into the future of digital audio, where audio and MIDI data seamlessly relate to one another in a timely fashion, accurate editing provides the key to unlocking many of these powerful new features. The advanced audio editing tools included in Pro Tools 7 can chop up audio regions collectively and precisely to take full advantage of the new and improved tempo grid. This chapter will give some in-depth approaches to using and understanding the editing tools that make this all possible.

Chapter Contents

Strip Silence

Beat Detective

Grouping and Looping Regions

Tick-Based Regions

Pro Tools 7 and REX Files

In addition, this chapter will focus on looping recipes, hidden power-user editing commands, and getting the most out of the four different editing modes to enhance productivity and speed. Time to slice and dice!

Global and Session Settings

Every program has its pros and cons and Pro Tools is no different. It helps to be aware of what functions are global Pro Tools preferences that control settings for all sessions and what preferences are session-specific. Pro Tools stores global user settings in a preference file located for Mac users in User\Library\Preferences. On Windows systems, the file is located at C:\Documents and Settings\[your directory]\Application Data\Digidesign. Pro Tools can be configured in many different ways to accommodate the different types of jobs you throw at it. Here's a list of some crucial global user settings that can make or break your session:

Link Timeline and Edit With Link Timeline and Edit enabled (see Figure 3.1), the edit cursor or selection dictates where playback begins unless you use any pre-roll. The quick keys to enable Link Timeline and Edit are Shift+/ for Mac and Windows. With Link Timeline and Edit deselected, your playback will start from the number indicated in the Main Counter. When the Edit and Timeline are unlinked, the session will play from this position no matter where you click your edit cursor in the track.

Figure 3.1 Link Timeline and Edit enabled

Timeline Insertion Follows Playback (Setup > Preferences > Operation tab) Enable this and the cursor plays from where you stopped playback, just as a tape deck would. It also will deselect your selection after every playback; it's not the mode you want if you are editing the same selections over and over, but it's great if you are charting a song or auditioning entire tracks. (See Figure 3.2.)

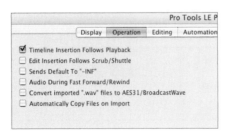

Figure 3.2 Timeline Insertion Follows Playback

Scrolling options In LE you have three options: None, After Playback, and Page. The scrolling options are found by choosing Options > Scrolling.

None turns scrolling off and is useful if you are working on a particular selection and don't want the screen to move but you can still hear other parts of the track.

After Playback scrolls to the cursor after playback stops.

Page is a common setting that allows the screen to follow the playback cursor.

On HD systems you have two more options—Center Playhead and Continuous:

Center Playhead makes the playback cursor turn into a blue playhead. During playback, all tracks visually move under the playhead. The edit cursor is not linked at all to playback. Film mixers like this scrolling option because it allows them to see what is coming up.

Continuous is like center playhead, only the edit cursor and selections are linked to the playback.

Auto-Name Separated Regions (Setup > Preferences > Editing tab) When you cut or capture a new region, this preference tells Pro Tools either to name the new region automatically (checked) or to display a prompt box for you to label the region manually (not checked). (See Figure 3.3.)

			Pro Tools LE Preferences				
Display	Operation	**Editing**	Automation	Processing	MIDI	Machine Control

☐ Recall Memory Location Selection at Original Track
☐ Auto-Name Memory Locations When Playing
☑ Auto-Name Separated Regions
☐ Region List Selection Follows Edit Selection
☐ Edit Selection Follows Region List Selection

Crossfade Preview Pre-Roll: 3000 msec
Crossfade Preview Post-Roll: 3000 msec

Figure 3.3 Auto-Name Separated Regions enabled

Screen setups Tools remembers the setup of your screen when you last saved the session. This includes pop-up windows like the Transport bar. If you close the Edit window and leave the Mix window open, then the next time you open a session that will be the arrangement.

AutoSave (Setup > Preferences > Operation > AutoSave) Why not? Survey says leave this on at all times (see Figure 3.4). You can tell AutoSave how often to back up and how many backups to keep. This has saved so many engineers and producers it's like digital penicillin.

AutoSave
☑ Enable Session File Auto Backup
Keep: 10 most recent backups
Backup every: 5 minutes

Figure 3.4 AutoSave preference

Levels of Undo Multiple levels of undo are pretty much standard in this day and age in most computer applications. Pro Tools gives you up to 32 levels of undo (see Figure 3.5) in the Setup > Preferences > Editing tab, but beware; sometimes undoing back too many steps is not worth losing the other work you have just undone. Choose wisely, grasshopper.

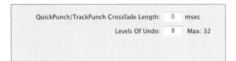

Figure 3.5 Levels of Undo in Pro Tools

Input Quantize You can access this setting by choosing Event > MIDI > Operations Window > Input Quantize. When enabled, it quantizes your MIDI performance on the way into the computer. If you don't know that Input Quantize is enabled, the part you play will be quantized to whatever the current grid value is set to. Undo just takes away the recording, not the quantizing (ouch). Like all of these listed preferences, this is a global preference and will stay turned on from session to session, so beware.

Keyboard Focus

In the world of professional audio, "Time is money" is not just a cliché. Even if you work at home without a producer breathing down your neck, the faster you can act upon what you are thinking, the more creative you can be. Your workflow efficiency and therefore your creativity and productivity can be greatly enhanced with a thorough knowledge of the computer keyboard and keyboard commands. Going a step further, a function in Pro Tools called Keyboard Focus allows the user to bypass the modifier keys altogether and perform commands with a single keystroke. Keyboard Focus determines how the QWERTY keyboard functions and what it controls. It works on the Edit window, Groups List window, and Regions List window. Keyboard Focus is always enabled in one of the three areas and can control only one area at a time.

The Keyboard Focus button for the Edit window (Option+⌘+1 / Alt+Ctrl+1) is located at the top of the Edit window between the Tab to Transient button and the Link Timeline and Edit button.

Continues

Keyboard Focus *(Continued)*

It controls key commands in the Edit window. A need-to-know for power users in Pro Tools: You can perform many of the most common edit functions with a single keystroke. Here's a best-of list (for the entire commands list, look in the Pro Tools 7 manual):

E explodes the selection, blowing it up to full screen and simultaneously turning track size to large. Hit E again to return to normal view.

T zooms in.

R zooms out.

X performs a cut operation.

- (the hyphen key) toggles between waveform and volume view on any audio-based track your edit cursor or selection is in, and toggles between region and note on any instrument track or MIDI track your edit cursor or selection is in.

P moves the selection or cursor up.

; (the semicolon) moves the selection or cursor down.

The numbers 1 through 5 on the QWERTY keyboard recall the five zoom presets.

The Group List Keyboard Focus (Option+⌘+3 / Alt+Ctrl+3) is located on the top right of the Group List pop-up, and when it's enabled, it lets you toggle groups on and off by pressing the group letter on the QWERTY keyboard.

The Region List Keyboard Focus (Option+⌘+2 / Alt+Ctrl+2) is located on the top right of the Region List pop-up, and when it's enabled, it allows you to select regions in the Region List with the QWERTY keyboard. Just type the first letter of any region you wish to select, and that region will become selected. If there is more than one, then type the second letter of the region name, and so on. These three keyboard focuses can be enabled only one at a time.

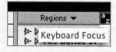

Note: If you work in a facility that has multiple users of the same system, you can set up individual profiles with different preference settings. Because Pro Tools preferences are stored separately in individual user accounts, each user can log in to their personal settings.

Creating the Vital Loop

What does the music on popular radio, your favorite new records, and current film and TV soundtracks have in common? The loop—a short piece of audio that repeats so seamlessly, it sounds like one continuous, well-played performance. In today's digital audio arena, the loop is the most accepted form of musical currency. Loops of all shapes and sizes can be copied and pasted, stretched and shrunk, repeated endlessly, or dropped in just at the right moment. What makes this all possible is the quality of the loop. If edited correctly, a good loop can be thrown into any Pro Tools session and fit right in. Starting with loop selection techniques, then covering loop extraction, and finally loop management, the following sections demonstrate all the important techniques to help you make the perfect loop.

Note: When working on loops, it is best to have Insertion Follows Playback disabled. Uncheck it in the Pro Tools > Preferences > Operation tab. Now your selection will hold when you stop playback and the edit cursor will remain at the start of your selection.

Loop Selection Techniques

The jumping-off point before any loop can be created is the selection. Without a selection, you can't isolate the audio in order to make a loop. Remember that if you are in grid mode, you may not have enough resolution to edit as precisely as you need. Slip mode gives you the finest resolution offered by Pro Tools.

Note: Use the tilde key (~) to toggle between the five editing modes: Slip, Shuffle, Spot, Grid, and Relative Grid.

Shift Selecting

The simplest way to select is to click and drag visually with the Selector tool into your target track(s). Use this technique to get your initial selection for the loop started; however, it is not usually accurate enough on its own.

The Shift key is the most important selection modifier. Once you make your initial selection, hold the Shift key while you click and drag on the left or right side of the selection to move the beginning or end of it earlier or later.

If you want to listen as you select, you can use Shift in combination with the Scrubber tool as you alter the selection. Change your cursor to the Scrubber tool by clicking the Scrubber icon or by pressing the F9 key (see Figure 3.6). Hold Shift as you click and drag left and right on the beginning or end of any selection to move it earlier or later. Additionally, pressing Option/Alt turns the scrub into the Shuttle mode, where it can move faster than real time. The closer you zoom in, the finer the resolution of the Scrubber will be. This method is preferable for those cases when visually selecting the audio just isn't enough. We are working with sound here, after all!

Figure 3.6 The Scrubber tool enabled

Note: When selecting with the Scrubber tool, it is best to enable Insertion Follows Scrub in the Pro Tools > Preferences > Operation tab. This will make your timeline cursor move wherever you scrub.

Numeric Selection

The Edit Selection Indicators are located at the top of the Edit window next to the Main Time Scale (or in the expanded Transport bar). Use these to make or alter a selection by manually typing in a numeric position that describes where you want the selection to begin or end. Double-click any number to highlight its field, and type the new number in. You must press Return or Enter to lock the number in when done. If you know only the begin point or end point, you can type in one of these numbers and then the total length of the selection. For example, if you know that the point at which you want the selection to end is bar 6, beat 3 and you know the total length is 8 bars, enter only those values. Pro Tools will automatically fill in the blank and position the start time accordingly. The units of measurement can change from Bars/Beats, Minutes/Seconds, Samples, or (Timecode, Feet/Frames for HD), depending on what the Main Time Counter is set to. Open the pull-down menu next to Main Time Counter to see the list of options.

Note: Here's a very fast way to change the current selection using your keyboard and the Edit Selection Indicators: Type Keypad/ on the keypad to automatically highlight the first field of the Edit Selection Indicators. Then use the decimal point (Keypad.) to move from field to field. To move down a field, type Keypad/ again. Hit Enter to lock in the changes. These key commands work for the Edit Selection Indicators in the Edit window only. To make these key commands enter values into the Edit Selection Indicators on the Transport bar, you must click on a field before applying the / or decimal keypad shortcut.

Another useful tool embedded in the Edit Selection Indicators box is a calculator. Addition and subtraction gets difficult when dealing with units like Bars and Beats or Timecode, so it can be a lifesaver to have this functionality built right in the same place you can change the selection. To activate the calculator, follow these steps:

1. Highlight a field in the Edit Selection Indicators box by clicking or typing Keypad/.

2. Type Keypad+ to add or Keypad- to subtract.

3. Enter the amount you wish to add or subtract and press Enter to make the calculation.

4. Press Enter a second time to lock in the changes.

Tab to Transient

Tab to Transient mode is a powerful secret weapon in Pro Tools's looping arsenal. It is especially effective when creating loops since the quality of your loops depends on accurately editing to rhythmic transient points.

In the audio world, a *transient* is a sudden change in the amplitude of sound. Visually you will see this reflected as a spike in an audio region in a Pro Tools audio track.

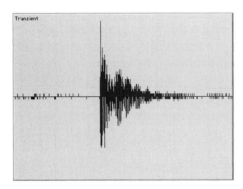

Examples of audio with significant transients are drums, clavinet, gunshot sound FX, congas, hand claps, and plucked strings. Examples of nontransient audio are bowed strings, airplane sound FX, synth pads, and flute.

For looping beats, there is nothing faster and more accurate than selecting with Tab to Transient.

Here's how to use Tab to Transient to make a loop selection:

1. Click the Tab to Transient button beneath the Edit Modes icons (see Figure 3.7). When the button is highlighted blue, Tab to Transient is active and regular tab mode (which moves the edit cursor to the nearest region boundary) is disabled.

2. Click into the target audio region before the point you wish to select.

Figure 3.7 The Tab to Transient button enabled

3. Press the Tab key until the edit cursor moves to the transient point you want your loop to start from. If you move past the point, press Option+Tab / Alt+Tab to move the cursor backward to the desired transient point.

Note: Tab to Transient finds transient points with a nonadjustable threshold. It may find more transient points than you expect, but it rarely misses them. It may be necessary to press Tab repeatedly until the cursor moves to the one you want, but when it gets there, its timing is incredibly accurate.

4. Hold Shift+Tab to move the cursor ahead while making a selection. If you go too far while making a selection, the trick is to Shift+click before the desired end of the selection with the Selector tool and then press Shift+Tab to move it back.

Note: If audio was recorded to a click, or if you used Beat Detective (see the section "Pro Tools on Acid: Tripping with Beat Detective" later in this chapter) to match the tempo grid of your session with the BPM of the target audio, you will find it helpful to create bar-specific loops when selecting with Tab to Transient. If the Main Time Scale is set to Bars and Beats, you will be reminded when you are nearing a 2-, 4-, or 8-bar loop since the time of your selection will be reflected in the total-length box.

Nudge Selecting/Trimming

Nudging in Pro Tools refers to hitting Keypad+ or - to move the cursor, a selection, or a region forward or backward by an amount of time set in the Nudge value pop-up menu (see Figure 3.8).

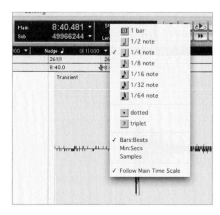

Figure 3.8 The Nudge value pop-up menu showing bar and beat values

Depending what you have selected, Nudge works in different ways. For example, if you have an entire region or multiple regions selected, hitting Keypad+ or - will move the region forward and backward. If you have made just a selection that is shorter than a region, hitting Keypad+ or - will move only the selection forward or backward. However, if you have a selection that is larger than a region, hitting Keypad+ or - will move the enclosed region forward and backward. Here are some ways you can use Nudge in accordance with key commands to make precise selections:

- ⌘+Shift+Keypad+ or - / Ctrl+Shift+Keypad+ or - moves the selection end point forward and backward by the Nudge value.

- Option+Shift+Keypad+ or - / Alt+Shift+Keypad+ or - moves the selection start point forward and backward by the Nudge value.

   You may also use Nudge to trim a region's start or end point by the Nudge value:

- ⌘+Keypad+ or - / Ctrl+Keypad+ or - trims the end point of entirely selected regions.

- Option+Keypad+ or - / Alt+Keypad+ or - trims the start point of entirely selected regions.

- Control+Keypad+ or - / Start+Keypad+ or - moves the media forward or backward inside an entirely selected region. This one is especially useful for dialog editing—try it out, but make sure there is enough underlying media to shift by your Nudge amount or else it will not work.

Selecting on the Fly

It's possible to select audio and make regions while listening to the playback of a track. This method is great for grabbing lots of regions on the fly to work with later. To capture the selection during playback, hit the down arrow ↓ on your keyboard to begin the selection and the up arrow ↑ to end it.

Auditioning Your Selection

No matter what method you use to select your loop, it is essential to efficiently audition your loop while you are creating it. With short loops this is easy; just make sure Loop Playback is enabled in the Options menu and press play. Your selection will loop and it you will be able hear if the loop works.

   If you have a longer loop, it will become tedious to always have to listen to the entire loop to see if the end matches up with the beginning. Selection auditioning actually works in conjunction with your Pre- and Post-Roll settings and the keyboard arrow keys. Using the following key commands, you can cut right to the chase and hear what's going on exclusively at the start and end of your selections:

- Hit ⌘+Keypad1 / Ctrl+Keypad1 to show the Transport bar and enter in a pre- and post-roll amount that is sufficient (start with 1 bar for each). It doesn't matter if Pre-/Post-Roll is actually enabled for this to work.

- $\mathcal{H}$+← / Ctrl+← will play from the start of your selection for the length of the post-roll time you entered.

- $\mathcal{H}$+→ / Ctrl+→ will play after the end of your selection for the length of the post-roll time you entered.

- Option+← / Alt+← will play before the start of your selection for the amount of pre-roll time you entered.

- Option+→ / Alt+→ will play up until the end of your selection for the amount of pre-roll time you entered.

- $\mathcal{H}$+Option+← / Ctrl+Alt+← will play through your selection before and after its start point by the amount of pre- and post-roll time you entered.

- $\mathcal{H}$+Option+→ / Ctrl+Alt+→ will play through your selection before and after its end point by the amount of pre- and post-roll time you entered.

Note: If you are having a hard time telling if your selection is looping properly, try looping playback and leaving the room. When you come back, don't look at the screen, and try to hear the point where the audio repeats (called the loop point). If you can't tell where it begins or ends, you made a good loop. If you can still hear it, you've got more editing to do!

Loop Extraction Techniques

Once you've nailed your loop selection, its time to liberate it from its region. For loop extraction, you have two options:

- Capture Region: $\mathcal{H}$+R / Ctrl+R or Region > Capture. This method does not alter the original audio region in any way. It will prompt you to rename the new region and it will then appear in the Regions list in the right column of the Edit window. Use this if you want to leave the original audio alone and use the loop elsewhere, even in another session.

- Separate Region: $\mathcal{H}$+E / Ctrl+E or Edit > Separate Region > At Selection. This method splices the original audio region at the boundaries of your selection. Pro Tools will prompt you to rename the region and it will also appear under the name you choose in the Regions list. You can make Pro Tools automatically name separated regions by enabling Auto-Name Separated Regions in the Pro Tools > Preferences > Editing tab.

Note: Here's a fast way to separate a region and move your selection: Tap F8 twice or click and hold on the Grabber tool and choose the Separation Grabber (see Figure 3.9). Click and drag your selection to a new location. Pro Tools separates and autonames the new region.

Figure 3.9 The Separation Grabber enabled

Pro Tools 7 has a few new Separate Region options found only in the Edit menu. You can use Edit > Separate Region > At Transients to splice your selection right on the nearest transient points. This uses the same algorithm as Tab to Transient, so if you already made your selection using Tab to Transient, this is redundant. Additionally, you can choose Edit > Separate Region > At Grid to splice your selection on whatever grid resolution you have set in Grid mode.

Note: With Auto-Name Separated Region enabled in the preferences, you'll be able to separate a lot of little regions (like individual drumbeats) very quickly without stopping to rename them all. Pro Tools will give each new region a numeric suffix.

Now that you have your loop separated, you can use it in your current session by dragging it out into an audio track from the Regions list.

Export Selected

Using loops in your current session is cool, but you may wish to dump them out of Pro Tools altogether. Why do this? Because now that you have a perfect loop made, you can bring it into Propellerhead's Recycle (Pro Tools 7 has direct REX file support) or even make it into an Apple Loop for use in Logic Pro or GarageBand.

Follow these steps to get your region out of Pro Tools and into a new location on your hard drive:

1. Select your entire separated looped region.

2. Press Shift+⌘+K / Shift+Ctrl+K to get the Export Selected dialog (see Figure 3.10). This can also be found in the Region List pop-up menu under Export Regions as Files.

3. Choose the appropriate file type, format, bit depth, and sample rate for your exported region.

The best thing to think about here is, what are you planning to do with your loop? For example, if you wish to use it in another Pro Tools session, then you should keep the stereo files multi-mono since Pro Tools cannot directly support stereo interleaved files. Soundtrack Loop Utility and Recycle, however, both have direct support for stereo interleaved files. You will see the conversion quality pull-down menu here only when you are changing sample rates. The options range from Low (Fastest) to Tweak Head (Slowest). The best option takes the longest here, but not by much. Unless you are in a crazy rush and don't care about audio quality, we suggest you always set this to Tweak Head. If you weren't already a Tweak Head, you wouldn't be reading this book.

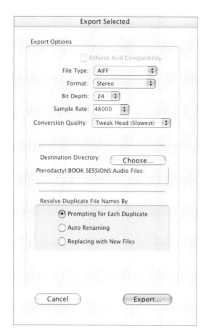

Figure 3.10 Export Selected offers a myriad of options for exporting regions.

Note: A pro user tip for Export Selected Regions: Use it to convert and export multiple regions after recording a large number of drum samples, hours of VO recording, or even sound FX recording sessions—anything with a lot of separated regions involved. Exporting Selected Regions allows you to convert on export *without* bouncing in real time. It will also apply Dither and Noise Shaping if you are moving from 24-bit down to 16-bit audio. So if the client needs a reference CD at 44.1kHz, 16 bit and you recorded your session at 96 kHz, 24 bit, Export Selected Regions will take a fraction of the time and cause none of the labeling headaches that bouncing to disk would cause.

Now that you've got your loops separated, captured, or exported, it's time to rock them to their fullest potential.

Looping Regions in Pro Tools 7

If you wish to repeat your looped regions in the old-school way, you have a few standard options. You may select your entire looped region, copy it, and paste it after itself. You may also choose Edit > Repeat Regions or Option+R / Alt+R. You will get a dialog that asks how many repeats you want. These methods are the tried-and-true standby ways to loop.

However, Pro Tools 7 offers elaborate new looping functionality under the Region menu for greatly enhanced loop flexibility.

Loop Your Regions

Follow these steps to loop your regions the Pro Tools 7 way:

1. Using any of the methods outlined in this chapter, select a loop and create a region out of it.

2. With your looped region selected, choose Region > Loop or hit ⌘+Option+L / Ctrl+Alt+L.

3. In the Region Looping dialog that appears (see Figure 3.11), select Number of Loops to type in how many times you want the loop to repeat, or select Loop Length to designate a total time (or bars) for your loop to repeat. You can also check the Loop Until End of the Session or Next Region option to make your loop repeat only until there is a region in its wake or until the end of your session if there is nothing in its path. If you need to make a crossfade at each loop point, you can check the Enable Crossfade box and adjust crossfade settings by clicking the Settings button. (See "Getting the Most out of Your Fades" later in this chapter for more info on fades.)

Figure 3.11 The Region Looping dialog

When you click OK, you will see a little loop icon in the bottom right of each looped region (see Figure 3.12). This symbol indicates that the region is a *Loop iteration*. The original region remains the *Source region*.

Edit Your Looped Regions

Once regions are looped, they operate very much like grouped regions. Here are some intelligent editing options available to you in Pro Tools 7.

- To make your loops repeat more times, simply use the Trimmer tool in the normal way. Instead of trimming a region's length, for looped regions the Trimmer tool will make more Loop iterations as you drag a looped region boundary to the left or right.

- To increase the size of every Loop iteration in a looped region, position the Trimmer tool in the bottom right of a looped region so that the Trimmer icon changes to show a Trimmer loop icon. As you drag the looped region boundary to the left or right, you can resize all of the regions contained within the loop at the same time.

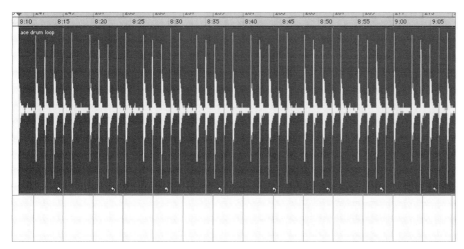

Figure 3.12 Looped regions showing the loop icon

Note: Looping regions does not copy any automation data along with each loop. To do this, select the automation you wish to copy and choose Edit > Copy Special and select additional loops you wish to extend the automation over. Then Choose Edit > Paste Special > Repeat to Fill Selection.

- To turn each Loop iteration into a real region that you can work with independently, select the looped regions. Choose Region > Unloop. In the Region Loop dialog, choose Flatten. This will create real regions out of all the iterations. If you wish to remove all loops and return just to the original source loop, choose Remove (see Figure 3.13).

Figure 3.13 The Unloop Regions dialog

Note: If you are working in postproduction, you will find the new looping region functionality extremely useful for quickly filling in room tone where it is needed.

Take Advantage of External Loop Software

A huge advantage for Pro Tools 7 users is the ability to drag and drop REX loop files (.rx) directly into audio tracks and use the relative tick-based functionality offered by Recycle's slice technology. (See "The Magic of REX" later in this chapter.)

The Many Modes of Pro Tools

Editing in Pro Tools is always done in one of the four edit modes. These different modes control the placement and movement of audio and MIDI regions as well as edit commands like Copy, Paste, Duplicate, and so on. A thorough knowledge of these modes and their uses is a must to edit efficiently. Each mode is tailored to a certain type of editing, but in the real world, you find yourself moving between modes for most types of work.

In **Shuffle mode (F1)**, editing is based upon the fact that other regions in the track control region placement and movement. Imagine a rubber band that is running through all of the regions and anchored to the beginning of the track. Every time you delete a region, the tracks later in time snap to the left. In Shuffle mode, if you drag a region from the Regions list into a track with no other regions, the region will be placed at the beginning of the track. If there are regions already in the track, the new region will be snapped to the last region in the track. When there is more than one region in a track, the regions "snap" together and cannot be separated, but they can be shuffled into different orders. Be aware when you are in Shuffle mode that your edits will affect every other region in the track. In other words, in a music track, change modes when you are done with Shuffle or when you make an edit, and your track will get moved out of time!

Slip mode (F2) allows free-form editing. There are no rules, no restraints, no grid. You can move regions freely on the timeline and drop them at any point, even if you cover part of or an entire existing region. If you are editing music that is on the grid, you could still switch to Slip mode to move regions earlier or later in time for feel and then switch to Relative Grid mode to maintain consistency. Slip mode is accurate to the sample level, giving it the finest resolution of all of the modes.

Spot mode (F3) places a sample at an exact point on the timeline. When you drag a region into a track or move a region with the Grabber tool, the Spot dialog box opens, and using any of the Time Scales , you enter the exact placement for the start, end, or user-defined sync point of the region.

Grid mode, Absolute (F4) and Relative (F4 toggle), rules the land of Bars and Beats–based information such as click-based music. This sets up Pro Tools to quickly and precisely perform functions like Quantize, Duplicate, Copy, Paste, and many more on whatever grid you assign. This is the main mode for most modern music production. Absolute Grid places regions exactly on the user-defined grid and keeps your edits right on it. Relative Grid mode allows you to take a region that is offset from the grid and edit it consistently, keeping its same offset relationship to the grid. This is a great trick to induce a little timing feel to a track but still use edit functions like Duplicate and Repeat.

Using Strip Silence to Quantize Audio Regions

Strip Silence can be used to create new regions out of an audio track or tracks in order to manually move the regions in time or apply a quantize value to place it on a grid. You can manually separate regions many ways in Pro Tools, but Strip Silence allows you to slice up a selection very quickly and precisely:

1. Select the audio you wish to work with and choose Edit > Strip Silence (⌘+U / Ctrl+U) to bring up the Strip Silence dialog box (see Figure 3.14). There are only four parameters to adjust and four buttons to select in the Strip Silence box, so it is pretty straightforward to control.

Figure 3.14 The Strip Silence dialog box

2. Dial up the Threshold slider until you see rectangles appear in your selection. The Threshold slider is the most dynamic control in the Strip Silence function. Adjust it until your basic selections include your desired audio but exclude most of the silence or noise or whatever else you might want to get rid of on the track. The Threshold command is an amplitude-based command, so it is looking at the waveform to figure out where to make the division.

3. Adjust the Minimum Strip Duration slider to decide what the smallest slice will be in milliseconds. If you set the duration to 1000 msec, the smallest new region you could create would be 1 second.

4. Adjust the start and end pads to extend your selections to get the audio that is left outside of the threshold-based selection. After you make your adjustments with the first two settings, you can fine-tune your selections with even more detail. This allows you to capture softer parts, like a breath at the beginning of a phrase or the reverb tail at the end of a note.

5. Click the Separate button in the bottom right of the Strip Silence box when you are happy with your settings. This cuts your selections into multiple new regions that are then fair game to move about the timeline.

6. Quantize the regions: Choose Region > Quantize to Grid or type ⌘+0 / Alt+0. This will quantize your regions to whatever is the current grid setting.

7. To tweak the settings far beyond the capabilities of the basic grid quantize, choose Event > MIDI > Grid/Groove Quantize or type Option+0 / Alt+0 (see Figure 3.15).

Figure 3.15 The MIDI Operations Grid/Groove Quantize window

Your regions can now be quantized with different grooves or different strengths, randomized, or made to swing like a well-oiled gate!

8. As an alternative to Strip Silence you can use Separate Regions at Transients or Separate Regions on Grid. This lets you cut regions at transients or on your grid, making many beat-based regions in a hurry.

 Note: If you create too many regions to manage effectively with any of the methods available in Pro Tools, you can deselect Show > Auto-Created in the Regions List pop-up window.

Ticks vs. Samples, Part II

There are two ways to think of time in Pro Tools: absolute and relative. When you measure time with a Main Time Scale of Minutes and Seconds, Timecode, or Samples, you are working in *absolute* time. In other words, a second or minute is always the same length, no matter what. In contrast, Bars and Beats is a *relative* time scale, so the lengths of the units change depending on the tempo you have set. For example, a quarter note will be a longer period of time at a tempo BPM setting of 60 than it will be at 120 BPM. In the section "Ticks vs. Samples, Part I" in Chapter 2 ("MIDI with Confidence"), we discussed how MIDI takes advantage of a relative time scale by using tick-based time. The relative nature of tick-based time allows for MIDI data to stretch and shrink like an accordion in order to follow changes and fluctuations in tempo. Up until

Pro Tools version 6.7, audio regions could not take advantage of this type of relative movement. Sample-based audio was synonymous with absolute time, so you could make MIDI follow tempo changes but audio would never move in time. In the Pro Tools of today (version 6.7 and above), any type of track can be made tick-based. (See "Ticks vs. Samples, Part I" in Chapter 2 for an illustration.)

So why are tick-based audio regions such a big deal? Because now you can chop up rhythmic audio regions and make them lock to tempo changes, stretch nondestructively to conform to the tempo of your choice, and even redesign a performed drumbeat to follow another groove template. The following demonstration shows how you can take advantage of tick-based time to create a groovy drumbeat out of three sampled drum sounds:

1. From the Mac Finder, drag three discrete drum samples into the empty session. Pro Tools 7 on a Mac now supports dragging and dropping directly from the Finder. In this case, it was possible to ⌘+click / Ctrl+click all three samples to select them and drop them directly into the session. Pro Tools will automatically create tracks named after the regions you are dropping into it—a real time-saver! Windows users will have to import the files using File > Import > Audio to Track. For this exercise, we will use kick, snare, and hi-hat samples from the Native Instruments hip-hop samples. When the samples are in the tracks, name the tracks accordingly (see Figure 3.16).

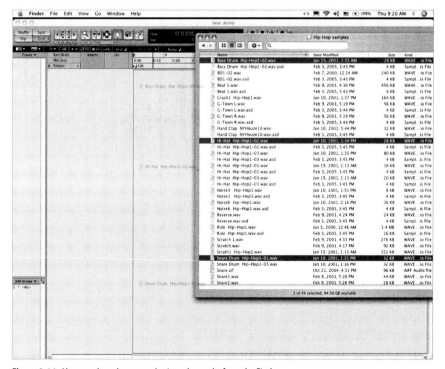

Figure 3.16 About to drop three samples into the tracks from the Finder

2. In a grid mode set to 1/16 notes, copy and paste the regions to make a one-bar beat. In this example, we made the hi-hat a syncopated pattern, emphasizing 1/8 notes. We placed the snare on the second and fourth beats and we put the kick in on the first beat and again a little later than the third beat to give it a less square feel—your basic hip-hop-style beat. (See Figure 3.17.)

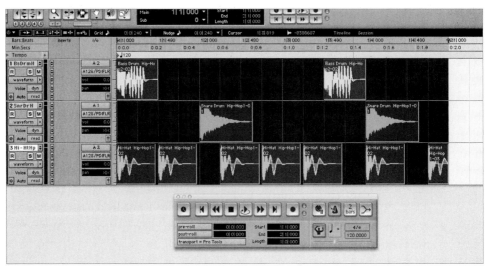

Figure 3.17 A simple one-bar beat

3. Change each track to tick-based time by clicking on the Time Base selector in the bottom left of each track's display:

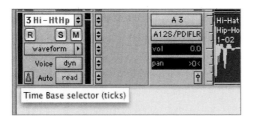

Because the elements of the drumbeat are discrete samples, you can take advantage of the tick-based track to alter the tempo any way you wish. Even though they are audio regions, these tick-based regions will act like MIDI notes when you alter the tempo of the session and conform to the changes automatically. Figures 3.18 and 3.19 show the same beat at tempos of 100 BPM and 200 BPM. Notice how the beat stretches and shrinks like an accordion to accommodate the tempo changes.

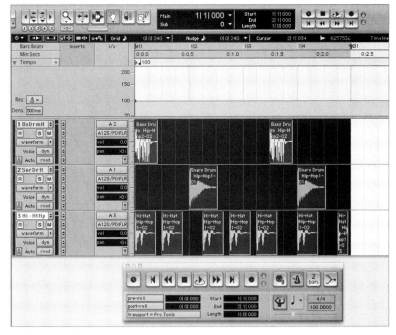

Figure 3.18 The beat at 100 BPM

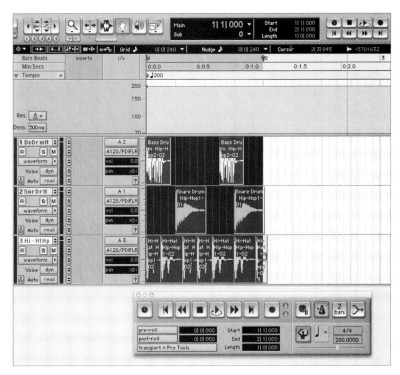

Figure 3.19 The same beat at 200 BPM

With tick-based audio regions, you can also take advantage of Pro Tools's Grid/ Groove Quantize functions. Even though the dialog box is chosen under a MIDI menu, the Grid/Groove Quantize functions will work on separated audio regions such as the hip-hop beat in this example. In addition to standard note-length quantizing options, Pro Tools offers more interesting and sophisticated Groove templates from Logic, Cubase, Numerical Sound's Feel Injector, and even the old-school MPC drum machine.

4. With the entire beat selected, choose Event > MIDI > Grid/Groove Quantize. This window will also appear if you hit Option+Keypad0 / Alt+Keypad0. Open the Quantize Grid pull-down menu to see a list of Groove templates. For this beat, we chose the MPC 65% 16th swing to give the hi-hat a groovier feel (see Figure 3.20).

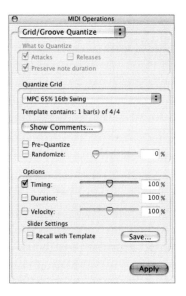

Figure 3.20 The Grid/Groove Quantize dialog

How can you take advantage of tick-based time and Groove Quantize for a rhythmic element that doesn't start at the beginning of the region? Easy. Use a sync point. For example, if you wanted to drop a DJ record-scratch sound into this beat, the rhythmic part of the scratch lies farther inside the region than at the beginning (see Figure 3.21).

Figure 3.21 The rhythmic sync point is not at the very start of this region.

Here's how to make a region sync up to the grid from a middle point correctly:

1. Go into Slip mode.

2. With the Selector tool, find the point you would like to sync up (usually Tab to Transient mode helps for beat-based regions).

3. Choose Region > Identify Sync Point or type ⌘+, / Ctrl+,. A little downward triangle will appear at the location. This is your sync point.

4. Go back to Grid mode. Reposition the region, which will now line up to the grid according to the sync point, not the region start point.

Figure 3.22 shows the complete one-bar loop with the scratch sample timed right using a sync point.

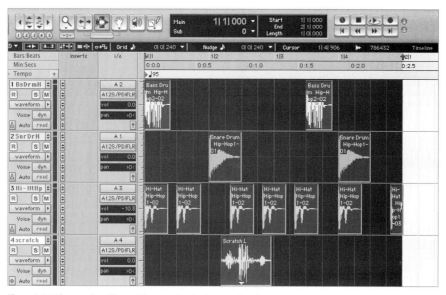

Figure 3.22 The completed beat with sync points in the scratch region

Pro Tools 7's New Region Groups

Region grouping is a powerful new editing feature in Pro Tools 7 that allows you to group multiple audio and MIDI regions in a track or across multiple tracks and work with them all as an individual unit. Once regions are grouped, it is also possible to *nest* region groups within other region groups. As an arrangement approach, region groups are an indispensable part of the new Pro Tools workflow. Region groups are ideal for edited sections of a tick-based region, just like the hip-hop beat created in the preceding section, "Ticks vs. Samples, Part II." The following illustrates how to create, manipulate, remove, and export region groups using the same hip-hop beat made of four discrete drum samples in a tick-based track.

Creating Your Region Group

To create your region group, follow these steps:

1. Select the entire contents you wish to group. In the example in Figure 3.23, it is a one-bar selection containing all the elements of the beat.

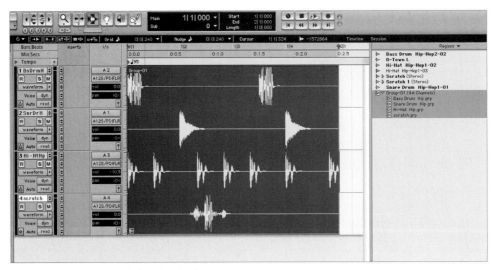

Figure 3.23 A region group made from the 1-bar drumbeat

2. Choose Region > Group or use the key combination ⌘+Option+G / Ctrl+Alt+G to create the group. The result is that all parts of the group are now uniformly color-coded and the original region boundaries are no longer visible. The region group icon in the lower left is an additional indicator of the region group. The group made in Figure 3.23 shows up automatically named as Group-01 in the Regions list column. Group-01's disclosure triangle is opened to reveal the four underlying groups, which were autonamed according to their individual track names.

This region group can now be moved as a unit—a great way to arrange a constructed beat across multiple tracks. The advantage of arranging this way is that each individual track can still have its own independent effect chains and the regions can be ungrouped at any time if you wish to get back in to the individual elements. You have the best of both worlds: the ease of group arranging and the flexibility of individual tracks and regions.

Editing Your Region Group

The method of editing region groups is very similar to editing any normal region, but the results are a little different. For example, you may use the Trimmer tool to lengthen the group, but all the regions contained will not be altered—just the group length itself.

If you use the Trimmer to shorten the group, only those regions near the trimmed region boundary will be shortened.

If you apply any kind of file-writing action to the group, such as using an Audiosuite plug-in or the TCE Trimmer tool, the end result will ungroup the regions and show all new files.

Crossfades can be placed on region groups just as they would be for any standard audio regions. If there is MIDI involved in the group, there will be no crossfade applied to the MIDI region.

Tracks of any group can be changed between tick-based time and sample-based time, although the group will be broken if all tracks are not changed together.

Nesting Your Region Groups

You can choose to take several groups and nest them inside another group. Then you could take that group and nest it with other groups in another group. Here's how to do this:

1. Select all the groups you wish to include in the next group.
2. Choose Region > Group or use ⌘+Option+G / Ctrl+Alt+G.
    This can get confusing, but it adds up to deep layers of arrangement possibilities.

Removing a Region Group

If you wish to remove a group, do this:

1. Select the entire group or groups you want to remove.
2. Choose Region > Ungroup or type ⌘+Option+U / Ctrl+Alt+U.

This will remove the group and return you to the original regions. If you have nested groups, this will only remove the top layer of groups. If you want to return to original regions of nested groups, then choose Region > Ungroup All.

If you chose Ungroup All for a nested group and wish to return to all of the nested groups, follow these steps:

1. Select any of the regions from the group you want to put back into the nested groups.
2. Choose Region > Regroup or type Option+⌘+R / Alt+Ctrl+R.

If you move or change a region element that was once part of a region group and then choose Region > Regroup, you will see the dialog in Figure 3.24.

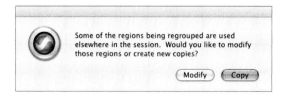

Figure 3.24 The Regroup Region dialog

Modify will change all other groups to mimic the changes you made. This is useful when you want to alter all instances of a grouped drumbeat. For example, you decide that the snare sample should move later in all of your copied drumbeat groups. This method allows you just to alter one and have them all change. Copy will make a new region group with the change reflected in only the new group. Use this when you want to change up a beat in only one region group or create a drum fill that happens only occasionally.

Separated Region Groups

If anything is done to alter the coherence of a grouped region, you will see a separated region icon in the bottom left of the region (see Figure 3.25).

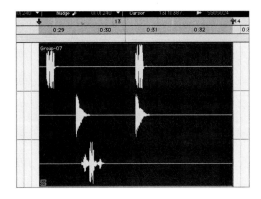

Figure 3.25 This region group was separated because a track was deleted.

A separated region group is caused by several things:

- Moving, deleting, or hiding a track that is a part of a region group
- Recording into a track in a region group
- Altering the playlists on tracks in a region group

The separated group symbol is there simply to visually indicate that the group is incomplete or altered in some way. A separated region group can still be moved as a unit like a normal region group. To delete or move a track and maintain a group, simply ungroup the regions, delete or move the track, and then regroup the regions.

Exporting a Region Group

Pro Tools 7 supports the import and export of region groups as files that can be read by other sessions (files with the .grp extension). This is cool because you can now export region groups created across multiple tracks and even include MIDI data to open in other sessions seamlessly. To export groups, follow these steps:

1. With a region group selected, choose Export Region Groups from the Regions List pop-up menu on the right column of the Edit window (see Figure 3.26).

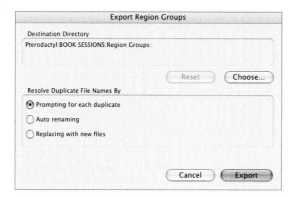

Figure 3.26 The Export Region Groups dialog

2. By default, Pro Tools creates a Region Groups folder in the session folder of the current session; however, you may navigate to a different location.

It is important to understand that an exported region group is only a reference to the original media. If you wanted to import region groups into a session on another drive, you'll want to copy over the associated audio files too. Follow these steps to include the original media along with your imported region groups:

1. Create a new session on the drive you want to contain the exported region group and the media associated with the groups.

2. Check Automatically Copy Files on Import in the Setup > Preferences > Operation tab.

3. Drag the region group file into the session. The new session folder will now contain the region groups and the media—in other words, your session is self-contained.

Moving Data between Sessions

Pro Tools allows just one open session at a time, so to share information between sessions, you need to use Import Session Data. This allows you to raid your other sessions to get just about anything that a track might contain. In addition to your tracks, the Import Session Data dialog box shows you settings under the headings Source Properties, Audio and Video Media Options, Time Code Mapping Options, Track Offset Options, and Sample Rate Conversion Options. To get to yhe Import Session Data window you first must chose File > Import > Session Data to bring up the Open File window shown in Figure 3.27.

This window lets you chose the session from which to import the data. After you open the session, the Import Session Data window opens. (See Figure 3.28.)

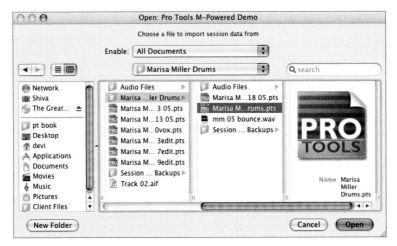

Figure 3.27 Open File window

Import Session Data

Source Properties

Name: gdd remix10
Created by: Pro Tools TDM/MacOS
Start time: 01:00:00:00
Time code format: 30
Audio bit depth(s): 24
Audio sample rate(s): 48000
Audio file type(s): AIFF

Time Code Mapping Options

Maintain absolute time code values

0:00.000

Track Offset Options

Offset Incoming Tracks to:

1| 1| 000   Bars:Beats

Audio Media Options

Copy from source media

Handle size 1000   milliseconds

Video Media Options

Copy from source media

Sample Rate Conversion Options

☑ Apply SRC

Source sample rate: 192000

Destination sample rate: 44100

Conversion quality: Tweak Head (Slowest)

Source Tracks	Destination
virus print.07 (Stereo audio)	New Track
bee swarm.07 (Mono audio)	(none)
main k riff.07 (Stereo audio)	New Track
ploy key break.07 (Mono audio)	New Track
jewsarp.07 (Mono audio)	(none)
at 1 (Stereo aux)	New Track
lobass (midi)	New Track
new lead.10 (midi)	New Track

Import:

☐ Tempo/Meter Map

☑ Markers/Memory Locations

Cancel   OK

Figure 3.28 Import Session Data dialog box

Import Session Data has a couple of different options for HD and LE systems, but both work basically the same way. In LE when you import a track, you import all aspects of the track with the option of selecting to bring in tempo/meter maps and markers/

memory locations. In an HD system, you can bring in all of the attributes connected to the track or just the aspects of the track that you need. No automation or just automation, your choice.

Here's how to import track data:

1. Choose your source track or tracks and assign them to a new track or tracks in the destination.

2. Select Tempo/Meter Map or Markers/Memory Locations to bring in to your current session if needed.

3. If you need to convert sample rates, check Apply SRC and tell Pro Tools which quality to convert with. Tweak Head is preferred and in a modern computer does not take that long.

4. Choose to copy the audio into the current session audio folder or use the audio where it is. It is a smart practice to copy if possible just in case the other session folder is moved, lost, or trashed.

5. Set up your Time Code Mapping and Track Offsets if needed and click OK.

Import Session Data is a great tool if different people work on a project simultaneously. You can keep a master session file and import tracks from the other sessions back into the original.

N o t e : If you use Save As to save different versions of your sessions, you can use Import Session Data to retrieve data from the other saved files if you accidentally delete or change something and then save over it.

Using Strip Silence to Get Rid of Annoying Headphone Bleed

The Strip Silence function allows you to remove noise, bleed, or any low-level ambient sound that you need to get rid of. Strip Silence is threshold-based, retaining everything that is above the user threshold level and removing everything under the threshold. Headphone bleed in a vocal track is a prime candidate for this technique. Headphone bleed is going to happen almost no matter what you do, but it can get worse depending on how deaf, er ... um, how enthused the performer is and the kind of volume driving their headphones. The style of headphone and other variables like the room and what kind of music is being played can factor in as well.

Here's how to use Strip Silence to remove unwanted noise from a selection:

1. Select the region(s) or track(s) you want to perform Strip Silence on.

2. Bring up the Strip Silence window shown in Figure 3.29 (⌘+U / Ctrl+U).

3. If you want to rename the regions, click the Rename button to open the Rename dialog box.

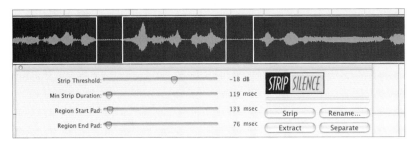

Figure 3.29 Strip Silence window and vocal track

4. Adjust the Strip Threshold slider to define your basic new regions. You want just the vocals and no bleed. If the new region is too small and you cut off part of the voice, you need to back off of the threshold level and go to step 5 to set the minimum strip duration.

5. Adjust the Min Strip Duration slider to set what the smallest region will be. This helps keep you from creating more new regions than necessary and from breaking up the track too much to be usable.

6. Adjust the Region Start Pad and Region End Pad values to fine-tune your selections. This lets you pull the selection a little before and after to get the attack or decay on a region that you would clip off otherwise just using the Strip Threshold and Min Strip Duration settings.

7. When your selection looks good, click the Strip button.

8. If your new regions are not cut exactly right on the front or back, Strip Silence is nondestructive and you can trim out the new regions to get back breath, room tone, or whatever is missing.

The Zero Crossing

Pro Tools audio editing is accurate down to the sample level. This means when you edit audio in a 96kHz sample rate session, you have the ability to cut a second of audio into 96,000 parts. This ultra-fine editing resolution allows Pro Tools editors to have their choice about where exactly to cut up an audio region. With all of this accuracy, should we be aware of where we cut? Yes! Editing should occur at the *zero crossing*.

When you zoom into a region closely in Pro Tools, there comes a point when the solid waveform view turns into a single curved line. This is when it becomes possible to view a very accurate graphical representation of the audio waveform. These graphics are representations, because when the sound becomes digital audio, it is only ones and zeroes, but Pro Tools is smart enough to draw a picture of what the waveform would look like if it were analog. Analog audio is continuous voltage, an electrical current that flows between the positive and negative charge. The null point

Continues

The Zero Crossing *(Continued)*

exactly between the positive and negative charge is known as the zero crossing. Visually, in a Pro Tools track, the zero crossing is the middle point, halfway between the top and bottom of an audio waveform.

Zero crossing:

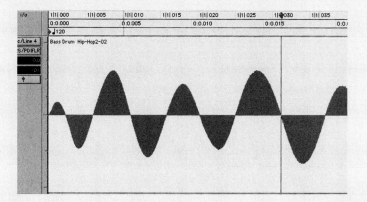

A closer look at a zero crossing:

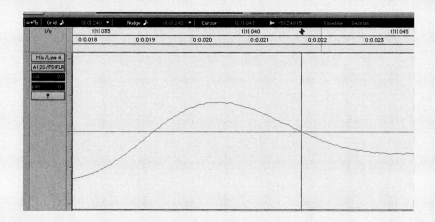

So what's the big deal? Why should you make edits on the zero crossing? If edits are not made at the zero crossing, there is a high potential that you will hear a loud digital click at the edit point. These clicks, called Fourier clicks, are usually undesirable sounds that disrupt the seamless edit.

To make the edit exactly on the zero crossing, it is usually necessary to go into Slip mode to edit at the sample level and zoom in enough to see where you are cutting. If it is absolutely necessary to edit two regions together where there is no zero crossing (this happens sometimes), a very fast cross fade can help smooth out the transition and remove the click. See "Getting the Most out of Your Fades" later in this chapter.

The Magic of REX

As Ron Burgundy said in the movie *Anchorman*, "I'm kind of a big deal." REX files might say the same. The ability to import REX files into Pro Tools has made producing music as easy as drag and drop. REX files are the original examples of elastic audio, audio files that can change tempo and pitch independent of each other. This is what a REX file icon looks like:

412*D&B1.REX

If you have a drum loop with a tempo of 128 BPM but you have a track that is at 137 BPM, you can Recycle the drum loop to change the tempo to match your session tempo without changing the pitch—way cool. This technology is finding its way into an increasing number of audio applications. The folks that brought us Reason, Propellerhead Software, created REX technology back in the 1990s with the program Recycle, and the rest, as they say, is history. There are thousands of REX libraries out there, containing almost every kind of sound you could ever think of—loops or one-shots, you name it. To go beyond any preexisting library, you can import your own WAV or AIFF files into Recycle and then slice and dice and save your own REX files (see Figure 3.30).

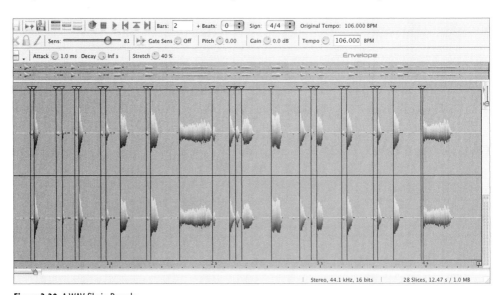

Figure 3.30 A WAV file in Recycle

This puts the entire universe of REX-based sound at your fingertips. Any type of loop that has some sort of definable rhythm in it—such as drum loops, bass lines, and rhythmic melodies—can be sliced up and made into a REX file. REX files are great building blocks for creating and producing music in the digital age. For the producer or composer who can't track a band or find someone to play the pan flute or zither, REX files can save the day. In the past, drum loops were the REX mainstay, but you can get loops of almost any instrument or grooves of almost any style. Pro Tools provides a number of ways to utilize REX files in version 7, giving great power and flexibility to your music-making endeavor.

There are more ways to get REX files into Pro Tools than on-ramps to the 405:

1. You can import REX files with the Import Audio to Track command and the Import Audio to Regions List command (Shift+⌘+I / Shift+Ctrl+I), drag a REX file from your OS onto a track, drag a REX file from your workspace onto a track, or drag a REX file into the Tracks List window from wherever. If you use Import Audio to Track or drag a file into the Tracks List window, Pro Tools will place the file at the beginning of the track and automatically make the track tick-based. If you drag a file from your OS, the workspace, or the Regions list, then you can place the REX file anywhere on the timeline, depending on the editing mode you are in. The REX file is dropped into Pro Tools as a grouped region. If you drag the REX file into a tick-based track, the grouped region will follow tempo changes. If you drag the REX file into a sample-based track, it will act like a normal audio region (see Figure 3.31).

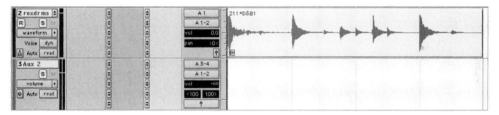

Figure 3.31 A grouped REX file

2. When you're working with grouped REX files in a tick-based track, even if you leave the region grouped, you can still change tempo and the region will follow the BPM like MIDI. If you don't need to quantize the REX files to the grid or alter the individual slices in any way, this is a fine way to work. This also is a little kinder on your region count in the Regions List window.

3. Working with ungrouped REX files in a tick-based track is the most flexible way to use REX files in Pro Tools. To ungroup the selected REX file(s), choose Region > Ungroup or type ⌘+Option+U / Ctrl+Alt+U (see Figure 3.32).

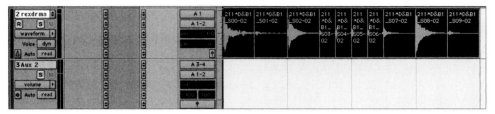

Figure 3.32 The same region shown in Figure 3.31, but this time it's ungrouped

Once the REX file is separated, the fun really starts. To quantize the newly created regions to the current grid, type ⌘+0 / Ctrl+0. To groove-quantize REX slices or to use quantize functions like Swing and Strength, bring up the Grid/Groove Quantize window from the MIDI Operations window (Option+0 / Alt+0). With the Quantize methods in the Grid/Groove Quantize window, you have maximum control over your REX files. In addition to being quantized, the individual slices can be reordered, deleted, have their tempo changed, and in general, thoroughly manipulated!

Note: Instead of deleting regions when reordering and remixing REX slices, try muting your regions. This will let you just un-mute a region if you decide the track was better with the part. Muting regions is a good way to try different ideas in a hurry and still get back to your original without massive undos.

Getting the Most out of Your Fades

Fades are elementary editing techniques used to get in or out of a region gracefully or to blend two regions together in a crossfade. Used simply, fades are fairly straightforward. Make your selection over the region boundary, type ⌘+F / Ctrl+F, choose a fade preset curve, click OK, and you've got a smoother transition. But fades are deceptively simple. The following advanced fade techniques will help you masterfully fade your way to a solid, airtight edit.

Auditioning Fades with Sight and Sound

When you are creating crossfades, it is sometimes helpful to see how the waveforms are going to overlap. The buttons on the left side of the Fades dialog can be selected to show the two regions overlaid, as in Figure 3.33, or on top of one another, as in Figure 3.34. The up and down arrow buttons can be used to magnify the waveform for further scrutiny. For a stereo region, you have the option of selecting buttons named 1 (left), 2 (right), or Both in order to change what elements of the region you are looking at.

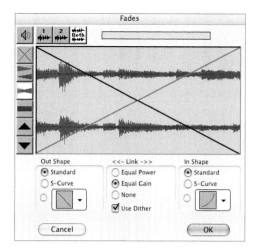

Figure 3.33 An Equal Gain fade

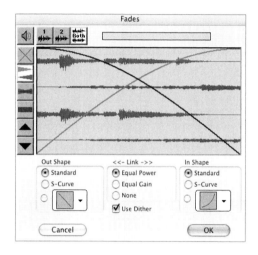

Figure 3.34 An Equal Power fade

Remember, we are dealing with sound here, so the most important way to check out your prospective fade is to click the audition button at the top of the Fades dialog. This button renders your proposed fade and auditions it for your approval in a loop before you actually commit to it.

Equal Power vs. Equal Gain Linking

Knowing when to choose Equal Power or Equal Gain linking is most pertinent when you are creating a crossfade. Equal Power works better for crossfading two regions comprising different-sounding material, such as an organ and a flute. This way, the volume does not potentially drop out during the crossfade. Use Equal Gain linking for crossfading regions with identical-sounding material, such as room tone or two regions of the same bass guitar. Equal Gain will avoid any doubling or canceling of identical waveforms during the transition. (See Figures 3.33 and 3.34.)

Need to take the *ill* from *will* and combine it with the *p* from *paint* to create the word *pill*? An asymmetric fade may be the only way to make it sound real. Choose None in the <<-Link->> box. With no link, little black boxes will be displayed in the corners of each fade slope (see Figure 3.35). These boxes allow the in and out slopes to be dragged independently with the mouse for creating asymmetrical fades of endless possibilities. A musical use for an asymmetrical fade is to take the transient from one snare sample and combine it with the decay of another—a very cool technique to create an original sound.

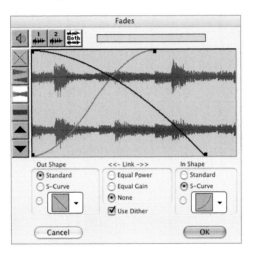

Figure 3.35 An asymmetrical fade with no link

Here are some helpful key commands to navigate through different fade slopes and links in the Fades dialog:

- Ctrl+← → / Start+← → toggles the presets of the outgoing slope.
- Option+← → / Alt+← → toggles the presets of the incoming slope.
- Ctrl+↑ ↓ / Start+↑ ↓ toggles incoming slope between Standard, S-Curve, and Presets.
- Option+↑ ↓ / Alt+↑ ↓ toggles the outgoing slope between Standard, S-Curve, and Presets.

Batch Fades

If you are cutting regions right in the middle of audio waveforms, you should always try to make edits on the zero crossing (see the sidebar "The Zero Crossing" earlier in this chapter). Sometimes to get that perfect loop or cut, editing on the zero crossing just isn't possible. Batch fades can fix any digital clicks (Fourier clicks) that may occur between sloppy edits. To get the Batch Fades dialog to appear, you must make a selection that covers more than one region boundary. Here's an example:

1. Select all instances of a duplicated looped beat that has problematic clicks in between each region.

2. Type ⌘+F / Ctrl+F. Because there is more than one region selected, the Batch Fades dialog appears (see Figure 3.36).

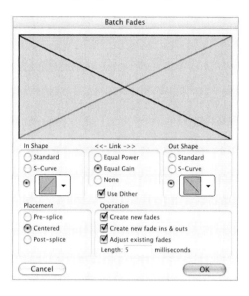

Figure 3.36 The Batch Fades dialog

3. The Batch Fades settings shown in Figure 3.36 are usually sufficient for removing the digital click while maintaining a quick chop edit absent of any audible crossfades.

Pro Tools HD users can go to the Setup > Preferences > Operation tab and manually type in an amount from 0 to 10 milliseconds under AutoFade Value. This creates an automatic fade over all region boundaries in the entire session in real time without saving them to the disk. It will put a larger load on your HD rig, but it will prevent any digital clicks from ever occurring in your session.

Lose Those Fades on Purpose

Pro Tools saves all fades as unique files in the Fades folder in your session folder. The creation info of these files is stored in the session file itself when you click Save. It is therefore possible for Pro Tools to rewrite fades should they get corrupted or lost. One technique to downsize your session before FTPing it over the Internet, or taking it with you to another studio on your iPod, is to *purposefully* throw away your Fades folder. All fades can be re-created when you load the session again.

Fades without All the Dialog

For lightning-fast fade creation, there are a few powerful ways to create fades and crossfades without having to go into the Fades dialog. Here's how:

1. Choose the Setup > Preferences > Editing tab.

2. Click the buttons named Fade In, Crossfade, and Fade Out Slopes under Default Fade Settings and selecting your desired slope for each (see Figure 3.37).

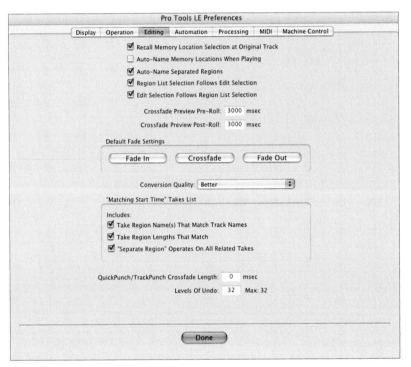

Figure 3.37 Default fade settings in Preferences

3. Enable Keyboard Focus mode (⌘+Option+1 / Ctrl+Alt+1) to get one-stroke key commands.

4. Make a selection over a region boundary.

5. Type F to create a fade.

    For quick fade-in of a region using Default Fade Settings and the Keyboard Focus mode, do this:

1. Place the selector where you want a region to be at full fade-in volume.

2. Type D.

    For quick fade-outs, follow these steps:

1. Place the selector where you want a region to start fading out.

2. Type G.

Arranging Pro Tools 7 Style: Insert and Cut Time

The new editing workflow of Pro Tools 7 allows for arranging techniques that were never before possible. This ain't your older brother's Pro Tools system. If you have regions looped and grouped, tick-based and timed together with MIDI in a variable-tempo grid, there comes a point when a complete arrangement can be adjusted from a global standpoint. This is the fun part; you've sweated to get perfect loops, fine-tuned your MIDI data, and grouped together regions across multiple tracks. You can now arrange whole grouped regions to try out different sequences and versions of your song with the Grabber tool in a grid resolution of 1 bar. Insert and Cut Time are two new ways to globally insert empty bars or remove bars of your arrangement.

Insert Time

To insert blank bars in the middle of an arrangement in order to add another verse or double up the chorus section of a song, for example, follow these steps:

1. Choose Event > Time > Insert Time. Or type Option+Keypad1 / Alt+Keypad1. The Insert Time Operations dialog will open (see Figure 3.38).

2. Manually enter Start, End, or Length values of the amount you want to insert. If your cursor is already at the designated point before you open this window, the Start value will update to show your current location.

3. To insert the time globally across all regions, choose Meter Tempo Rulers, All Tick-Based Markers & Tracks, and All Sample-Based Markers and Tracks.

4. Click Apply to have the new time inserted.

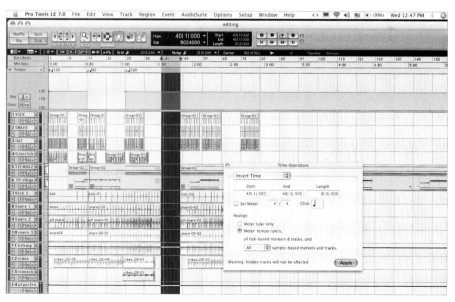

Figure 3.38 Using Insert Time to add eight bars to the arrangement

Cut Time

Here's how to globally remove an amount of bars or time from your arrangement:

1. Type Option+Keypad1 / Alt+Keypad1 to open the Time Operations dialog (see Figure 3.39). Choose Cut Time from the pop-up.

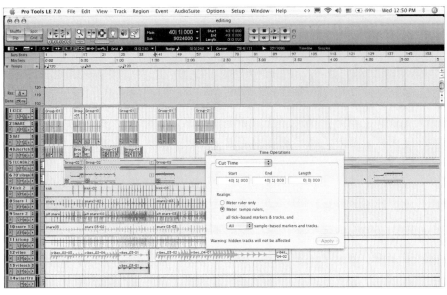

Figure 3.39 Using Cut Time to remove eight bars from the arrangement

2. Manually enter a Start, End, or Length value of the amount you want to cut. If your cursor is already at the designated point before you open this window, the Start value will update to show your current location.

3. To cut the time globally across all regions, choose Meter Tempo Rulers, All Tick-Based Markers & Tracks, and All Sample-Based Markers and Tracks.

4. Click Apply to cut out the designated time.

Pro Tools on Acid: Tripping with Beat Detective

Beat Detective is an incredibly powerful and sexy tool in the Pro Tools arsenal. It slices, it dices, it makes julienne files—ouch. While this is not a magic cure all for all of your rhythmic maladies and chores, it's sure close! One word about Beat Detective: Like MIDI, it can be a bit quirky and mysterious, so get to know it and practice, practice, practice.

Readymade loops and samples are fine and dandy for some things, but the more control you have over your audio, the more flexibility you have when you are producing your tracks. Beat Detective gives you the ability to adjust and manipulate your audio in ways that were unheard of in Pro Tools until recently. With a tick-based track, you can adjust tempo and the separated audio regions will follow right along the same way a REX file does. It is almost like working with MIDI! Raid your Apple loops libraries and bring them in to Pro Tools with the ability to change BPM, rhythm, and feel. Do I hear a GarageBand, Acid, or Recycle from the choir?

To slice, dice, and conform existing audio regions, loops, or tracks, follow these steps:

1. Make sure your tracks are tick based.

2. Make your selection based on the exact number of bars you want to work with in the region(s) or track(s). It has to be an even number of bars and consistent meter to work. This is the most important part of the entire process. If you don't get your selection right, you are doomed from the get-go. (See the selection techniques in "Creating the Vital Loop" earlier in this chapter.) If your selection is a loop, then you can double-click with the Selector tool to select the entire region or single-click with the Grabber tool.

3. Bring up Beat Detective by typing ⌘+Keypad+8 / Ctrl+Keypad+8 (see Figure 3.40).

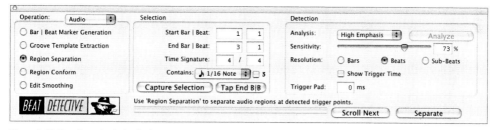

Figure 3.40 Beat Detective in Pro Tools 7

4. Select the Region Separation radio button on the left side of the Beat Detective window. The first two buttons are for generating bars and beats markers and for extracting grooves from selections.

5. Click Capture Selection if you know the BPM of the loop; this should automatically enter in the start and end points for your selection. If you don't know the tempo but the tempo is consistent, use Identify Beat (⌘+I / Ctrl+I) with the Tempo Ruler enabled to figure the BPM. Identify Beat is a valuable tool in Pro Tools even though most loops identify their BPM.

6. Click the Analyze button to have Beat Detective figure out where the transients are in your track. This starts the slicing process, and in a combination of the next three steps, you will get the slices you desire.

7. Choose your resolution in bars, beats or sub-beats. This will tell Beat Detective how finely to slice up the regions made by analyzing.

8. In the Contains box, pick the note value that will represent the value of the sub-beat if used.

9. Slide the Sensitivity bar until you get enough slices in your track(s) to get the control you desire. The higher up you move the slider, the more slices you will get and the finer the resolution will be. When you are satisfied with the slicing, move to the next step. (See Figure 3.41.)

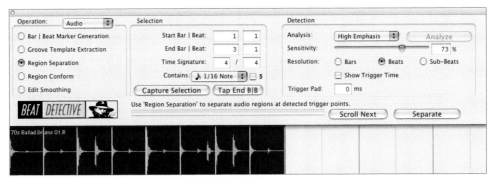

Figure 3.41 A region sliced by Beat Detective with a resolution of beats

10. Click Separate if you need to separate more than one region; then in Edit Keyboard Focus (⌘+Option+1 / Ctrl+Alt+1), use the up and down keys. (P is up. The semicolon (;) is down.) to move the same selection to whatever track you want to separate. (See Figure 3.42.)

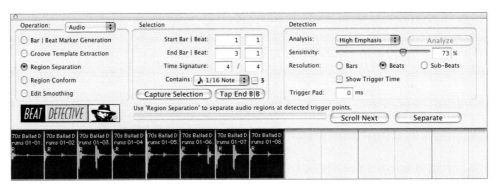

Figure 3.42 The same region after being separated

11. Choose Region Conform in the left column and then choose one of the two options in the Conform pull-down menu, Standard or Groove.

Standard Conform lets you select the different settings. The strength of the quantize lets you choose how much of the quantize you want to apply. 100%

Strength means that your selection has been moved completely to the Grid setting. Dial it down and you will get some of the original feel with some movement toward the grid. You can induce Swing by checking Swing and moving the slider up. Swing moves the sub-beats and will put a little shuffle of feel in a track.

Groove Conform is preset based and loads of grooves from the Clipboard or from the presets located in the Grooves menu. The grooves all have subtle differences that will change the feel of the regions when applied. Digidesign has more free grooves to download from its site in the DISK section.

12.   You can go outside these two options altogether and go straight to the MIDI quantize window, Option+0 / Alt+0. This window gives you the whole bag of tricks. All of the different quantize modes in Pro Tools are here. You can also move the regions manually to place them outside of the grid. Select Slip mode (F2) to move things off the grid.

Getting your loops and samples "REXed" up gives you great flexibility with tempo and rhythm as you arrange your track.

Note: When creating large numbers of new regions with Beat Detective, turn off the auto-created names in the Regions List pop-up to avoid unnecessary clutter.

The Way of the Insert: Inserts and FX

Cool plug-ins seem to make all of the headaches you get working with a computer-based system go away. Anyone who missed the past few years of plug-in development would be stunned at the sonic quality and diversity of software-based FX.

Plug-ins come in all shapes and sizes for all formats and platforms. Most pro studios use a combination of hardware and software for signal processing, so it's good to know your way around the working of both platforms. This chapter will cover the fundamentals of how inserts work in Pro Tools and throw out some cool recipes for plug-ins and hardware-based FX.

Chapter Contents

TDM vs. RTAS vs. AudioSuite

Plug-ins are certainly a key log in the logjam known as digital music production, so it's a good idea to know exactly what type of plug-ins your system will run. In Pro Tools version 7, there are three native types of plug-ins: TDM (Time Division Multiplexing), Real Time Audio Suite (RTAS), and AudioSuite, or AS. Figure 4.1 shows the menu options for TDM and RTAS plug-ins.

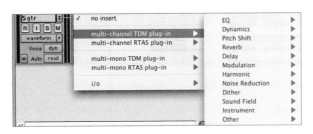

Figure 4.1 Plug-in types

The main difference between the plug-in types is where the processing is done and whether it's real time or rendered.

RTAS (HD and LE) plug-ins get their power exclusively from your computer. The more plug-ins you are running in a session, the more impact it will have on your system. If you need more power to run a session or need just one more little plug-in to get the job done, then increase your Hardware Buffer size (Setup > Playback Engine > H/W Buffer Size) and you will get more resources. You get more power but at the cost of speed and latency, so use this trick after your tracking and composition is done. ReWire is an RTAS plug-in in Pro Tools. Virtual instruments such as Reason, Trilogy, Stylus RMX, and others also use the RTAS ReWire platform as their portal into Pro Tools.

TDM (HD only) plug-ins use system resources from a separate dedicated Digital Signal Processing (DSP) card when they are inserted on a track in a Pro Tools session. Because the number and type of DSP cards varies from system to system, everyone's capabilities are a little different. Check out the appendix of this book for more information on system capabilities. Some of the finest plug-ins ever programmed roam in this TDM realm. Be warned, however, that TDM is is the land of more-expensive HD systems, so get your checkbook out.

AudioSuite (HD and LE) plug-ins are selection-based, non–real time, and need to be rendered to the region(s) or track(s). Because they're selection-based, you have the added capability of affecting just part of a track or region. AudioSuite plug-in types mirror your RTAS and TDM plug-ins but also give you a few different miscellaneous FX that are only found in the Audio Suite, such as Reverse. AudioSuite plug-ins give you the ability to normalize, gain change, reverse, and perform other useful audio tricks. Even though these effects are not done in real time, with a Quad processor Mac you might think they are! AudioSuite plug-ins can be handy if you know that a setting is right and you won't need to ever change it. When you hit Process, the effect is permanently written either over the original file or to a new file, saving the original. This is a great way to reduce the load on your CPU or HD cards.

Finally, for the more adventurous FX users out there, you can also run VST plug-ins using a VST-to-RTAS wrapper. (Wrapper, not rapper; we're not talking about Jay-Z here.) Wrappers can be problematic, so use with care.

Note: The HTDM format has been phased out in version 7. If you open a pre–version 7 session that contains HTDM plug-ins, the HTDM plug-ins will automatically convert into RTAS. If they cannot convert, they will appear grayed out as inactive and you should check for updates of the plug-ins.

Build Your Own Effects Library

"Presets are for suckaz, so program your own damn FX!" Okay, so maybe sometimes you start with a preset and tweak it to fit your needs. That's fine. Factory presets can serve as a starting point for your own library, but turning knobs and sliding faders is half the fun, so customize, don't comform to the manufacturers ideas about how your audio should sound.. However you get there, having folders full of custom presets tailored to your needs can keep the session rolling smoothly. Once you have amassed your libraries of effects for all of the different plug-ins, you can scroll through and audition them right in the plug-in window just as you scroll through sounds in a MIDI keyboard. In addition to the Plug-ins Settings select window (where you audition patches), plug-in windows contain many shortcuts and functions that are often overlooked (see Figure 4.2).

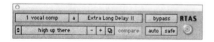

Figure 4.2 Global plug-in parameters

From the Global plug-in parameter buttons on the top of every plug-in, you can conveniently navigate between Librarian and Settings menus, Insert Position selectors, and Plug-In selectors, or select any non-MIDI track in your session. You can also enable automation parameters here.

Before you save any of your plug-in settings, decide whether you want them to be accessible to every session on your system or limited to the session you are in. If you work in different studios, saving your plug-in settings to a session folder will allow you to move your FX presets along with your Pro Tool session. By default, your plug-ins are saved to an OS location called the Root Settings folder. This makes the settings available to every session. On a Mac, this is found in Hard Drive\Library\Application Support\Digidesign\Plug-In Settings. On a PC, it is found at Program Files\Common Files\Digidesign\DAE\Plug-In Settings.

To save your plug-in settings to a session folder, follow these steps:

1. Navigate to Settings Menu > Settings Preferences > Save Plug-in Settings To.

2. Change the setting to Session Folder (see Figure 4.3). In your session folder, Pro Tools will create a plug-in settings folder just like an audio or fades folder.

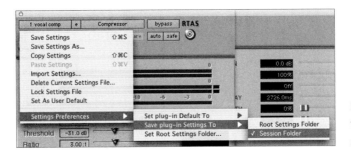

Figure 4.3 Changing the default plug-in settings folder

Once you have created a session settings folder, you will see the folder in the Librarian menu above the Factory Settings folder. You then have the option of loading settings from either location. Once you know where your saved settings are going, it's time to build a library!

Here's how to save your plug-in settings:

1. Click in the Settings menu to open the menu (See Figure 4.3).

2. If you want to save over the existing setting, just press Shift+⌘+S / Shift+Ctrl+S or select Save Settings.

3. If you are modifying a setting, always chose Save As. Save As will save a copy with a different name and keep the original. This is a great way to build different versions of effects settings for different applications.

Note: Copy your settings file on the Finder level to the session folder and the root folder to make them both global and session-specific.

Once they're saved, you can import the settings into any session.

Dealing with Plug-in Latency in Pro Tools

There is no denying it: plug-ins cause latency. You want to know how much? Simply ⌘+click / Ctrl+click the green Audio Volume Indicator numbers in the Mix or Edit window twice. Figure 4.4 shows a track with this view.

Figure 4.4 Plug-in delay is shown in samples after ⌘+clicking / Ctrl+clicking twice on the green numbers at the bottom of a mixer channel.

The number shown is a measurement in samples of how latent the audio on the track is after it runs through the plug-ins inserted on its track. Look-ahead compressors and gates are notorious for causing enough latency to throw a track out of phase with its neighboring tracks.

Since Pro Tools version 6.4, HD systems have a robust automatic system for dealing with this type of latency. It is a streamlined and beautiful system called the Delay Compensation Engine, and it is coveted and yearned for by LE users. This engine runs slyly in the background (with quite a bit of system resources used, mind you) and automatically equates latency caused by software plug-ins and shifts audio later in time to compensate. The Delay Compensation Engine must be activated in the Options menu. It can be set to either long or short in Setup > Playback Engine, depending on your plug-in demands and how much processing power you wish to dedicate to it.

Pro Tools LE users must manually compensate for these delays. One way to accomplish this is by shifting audio regions in a track earlier to compensate for the plug-in latency. To manually compensate, do this:

1. Select all audio regions on a track by triple-clicking any region with the Selector tool.

2. Choose Edit > Shift or type Option+H / Alt+H. Select Earlier and type in the amount of plug-in delay. Click OK.

Remember to do this only after you have decided for good on the plug-ins on a track, because if you change plug-ins, the latency will change and your audio will once again be out of sync.

Work with, Not against, System Resource Shortcomings

No matter what flavor Pro Tools system you are on, if your session calls for a lot of processing, you must know how to manage your system resources wisely to avoid a meltdown.

Deactivating Unnecessary Tracks and Plug-Ins

Many Pro Tools users are unaware that you can make selected tracks inactive from the Track menu. Select the tracks that aren't necessary for the current tasks you are working on and choose Make Inactive from the Track menu. You can also click the track type icon located at the bottom right of each track in the Mix window and choose Make Track Inactive. Holding Option+Shift / Alt+Shift while choosing the menu selection will deactivate all selected tracks (see Figure 4.5).

Note: On a Mac, the Make Inactive key command combination is easy to remember. Just make the "Rock On" symbol, aka the "Devil Sign," with your forefinger and pinky. Use this hand to simultaneously hit the Control and Command keys while clicking the track type icon, plug-in, or automation playlist to make them inactive. On Windows, press the Ctrl and Start keys. Pressing all three modifier keys will disable all tracks. To disable only selected tracks, use Option+Shift / Alt+Shift as you click.

This trick will release the system resources from having to deal with the mixer resources and the plug-in processing of those tracks if they have any active plug-ins on them. This can be a huge help to lower the necessary processing on your computer. Some Pro Tools users think that just by bypassing a plug-in, they are deactivating it from the host processing. This is incorrect; actually, you must make the plug-in inactive to do this. Similar to deactivating a track, deactivating a plug-in can be done with a quick key combination (⌘+Control+click / Ctrl+Start+click) on the closed plug-in in the inserts panel. See the aforementioned "Devil Sign/Rock On" tip). Open the system usage window located in the Window menu to monitor the system performance (see Figure 4.6).

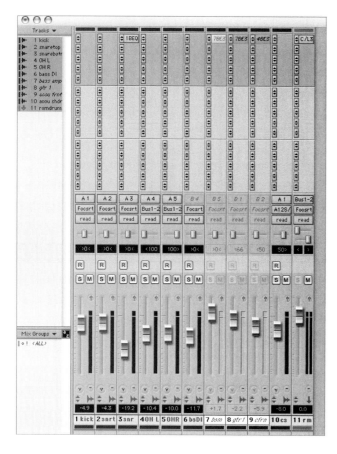

Figure 4.5 Tracks 7, 8, and 9 have been made inactive.

Figure 4.6 The LE system usage window

The CPU level is what you should watch out for because when that spikes, you are cooked. Playback will stop and you'll get hit with the dreaded "running out of system usage" dialog.

Recording through a Plug-In

If you would like to take advantage of Pro Tools RTAS or TDM plug-ins as you are recording, you will realize that the plug-ins affect the audio in a track only *after* it has been recorded to the hard drive. In other words, inserts affect only the audio downstream, on the output of an Audio track. For example, you are recording that wild, dynamic singer who unpredictably goes from whisper to scream and you would like to put a limiter in place so you can stop the audio from clipping before it hits the hard drive. There is a way to use Pro Tools insert plug-ins to achieve this, but if you are tracking on an LE system, you have to be a bit crafty about that dirty word again, *latency*.

The signal chain for both TDM and LE goes as follows:

1. Make a mono Aux track and a mono audio track. LE users remember to turn up the Aux Input track because it defaults to -∞.

2. Set the Aux's input to the input channel that your mic or recording source is attached to. Set the output of your Aux track to an available bus, such as Bus 1.

3. Insert the plug-ins you would like to use on the Aux track.

4. Set the input of your audio track to Bus 1, record enable, and voila, the signal is now routing through the plug-ins.

On an LE system, these plug-ins are going to introduce some latency. This can be tricky while tracking; for example, the singer may hear their own audio coming back as an echo. If you are working on a 002, the best you can do here is switch to low-latency mode in the Options menu and hope for the best. If you are on an Mbox, the trick is to mute the track you are recording to and turn the input/playback knob until the proper mix is achieved. Once the audio is recorded, however, you can use the following tip to test how latent the signal is and then shift it back in time:

1. Make a 1-second selection in a new audio track named test. Using the signal generator plug-in from the AudioSuite menu, process a 1kHz tone at -20 dB for this second-long selection.

2. Set the test audio track's output to go to any available bus, say Bus 2. Busses already being used will be in boldface type.

3. On the Aux input you made previously to record into, change the input to Bus 2.

4. Make sure the original audio you were recording to track is still record-enabled. Place the selector before the beep you just made and hit record and play. The beep should get recorded onto the audio track you have the Aux track routed to.

5. Switch to samples by opening the main counter selector pull-down next to the Main Time Scale in the Edit window.

6. Zoom into the timeline and select the exact distance between the beginning of the original beep and the beginning of the newly recorded beep. You may need to zoom in very close to make this selection accurately. Use the Edit Selection Length counter in Samples to see the total length of this selection. This is the amount of latency your routing is creating in Samples! Write this magic number

down and make sure you remember to switch the Aux input back to the recording source input.

7. Whenever you record anything through this signal chain, simply select the audio you just recorded and select Edit > Shift. Select Earlier, type in that magic number in the Samples field, and press Return/Enter. Your recording will now be perfectly in time!

If you've got an arsenal of cool vintage hardware EQ filters, tape echoes, and Leslie cabinets, you will want to use them as hardware inserts or hardware sends to augment your Pro Tools recordings. For LE systems, running through these types of devices spells out that nasty word again: *latency*! You can record a test tone and measure the distance to deal with this problem too. The previous method, in which you made a test tone, is precisely how you can deal with this problem. Just make a 1-second beep in an audio track and then route that audio track's output through the hardware via the hardware I/O on an insert or send and record its latent signal back on to a second audio track. The difference in samples between the original beep and the new beep is the magic number you can punch in to shift your audio earlier.

External Processing Latency in Pro Tools TDM

Pro Tools HD systems are equipped to deal with plug-in latency automatically with the use of the Delay Compensation Engine; however, it still can't go outside the box and determine how much latency your external processing might be causing. Especially if you are using digital devices, you may want to run the signal test and record tip detailed in the preceding section. The difference in TDM is that you can enter these amounts in the H/W Insert Delay window located by choosing Setup > I/O Setup > H/W Insert Delay (see Figure 4.7).

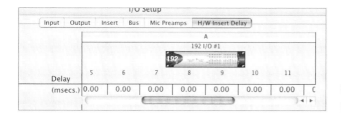

Figure 4.7 The H/W Insert Delay window on TDM systems

Once you determine how much latency your hardware insert causes, you may manually enter the amount in milliseconds into the insert or bus you plan to run the hardware through. The Delay Compensation Engine will then figure that into its equations and automatically compensate when you are using that particular insert slot or hardware send.

Automating FX

One of the most powerful features of any computer-based music system is automation. The ability to automate plug-ins, volume, pan, mute, and countless other functions is what separates us from the animals. Well, it seems that way sometimes. Pro Tools has high-resolution audio automation, which allows you to sculpt and tailor songs in ways impossible when working without automation. Disney had an army of engineers on the board to mix *Fantasia*, yet two or three people could perform the same tasks today. Technically speaking, at least, those Disney folks were pretty talented. Each automation parameter has its own playlist, which can now be copied and pasted between tracks in Pro Tools 7. Plug-in automation works on the same principle as any automation in Pro Tools except you need to enable the plug-in parameters that you want to automate before you can use them. There are two ways to enable plug-in parameters for automation. Here is how you do it:

1. Open the plug-in you want to automate and click the auto button in the upper-right corner. The Plug-In Automation window opens and shows you a list of the available functions you can automate (see Figure 4.8).

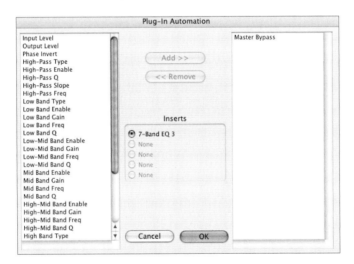

Figure 4.8 The Plug-In Automation window with Master Bypass chosen

2. Choose any of the parameters you want to automate by double-clicking or single-clicking, and clicking the Add button. You can add multiple functions simultaneously by using the ⌘ key or Shift key while choosing.

3. The other method to choose automation parameters is to use the old three-finger "Scouts salute." In the plug-in, click on the function you want to automate as you hold Control+Option+⌘ / Start+Alt+Ctrl. You will see a prompt that asks you to either turn the automation on for that feature or to open the Plug-Ins Automation box. For the shortcut, chose to enable the automation and then you can get at it in the track automation playlist (see Figure 4.9).

Figure 4.9 Shortcut to
enable Plug-In Automation

4. In the automation mode selector in your track, change the mode from Auto Read to Touch or Latch, depending on how you want the automation to act and if you already have any automation in the playlist.

5. If you want to automate your plug-in in real time by moving the controls to the music, you should do so on the plug-in window. You can do real-time automation with the Pencil or Grabber tool directly in the automation playlist in the track window, but you might not get the same sense of the effect. Make sure the parameter you want to automate is enabled and start playback. As the track plays, you can move any knob, slider, or button that you have enabled. You can automate multiple settings at once or do each setting in different passes. This is a great way to make musical moves with automation. You can feel the vibe of the track as your tweak the settings. Unlike the Disney folks in the '40s, you have undo, and the quest for automation perfection can be achieved in your bedroom studio.

Note: Control+⌘+← → / Start+Ctrl+← → can be used to toggle between automation views on a tr...

in your plug-in automation or fine-tune a pass of real-time automation
y, you need to break out the Pencil or Grabber tool. With this method,
itomate the parameters with incredible precision. If you want to do
rameters in one pass, automate in the plug-in window with multiple
enabled. In the track view selector, choose one of your enabled
...omation parameters and get the Pencil or Grabber tool.

7. Drawing in automation with the Pencil tool will be constrained to the Grid mode you are in unless you use Freehand or Line.

8. To cut, copy, paste, and clear automation, there is a new Special section in the Edit menu (see Figure 4.10).

You can choose what type of automation to edit. When you use Paste Special > To Current Automation Type, you can copy a volume curve from a guitar track and paste it into the automation playlist for a reverb decay. Go crazy. From any type of automation to any other, copy, paste and enjoy the results.

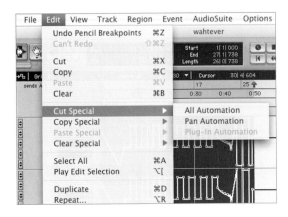

Figure 4.10 The Special functions in the Edit menu

Channel Strip Import

It's easy to create your own preset style channel strips in Pro Tools and import them into any session using Import Session Data. Chock-full of FX for processing vocals, guitars, drums, and stems, channel strip inserts can contain very complex FX chains. The idea of the virtual channel strip comes from the channel strip found on hardware mixing consoles where you see volume, pan, EQ, routing, and sends and returns. Pro Tools tracks can be configured like this and saved for later use. Any kind of track other than a pure MIDI track will work: an audio track guitar channel strip with Amp Farm, Echo Farm, Q10, and BF 3A; a mastering Master Fader track with L3, C4, or Maxim; or an Aux track to bus vocals to with TL Space and ReVibe with a little extra EQ III. You can import any track into any session using Import Session Data, but by creating a master FX session, you will always know where every channel strip is. If you have created other template sessions, you may want to save the FX session with them.

Here is a technique to create and access FX channel strips in any session:

1. Create a new session that will act as the master file holding the tracks with the FX insert chains.

2. You can go two ways here. Either you can make new channel strips from scratch fresh in this document or you can import channel strips from existing sessions. For example, if you already have a killer guitar FX chain on a track in another session, go ahead and bring it into this document. Create your track(s) to hold the inserts, thinking about mono vs. stereo and audio vs. Aux., and build your channel strips. Remember, plug-in ordering matters.

3. Label your tracks appropriately because that's how you will see them when you use Import Session Data to bring them to your new session.

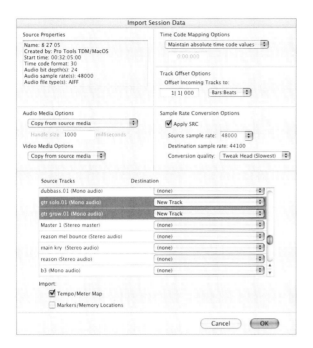

4. After you place your inserts, you can create sends in the tracks if you want to bus them to an Aux for more processing.

5. In addition to the audio channel strip, you can create Aux tracks that are bus destinations. A typical Aux track would hold reverb. You can import your I/O as well so you can have all of your original bus assignments.

6. In the master FX file, you may want to keep your insert-laden tracks inactive until you need them so as not to bog down your system resources. In any session, if you create lots of tracks with lots of plug-ins, you may want to print the tracks with the FX to release the system resources. After you print the tracks, you may want to make the tracks inactive (Track > Inactive). You can paint yourself into a proverbial corner by overloading the system resources: too many active inserts and you can crash and burn! Having a session that cannot be reopened because the system resources can't handle the load is not cool. To make tracks active, select the track or tracks and choose Track > Make Active.

Note: The Pro Tools HD system's Import Session Data dialog has more options for which track attributes you wish to import. For example, you can choose not to import any audio with a track. This can be useful for importing just certain complex mixing signal flows.

Once you have your FX session loaded up with cool FX chains, you can import your fine work into any new session.

Understanding Equalization: The Five EQ Shapes

Just as compression processing helps control variable sound levels and amplitude, equalizing helps control the way we hear the pitch and frequencies of the sounds we work with. EQ is an essential processing tool that can help shape the tonal characteristics of individual sounds and assist in the blending of many combined sounds in a multitrack situation. Your mix is like a sonic painting. Use EQ to make your palette rich with evocative and complementary sounds to paint with.

Frequency Response Graph

To fully understand EQ shapes, you must first be familiar with the frequency response graph. This graph shows what frequencies are being affected and how much of those frequencies are being added or subtracted. The graph has an X access across the horizontal bottom labeled with frequencies measured in hertz (Hz). Most graphs range from 20Hz to 20,000Hz or 20kHz, since this is the range of human hearing. The Y access is labeled vertically with decibels (dB). The middle point is 0, representing a flat line, no change. When the graph line extends above the zero line, it means decibels are added; below the line means decibels are being taken away.

The following graphics show the five EQ shapes in the frequency response graph along with some examples of how they are typically used. These shapes are extremely important because most EQ plug-ins and hardware will refer to different EQ types with icons reflecting these shapes.

- High shelf
- Low shelf
- High cut (low pass)
- Low cut (high pass)
- Parametric

The Shelving Filters

Everyday people use these EQs regularly. These are the kind found on many typical home stereos or car stereos. They affect either the low or high frequencies (treble or bass on car stereos). These filters are usually very musical sounding and have a variable frequency control to determine where the shelf begins. The shelving filters can either add or subtract volume at the high and

Continues

Understanding Equalization: The Five EQ Shapes *(Continued)*

low frequencies they operate on. This is an example of a high shelf adding high frequencies and then a low shelf taking away high frequencies:

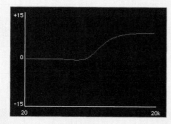 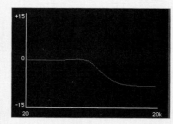

The high shelves could be used to brighten up a dark-sounding cello or to tone down drum overhead mics that are too brash-sounding.

Use the low shelves to boost a bass that is sounding too thin or to remove murky low end from an organ, for example. This is an example of a low shelf adding low frequencies and then a low shelf removing low frequencies:

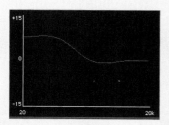 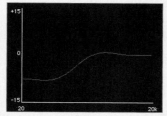

The Cut or Pass Filters

These EQ shapes only cut out frequencies. They are designed primarily to remove unwanted frequencies of sound. They are referred to as either cut or pass filters, so low pass would be the same as high cut. You are cutting the highs and allowing the lows to pass through. Although they work on high and low frequencies as the shelving filters do, these EQ shapes have different curves when graphed out, giving them a unique sound and purpose. This is an example of a low cut filter and then a high cut filter:

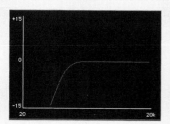 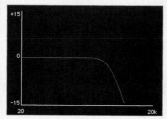

Continues

Understanding Equalization: The Five EQ Shapes *(Continued)*

You can use a low cut to remove low problematic rumble from wind or mic handling. You can use a high cut to remove tape hiss or to mellow a brass section. These filters can also be used for creative sound design. Since we associate presence with high frequencies, a high cut can be implemented to make a sound seem far away or in another room.

The Parametric EQ

The parametric EQ works in the middle of the frequency spectrum. It can be used to enhance a range of frequencies or to lower undesirable aspects within a sound. The parametric has three variables: the frequency at which it operates, the gain (how much added or subtracted), and the Q-factor. The Q-factor, or Q, is a measure of how wide the bell shape is. A lower Q value will mean a wider range, while a high Q means a narrow bell. Once the Q is very high, this EQ is sometimes referred to as a Notch filter because it can be used to "notch out" a very specific frequency. Here are two examples of parametric EQs adding and subtracting frequencies around 2kHz:

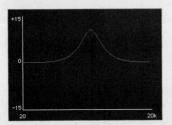 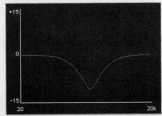

Use a slightly wide Q boost at 5kHz to enhance the presence of a vocal performance, for example. Or remove a bit around 300Hz to take away some of the muddiness of an acoustic guitar. Also, use a very high Q to remove unwanted hum from an air conditioner or electronic noise. Here is a parametric EQ with a higher Q:

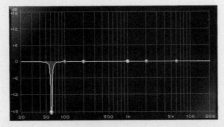

Now that some of the EQ shapes have been spelled out, you should have no problem understanding and using any of the different EQs that are available as plug-ins on Pro Tools systems. Waves's Renaissance, Filter Bank, Focusrite, and the Digidesign EQ 3 all use graphics referring to the aforementioned graph shapes.

Use EQ to Find and Remove Problematic Noise

There is a whole range of noise removal plug-ins on the market. Bias's SoundSoap, DINR, and Waves's X-Noise are a few that come to mind. But you would be surprised how a regular old EQ can be used to locate and remove unwanted noise from an audio recording. As long as the noise is constant and in a specific frequency range that isn't absolutely vital to the sound you are trying to keep, it can be done. Sounds like refrigerator noise, air conditioner hum, and even the electronic hum of an old organ can be dealt with. The free Digidesign EQ 3 has some effective notch filters that can get the job done. Here's how to go about finding the unwanted noise and removing it:

1. Insert an EQ 3 plug-in on the track with the problematic noise.

2. Make an edit selection of the problematic audio in the track and press Shift+⌘+L / Shift+Ctrl+L to turn on Loop Playback.

3. With the audio looping, turn up the Q value all the way to 10 on the LMF (low mid filter), MF (mid filter), or HMF (high mid filter), depending on the general area in which the problematic audio exists in the frequency range.

4. Turn the gain all the way up on the same filter (see Figure 4.11).

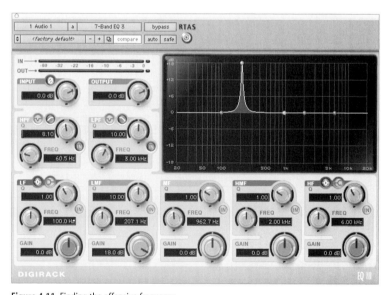

Figure 4.11 Finding the offensive frequency

5. Sweep the FREQ (frequency) knob back and forth until the problematic noise is as loud and pronounced as possible. Make sure your monitor speakers are not too loud when you do this because it could get nasty!

On the DigiRack EQ 3 plug-in, there are some awesome shortcuts that are useful for finding and sweeping your EQ curve.

Control+click / Start+click on the round dot associated with the band you are adjusting in the EQ's frequency display window and pull up or down to change the Q.

Shift+Control+click / Shift+Start+click on the dot to temporarily "solo" just that frequency and drag the mouse left or right to listen to only the frequency you are adjusting

6. Once you find the frequency you are looking for, move the gain of the same filter all the way in the negative direction. As long as this EQ is not affecting the original sound too badly, you can stick with this shape. If the good audio in the track is sounding too weird with this extreme EQ, you may need to decrease the gain as much as you can get away with.

7. If you have successfully found the frequency using this method, you can then move to the notch filters on the EQ 3 plug-in to get a more extreme EQ shape that will work on an even more specific frequency range. The notch filters can be activated by clicking the notch icon in the HPF or LPF section of the EQ 3 plug-in.

Remember, audio frequencies can be worked out mathematically so that you will find additional nodes of noise at ½, 2X, 3X, 4X (and so on) the original frequency. A final noise reduction EQ might look like Figure 4.12.

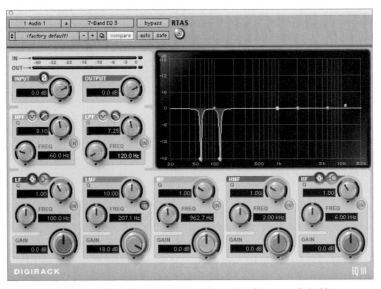

Figure 4.12 An EQ shape designed to remove air-conditioner hum from a specific building

Turn Your HD System into an AM Radio

One of the most sought-after effects in recent memory has been the AM radio or telephone sound on vocals. From a two-bar drop in rock and roll to emphasize a lyric to the double or triple track in hip-hop or the main vocal in an dirge track, the AM radio sound is a great trick to throw into a mix to give it some flavor and grit. There are a number of ways to get this sound and different levels of destruction you can do to the vocal:

1. Insert a distortion-type plug-in on the vocal track. Amp Farm, Sans Amp, and AmpliTube can all do this. You can get this effect without some distortion; it's just a little less "antiqued" or vintage-sounding. Some versions of Pro Tools come with the plug-in AmpliTube from IK Multimedia. This is a great amp simulator type distortion and general-purpose FX box. You can also download a fully functional demo version of AmpliTube from www.ampliTube.com that is good for 10 days. It's available for most systems and worth the effort to download it and test it out.

2. Set your preamp model and cabinet model to get the tone you want. AmpliTube has settings from pure tubelike clean tone to the hardest distortion (see Figure 4.13).

Figure 4.13 AmpliTube main screen

There is also a cool little springlike reverb that puts a classic sound on the track. AmpliTube and other new amp simulator plug-ins are very deep these days, so tweak the EQ, Tremolo, mic types, and gain. There is a separate FX page where you can pile on more reverb, delay, and EQ. The FX button to open the FX page is in the bottom-right corner of the AmpliTube Plug-In screen.

3. Insert an EQ of four bands or more after the amp plug-in. EQIII is a good default if you don't have anything else. On the EQ, you want to filter out everything below 500Hz and above 5kHz. Different voice types will need different treatment, so move the EQs around to find your sweet spots (see Figure 4.14).

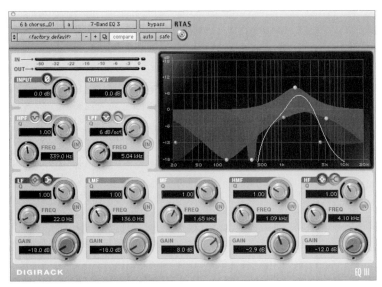

Figure 4.14 A basic EQ curve for the AM radio effect

4. Insert a compressor at the end of the chain. The free Bomb Factory compressors are pretty good and the new Digidesign Compressor III is good quality as well. This works with almost any compressor type.

5. For this effect, set Threshold to a lower level than you normally would. The lower you set the threshold, the more you crush the track (see Figure 4.15).

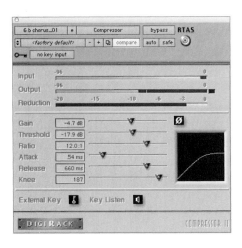

Figure 4.15 A basic compressor setting for the AM radio effect

6. Set Ratio above 10:1 to turn the compressor into a limiter. This means nothing gets out above your threshold setting. Squash squash, total control! Adjust to your own tastes.

7. Use Gain to make up the signal reduced by the compressing.

8. Adjust the Knee setting to determine how the compressor kicks in. The higher the setting the "softer" the Knee or the more gradual the compressor comes in. Soft-Knee is used most often for vocals, but interesting effects can be had with a Hard-Knee setting on a vocal track.

The compressor is being fed the vocal that has gone through the amp simulator and then the EQ first. This lets you really step on the track to flatten it out and give that classic old effect. The plug-in ordering is also a big deal. There is no one right way but many wrong ways, as they say. Experiment by dragging the plug-ins into different positions and listening back for the differences. For HD users, the only qualification is that RTAS plug-ins precede TDM plug-ins. Start your inserts in the second Insert slot and you have room to move your FX around. The combination of these three effects can be very powerful and versatile.

Parallel Compression

Most often, compressors and EQs are used directly in a track's insert slot so that 100 percent of the sound runs through them. The parallel compression technique breaks from that norm and uses a compressor on a send and return much as you would typically use a reverb effect. By blending in a little of the compressed sound with the original dry sound, you can achieve a unique mixing effect that works wonders for the low end of drums or even an entire mix.

Anthony Puglisi (aka Rollmottle), producer and owner of Sentrall Records, utilizes parallel compression on his mixes often. Here's what he has to say about the technique:

"I use parallel compression successfully to fatten up lows without mudding up the whole area. It works especially well for producing big solid kicks and low taut bass. It lets transients pass through untouched and broadens up the bottom. The technique works well for me on percussive elements, especially those sourced from analog equipment. In dance-oriented electronic music, this is key. I also find it nice to use conservatively across the master bus as it gives a track that extra oomph and power (not just makes it louder—there's a difference) through quieter portions of the jam without resorting to one of those horrific 'maximizer' plug-ins that squeeze the dynamics right out of your song. Lots of digital and electronic artists feel free to liberally use these maximizers across their master bus to 'make it louder!' But louder definitely does not always mean better."

Here's the recipe for parallel compression on drums:

1. Make a new stereo Aux Input. Name it Drums Comp. Assign it a bus input. For this example, Bus 1-2 is used.

2. Make a send on Bus 1-2 for all the drum tracks. Option+click / Alt+click all of the drum track send faders to set them to 0, or unity gain.

3. Insert an appropriate compressor plug-in on the Drums Comp Aux track. In this example, Focusrite's D3 Compressor is used, but you can substitute the free Dynamics 3 compressor if you don't have this one.

4. As a general guideline, the compressor can be set as follows: Threshold as low as it will go; you want to compress the whole signal. Start with a Ratio of 2.5:1, but this can go as high as to 4:1. Attack as fast as it will go. Start with a Release setting of 250 ms, but adjust this to taste. Output Gain can be increased to taste as well.

5. Bring up the Drums Comp Aux fader to blend in this compressed (wet) signal with the uncompressed (dry) signal of original drums audio tracks.

Figure 4.16 shows the Mix window routing and the Focusrite compressor.

Figure 4.16 Parallel compression at work

Compression

Compression is a vital part of the recording and mixing process and parallels the idea of how the human ear controls sound levels. The ear has a built-in compressor that will close down or open up to volume as need be. We can hear incredibly soft sounds but not as we hear incredibly loud sounds. We would be deaf in a second if we heard loudness at the intensity we hear lower levels of volume. The dynamic range of a human is 120 dB, and even in this day and age that is difficult for us to reproduce in a recorded media.

Compression can automatically control levels in recording, mixing, and mastering, transparently affecting the audio. It's like having hundreds of little engineers in your system constantly turning things up very quickly when they are too soft and then turning them down when they get too loud. The union fees alone would kill you. Compression can also be used as a powerful effect. Pumping drums or gating vocals can be a very dynamic technique. Since compressors reduce the dynamic range of a signal (the difference between the softest part and loudest part of the signal), you can boost the overall average level to create a seemingly louder track. These are the basic components of a compressor:

Threshold The Threshold setting is the level above which the signal will be affected. If you set this too low, you could overly compress your track and take the life out of it.

Ratio Compressors attenuate the output signal by the Ratio settings. If you set Ratio to 2:1 and raise the signal 10 dB past the Threshold setting, the output of the signal will be only 5 dB. A high Ratio setting turns a compressor into a limiter by reducing the output to the Threshold setting.

Attack Attack is the amount of time it takes for the compressor to kick in. Too long an attack and the compression won't kick in until after signal has passed through. This can also be a cool effect.

Release Release is the amount of time it takes for the gain to return to the threshold level. If the Release time is too short, you will hear the gain changing, known as the pumping effect. Try to set Attack and Release to match the rhythm of the music. Attack and Release affect each other, so often you'll need to work with them in tandem to get the desired result.

Soft-Knee The Knee function fine-tunes how the compressor will act on the audio it is compressing.

Continues

Selecting Soft-Knee will ramp the compression in gradually. Soft-Knee is often used for vocals and non-percussive sounds, where a transparent compression is needed.

Hard-Knee Selecting Hard-Knee will bring in the compression more dramatically so that it acts exactly at the Threshold point. Hard-Knee is typical for drums or any compression where you want the compressor's sound to be less transparent. Pro Tools Compressor/Limiter Dyn 3 compressors see a setting of 0 dB as the hardest setting.

Gain, aka make-up gain This allows you to make up the gain you lose by compressing by adjusting the output gain after compression has taken place. The higher the ratio and lower the threshold, the more gain you must make up to return your audio to the same peak levels.

The End of the Cardboard Kick

Revoicing MIDI tracks is a snap. You write a track with a grand piano sound and the next day you realize that the track just cries for a banjo sound instead—no problem. Just change the patch in your keyboard and you're done. Audio has never had this kind of luxury until the arrival of the AudioSuite plug-in SoundReplacer (see Figure 4.17).

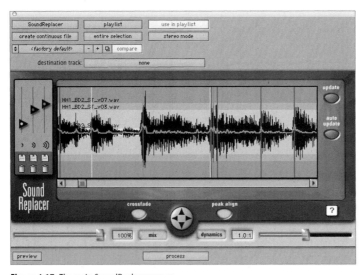

Figure 4.17 The main SoundReplacer screen

SoundReplacer analyzes and maps selected audio in a track so you can either replace the original with new audio of your choosing or print the new audio to a different track to mix the two together. SoundReplacer keeps the original performance but lets you use different sounds to voice it. SoundReplacer is a native Digidesign plug-in, so it runs in both the HD and LE environments, but it is not presently included with the basic software. You can get SoundReplacer a la carte or in the Digidesign Music Production Toolkit with a bunch of other cool plug-ins, sound makers, and expanded functions. Most studios, both pro and home, have large sample libraries containing hundreds if not thousands of samples. Finding just the right kick or snare is just a matter of time. The more separation you have in your audio tracks, the easier it is get an accurate replacement. If you have printed audio from MIDI and you need to revoice the sound without access to the original MIDI files, this is your fix. This plug-in works best for replacing drum sounds or for replacing sound effects and such in postproduction. Here's how to replace a kick drum from a track:

1. Select your audio to be replaced.

2. Open SoundReplacer (AudioSuite > SoundReplacer).

3. Press the load sound floppy icon to open the load sample dialog box (see Figure 4.18).

Figure 4.18 The load sample window

4. Choose your samples. There is no preview in this window, so you need to know what you want to import. After the samples are loaded, adjust the threshold controls to trigger different samples in the different zones. With three zones, you can trigger up to three different sounds based on your threshold settings. Try drums sampled at different velocities in the different zones to create realism.

5. Turning Peak Align on or off controls where SoundReplacer places the new audio in relation to the source audio. Turn Peak Align on for drum sounds and turn it off for drums with late peaks or for effects. Timing accuracy is very important for successful sound replacement.

6. Preview your replacement.

7. Depending on what you hear when you preview, adjust your Threshold, Dynamics, and Mix settings to fine-tune your replacement audio. You can tweak the trigger settings; follow track dynamics and balance between the source audio and the replacement audio. Some tracks are much harder to correctly replace than others. These three parameters are a powerful solution.

8. When you are happy with the new audio, chose how you want to apply the effect. You have a number of options as to how and where you apply the effect, just as with most every other AudioSuite plug-in. Pick which suits your needs (see Figure 4.19).

 Note: When replacing single drum sounds, always make sure to change from stereo mode to mono mode in the plug-in file mode pull-down menu for the best results.

Figure 4.19 File controls

Choose a destination track, click Process, and listen to your new creation.

Here is a technique that blends your original track with a new track of replacement samples. This technique is from Justin Phelps, a recording engineer at the legendary Hyde Street Studio C in San Francisco, California. Enjoy!

"I almost always use both the sample and the original drum track. To get one of each, I simply duplicate the drum track (Shift+Option+D / Shift+Alt+D) and process the duplicate. If the drum track is well recorded, I generally end up mixing them together with about 10 dB more original than sample. This adds a nice punchy, compressed sound to the drum track without losing too much of the natural dynamics.

"If the drum track is poorly recorded and/or horrible sounding, I will use a lot more sample. Sometimes in this situation, I'll use equal amounts or even more sample than original track. The sacrifice here is that the more sample you use, the more you move in the direction of your live drums sounding like a drum machine—unless, of course, that's what you were going for.

"When mixing the samples together, it is important to double-check the alignment of each sample to its trigger. As tedious as this can be, it can save you a lot of embarrassment later. Sound Replacer can be pretty inaccurate with its triggering, and drummers sometimes play things that are hard for a trigger to follow. The biggest stumbling blocks are flams and soft hits.

"When comparing your generated track to your original track, watch out for missed hits and hits that are out of phase. To my ear, it is more important that the sample is generally in phase with the original than for the attacks to be perfectly lined up. This is an aesthetic call, and if you disagree, well then go on with your thin-sounding drums! After generating the sample track, the first thing that I do is to go to the first substantial drum hit in the song, zoom in very close on the sample track and original track, and drag or nudge the sample track a little so that the waveforms are more in phase than out of phase. While doing this, keep the attacks as close together as possible. Occasionally you will notice that the tracks just seem generally out of phase. That's great news! Select the region of your sample track, go to AudioSuite, and invert the track. Presto! A nice full-sounding pair. At this point I begin the process of checking each hit for flaws in timing or missed hits, the solution for these problems being nudge or cut/paste. Enjoy. The end result will be worth it."

Reverb

Reverb is not an effect; reverb is a natural part of the sonic landscape. Reverb is so important in shaping the sound we hear that the absence of reverb would be like seeing without color and depth perception. In fact, only in an anechoic chamber can you hear sound without reverb. Listening to a sound, you hear the direct or dry sound and then the first or early reflections, which are the waves that find the quickest route to the listener after the direct sound and help the ear identify the size of the space. Then you hear the onslaught of the rest of the reflected waves coming later in time, with various levels of diminishing amplitude and differing frequency. The series of reflections that come after the original sound impulse and the early reflections are what we call reverb. Reverb is all about time and texture. The overall size and shape of a room and the type of its surfaces control the reverb time. Engineers and musicians have been very creative in attempting to create natural and artificial reverb over the years and have achieved different levels of success and believability. The very nature of modern recording eliminates most of the natural space around a sound wave and the associated reverb, so re-creating these spaces artificially is vital. Reverbs vary from company to company, and some of the newer, more sophisticated reverbs have more capabilities, but these parameters are typical:

Algorithm/Reverb Type Determines the type of the space you are modeling. You find choices like Room or Chamber.

Size Used to set the dimensions of the space you are re-creating. You see these values shown in meters or feet or by sizes like small, medium, or large.

Continues

Don't Stress, DeEsse

A DeEsser (included in the new Dyn3 plug-in bundle) is actually a side-chain processor all by itself. The DeEsser is like a selective volume knob that turns down sibilant high frequencies only when they happen. To accomplish this, it uses the audio of the track

Reverb (Continued)

Pre-delay Controls the amount of time before the reverb arrives. Pre-delay includes both the dry sound and the early reflections in most reverb units or plug-ins. Pre-delay can create the illusion of space in a close-mic-ed track. The bigger the pre-delay, the bigger the space you are simulating. Pre-delay can also keep clarity in your track even if you have a big effect going by separating the dry and the affected signal. Try using musical values for this setting.

Early Reflections These critical first or second reflections alert the brain as to what size of room or space you are in. Early reflections arrive before the main body of the reverb. Early Reflection settings are vital when creating room simulations.

Decay Sets the amount of time between the end of the sound and the end of the reflections, also know as reverb time. Technically the reverb time is the time it takes for the sound pressure to decay to $1/1000$ (60 dB) of the original intensity.

Diffusion Increasing the diffusion pushes the early reflections closer together, making a denser reverb. Too much diffusion can create muddiness in the reverb. Decreasing the diffusion pulls the early reflections farther apart, creating an echo-type effect. Percussive sounds tend to sound more natural with a higher diffusion level, while vocals and some sustained instruments work better with less diffusion.

Reverb Density Density determines the amount of space between the first reflections and the reverb. Lower densities have more space and higher densities have less.

EQ or Filters Shape the tone of the reverb. Make it big in the low end for drama or add some shine to your vocal verb.

Surface Not found on all reverbs, but it is very useful. This determines the reflective characteristics of the surface. This can be from spongelike absorption to tilelike reflectivity. Absorptive materials reduce the reverb time by diminishing the wave energy, while reflective materials increase the reverb time by passing the wave energy along. The reflective surface (tile) found in most showers or bathrooms is responsible for the old "I sound great singing in the shower" sound. Good thing showers aren't carpeted!

Reverb is very complex and somewhat difficult to understand, but knowing the basics can help you get the effect you're listening for. This complexity is also why believable artificial reverb has been so hard to develop and so painfully expensive until recently.

as a key input to trigger an EQ-filtered compressor that activates only when there are high frequencies present. It is a widely used tool of the pros to nondestructively remove sibilant "th" and "ess" sounds that some microphones amplify in a human voice.

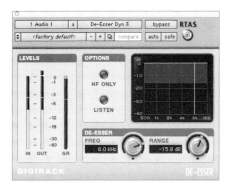

DeEssers are located in the Dynamics Plug-In folder. There is also a DeEsser preset in the DigiRack Compressor if the DigiRack plug-in doesn't give you the sound you want or if you need to work on a stereo track. To use the DigiRack or similar DeEsser on a vocal track, follow these steps:

1. Insert the DeEsser on a mono audio track in front of any compressors or limiters you may be using. DeEssers work best earlier in the chain and the DigiRack DeEsser is mono only.

2. Adjust the Threshold value so only the sibilants are compressed. Setting Threshold too low will compress the main body of your track.

3. Select the frequency at which you want the DeEsser to operate. If the frequency is too low, you will miss the sibilants and affect other parts of the frequency.

4. If necessary, you can automate the threshold to compensate for large volume differences in a track. (See the section "Automating FX" earlier in this chapter.)

A DeEsser can take some of the life out of your track, so use it with care and use it on individual tracks as opposed to entire mixes.

Demystifying the Side-Chain

Have you ever wondered what the side-chain, key input, and external listen buttons on dynamics plug-ins do? If you have experimented with third-party plug-ins like Waves's C-1 or the Focusrite compressor, you will have seen these buttons. Pro Tools 7 LE now offers frequency-controllable external side-chain processing on the new Dynamics 3 plug-ins. Side-chain processing is an advanced plug-in technique that takes the signal from an external audio track or bus and uses it as a control signal to trigger a gate or compress audio on a dynamics plug-in. You can use side-chain processing to tighten up a loose rhythm section, lower (duck) one sound when another occurs, or brighten a vocal, for example. The next three sections—"Key That Kick," "Brighten Those Vocals," and "Duck, You Sucker"—include recipes to get you started with side-chain processing and demystify those strange buttons once and for all.

Key That Kick

The most popular use of this side-chain technique is to key a loosely played bass line with the kick drum so that the two instruments become locked together. It can also be used to trigger a low-frequency tone on a track simultaneously with every kick drum hit—perfect for the boom in a hip-hop beat that will shake your bones.

To lock in a loose bass part with the kick drum, follow these steps:

1. Assign a send using an available bus for the kick drum track in the Mix window. Turn up the level of the send to 0 by Option+clicking / Alt+clicking the pop-up send fader.

2. On the bass track, insert a Expander/Gate Dyn 3 plug-in.

 Note: Side-chain techniques are shown in this chapter with the free DigiRack Dyn3 Compressor/Limiter, Expander/Gate Dyn 3, and DeEsser Dyn 3. If these plug-ins weren't installed with your version of Pro Tools 7, you can download them at www.Digidesign.com.

3. In the Expander/Gate plug-in window, open the key input pop-up window and select the same bus you used for the send of the kick track. In Figure 4.20, it is Bus 1. The plug-in is now set to listen to the kick to tell it when to open the gate.

4. In the Side-Chain portion of the plug-in window (upper right), activate the key button (the small key icon). This activates the key input.

5. Since you are keying a kick drum, use the low-pass EQ on the gate to filter out any unwanted high frequencies present in the kick drum track. In the example in Figure 4.20, the filter is used to filter out snare bleed so only the low kick frequencies will trigger the gate. This EQ could also be used if you were keying an already mixed drum beat in one track to key just the kick drum sounds. To listen to the sound you are keying, you may activate the Key Listen button (the speaker icon) next to the key icon.

6. Adjust the threshold low enough so that each kick beat will trigger the gate to open.

7. Adjust the attack as fast as it will go (knob turned all the way left) to make the gate open the instant the kick is heard.

8. Adjust the release to determine how long the bass notes will be held. Longer times (knob turned to the right) will leave each bass note in longer.

9. For optimum kick drum side-chain gating, adjust other knobs as shown in Figure 4.20.

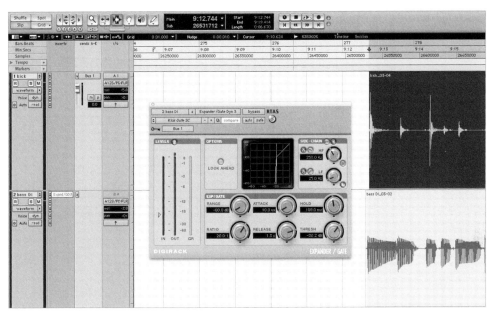

Figure 4.20 The Expander/Gate is set up here to key the kick drum on Bus 1 to trigger the opening of the gate.

You can use these same settings with some slight variations to key a low-frequency tone to play with the kick drum for that deep booty bass drum sound. Here's how:

1. Keep the same routing as mentioned in the preceding example (Figure 4.20). Instead of the bass track, make a new mono audio track and name it Tone.

2. On the Tone track, insert a Signal Generator plug-in (found in the Other category of the inserts list). Adjust the Signal Generator to play a sine wave at 50Hz and a level of -10.

3. Insert an Expander/Gate Dyn 3 plug-in on the Tone track below the Signal Generator. This plug-in must be inserted *after* the Signal Generator for this to work. Set up the controls as shown in Figure 4.21.

4. Adjust the Release and Hold knobs to make the tone last longer or be shorter.

5. Tune the frequency of the Signal Generator to match the tone of the original kick drum for optimum boom.

6. Try out the tune in a subwoofer-equipped ride and see if you make the neighborhood shake.

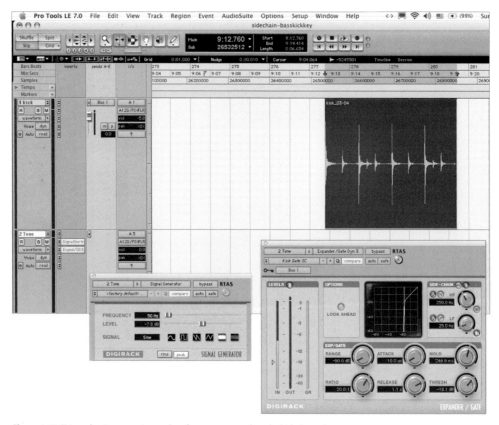

Figure 4.21 Using a key input to trigger a low-frequency tone when the kick drum plays

Brighten Those Vocals

Use this side-chain processing (in the form of a DeEsser) to brighten the vocals without EQing the entire signal. This technique allows you to blend in high frequencies keyed from the same source as the original to give the lead vocal a unique dynamic edge.

The following unconventional use of a DeEsser takes advantage of its Listen mode, using its filtered key input to blend with the original vocal:

1. Choose Track > Duplicate to make a duplicate of the Lead Vocal track.

2. Set the output of the original and duplicated tracks to an available bus. In Figure 4.22, this is Bus 3.

3. Create a mono Auxiliary track, name it Vocals Sub, and route its input to the same bus. Turn up the fader of the Vocals Sub Aux track.

4. Insert a DeEsser Dyn3 plug-in on the duplicated vocal track. Select the HF Only and Listen buttons on the plug-in. Adjust the frequency to somewhere between 5 and 12kHz and the range to around -35 dB. You are only hearing what the DeEsser is designed to remove.

5. Gently mix in the duplicated track with the original. Adjust the frequency to suit the vocalist's sound. (See Figure 4.22.)

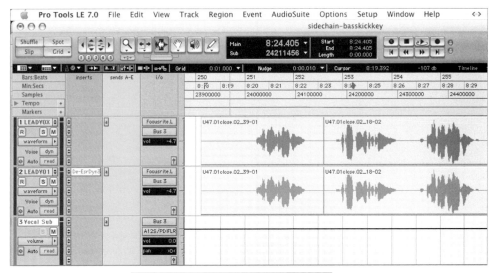

Figure 4.22 Using the Listen function on a DeEsser to blend in some high frequencies

Duck, You Sucker

Taking its name from a seldom-seen Sergio Leone spaghetti western, this technique is often used in film/video or radio postproduction to turn down, or *duck*, one sound while another plays. It is perfect for turning down music as a voice-over occurs or to lower background ambience when a principle actor speaks.

Here's how to use the duck recipe (foie gras) to lower music when a VO narrator speaks:

1. Assign a send on an available bus for the VO track in the Mix window. Turn up the level of the send to 0 by Option+clicking / Alt+clicking the pop-up send fader.

2. On the music track(s), insert a Compressor/Limiter Dyn 3 plug-in.

3. In the Compressor/Limiter plug-in window, open the Key Input pop-up window and select the same bus you used for the send of the VO track. In Figure 4.23, it is Bus 1. The plug-in is now set to listen to the VO to tell it when to compress the music.

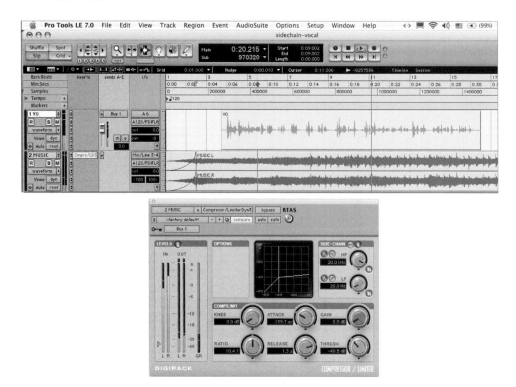

Figure 4.23 Using a compressor's key input to duck music under a VO

4. In the Side-Chain portion of the plug-in window (upper right), activate the key button (key icon). This turns on the key input.

5. Now set the compressor's threshold low enough to compress most of the music signal. Set Ratio to at least 10:1. Set the Attack time to a fast setting.

6. Play the VO audio. Notice that the compressor will activate only when the VO is happening. The Release time on the compressor will work best when it is set rather long, depending on the pacing of the VO. Work with the Release time so you don't hear the compressor pumping during speaking sections but the compressor lets the music level come back in a timely manner at the end of the VO passage. See Figure 4.23 for an idea of compressor settings.

Even the Pros Use Auto-Tune

With many artists using Auto-Tune on all of their tracks, it can't be wrong, can it? It's a fact that artists tune vocals all of the time. Auto-Tune and other tuning software may be most known for vocal tuning, but you can tune instruments with various degrees of success as well. Vocal tuning has been going on for years, but the technology has developed to the point where with a couple of mouse clicks, you can tune your track. Auto-Tune calculates the pitch of your selection in near real time by analyzing the amount of time between wave cycles. Auto-Tune needs to see the waves from a single sound to work like this, so you should use a mono- and solo-voiced track. A group of sounds like two voices singing the same note will not work because even though the notes sound the same, the waves produced by multiple instruments are too complex and random for Auto-Tune to figure them out. Auto-Tune can do more than just get your track tuned; it can be used (or overused) as an effect or it can add natural characteristics such as vibrato. Auto-Tune has two correction modes, Auto and Graphical. Within Auto Correction Mode, you will find both Key- and Scale-based entry and MIDI-based entry.

To tune a track using the Key and Scale functions in Auto Correction Mode, follow these steps:

1. Insert Auto-Tune into your track.

2. Select the region or track you want to tune.

3. Select an input type that matches your source track as closely as possible.

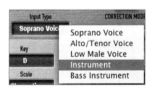

4. Pick your key. This sets the pitch of the first note.

5. Choose a scale. This is a powerful feature. There are 26 different scales to choose from. Ethnic or historic—take your pick. You can bypass or remove notes from your scale for more control.

6. Set the retune speed. This setting lets you choose how fast you take the original track to the new pitch. A low or fast setting will move the pitch in a hurry, making the track sound unnatural or effected (hint hint).

7. Set the tracking. This tells Auto-Tune how picky to be when analyzing the input pitch. Isolated tracks can be set to the default of 25 and usually find the pitch, but you will need to play with this setting to find the sweet spot.

Auto-Tune has amazing vibrato possibilities (see Figure 4.24), from natural styles on a voice to a more pronounced effect-type vibrato on an instrument track.

Figure 4.24 The vibrato section in Auto-Tune 4

8. Shape sets the motion of the vibrato. Use a sine wave for the most natural vocal effects and square or sawtooth for instrument tracks.

9. Set the rate for the speed of the vibrato.

10. Set the variation to randomize the rate and amount settings to give a more human feel to the track. A higher setting makes the vibrato more random.

11. Set the onset delay. This controls the amount of time before the vibrato kicks in.

12. Set the vibrato onset rate to control how long it will take the vibrato will get up to the full rate or speed.

For MIDI-based entry, to set pitch you need to be in Auto Correction Mode. You can play the notes on a MIDI keyboard and Auto-Tune will create a new scale based on those notes with Learn Scale From MIDI. You can also enter a scale in real time using your MIDI keyboard during playback with Target Notes Via MIDI (see Figure 4.25).

Figure 4.25 The MIDI modes in Auto-Tune 4

Here's how to tune a track using Learn Scale From MIDI in Auto Correction Mode:

1. Insert Auto-Tune into your track.

2. Select the region or track you want to tune.

3. Set your input to match the listed types as closely as possible.

4. Create a MIDI or instrument track, assign the output to Auto-Tune, and record-enable it.

5. Click the Learn Scale From MIDI button.

6. Play only the exact notes of the melody. As you play the notes, you see them all on the keyboard. This is not real time or recorded as to tempo, so you can enter the notes one at a time. When all of your notes of the melody are on the keyboard, you are good.

7. Deselect Learn Scale From MIDI.

8. Set the vibrato the same as in the Key and Scale example.

The other MIDI-based Auto Correction Mode is Target Notes Via MIDI via real-time MIDI input. You can control pitch from your MIDI keyboard as the track playback. This function is awesome for creating bizarre vocal effects as well as straight-up tuning. To tune a track in real time using Target Notes Via MIDI in Auto Correction Mode, follow these steps:

1. Follow steps 1 through 4 in the preceding set of steps (the Learn Scale From MIDI tip).

2. Click Target Notes Via MIDI.

3. Click record and start the track. Play your notes as you would play and record any MIDI track.

4. Deselect the Target Notes Via MIDI button.

5. Play back the track and use your MIDI editing tools if you need to make any changes. MIDI controls audio!

6. Set the vibrato the same as in the Key and Scale example.

Graphical Correction Mode allows you to see your pitch as a waveform and manually tune your track by drawing on a graph. This mode is a very precise way to tune your track regardless of scale or key. Whatever note you draw in is your pitch. What you see is what you get. This mode is also a great educational tool to show singers where they are in pitch (see Figure 4.26).

Here's how tune a track using Graphical Correction Mode:

1. Insert Auto-Tune into your track.

2. Select the region or track you want to tune.

3. Chose Graphical Correction Mode.

4. Under Playback, click Track Pitch.

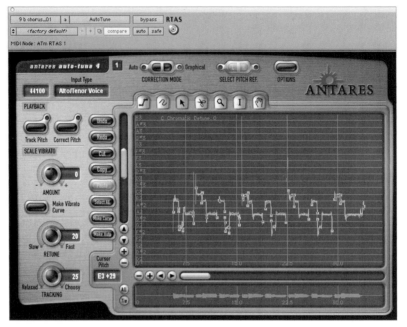

Figure 4.26 Graphical Correction Mode

5. Play the selection to capture your track. When you stop playback, you will see the waveforms of your track represented in a musical view, pitch and time. You can see just how in tune your track is, or is not.

Note: The length of the selection you can tune at one time is controlled by your buffer size. To get to the buffer, click the Options button at the top right of the Auto-Tune window.

6. Now it's time to get into your tools and start manually correcting your pitch. Look at the graph to see where pitch is and where it needs to be. With the Line tool, you can draw a series of connected straight lines on the graph to construct your pitch curve. With the Curve tool, you can draw in freehand corrections. You will see the track's original pitch against the grid and you can draw the new pitch in next to the original. If you know what the notes should be, that will make your life much easier and the editing quicker. You could know nothing about theory and just experiment until you found the right notes. but that would take much longer.

Study the Photoshop-like toolset to work in the most efficient manner. This is a very deep plug-in, so give it a thorough going over. The Graphical Correction

Mode offers familiar edit capabilities—like Copy, Paste, Cut, and Undo—and two not-so-familiar capabilities, Make Curve and Make Auto.

7. Make Curve and Make Auto can automatically generate pitch curves from the input data corresponding to your Key and Scale settings. If you don't like what you get, manually try this.

8. Enable Correct Pitch under Playback. This applies the pitch correction to the track. In most Pro Tools systems, starting playback will automatically kick in the pitch correction. This is a good plug-in to print to an audio track to free up system resources.

9. Set Retune and Tracking as described earlier in the Auto Correction Mode Key and Scale technique.

10. Scale Vibrato will let you increase or decrease the amount of existing vibrato in your track.

The ability to tune vocals quickly and correctly has generated more than one job in this industry. Ever heard of an Auto-Tune specialist? They exist. Draw in that perfect pitch and fool everyone. These are four very different ways to tune your tracks; experiment to find what works best in a given situation. Tuning is as much an art as a science, so practice, practice, practice!

The Power of Printing FX

Printing FX means running audio tracks through plug-ins, hardware effects processors, or any kind of effects chain and then recording the altered sounds back onto a Pro-Tools track. With all the benefits of real-time plug-ins in Pro-Tools, why do this? There are several reasons why printing FX is a working method of the pros:

•   If you are running audio through external hardware effects, you don't have to patch or set up knobs/program patches on those devices every time you open your session.

•   If you are manually automating your analog effects (a fun thing to do), you can capture your performance almost as if you are playing an instrument.

•   When using lots of resource-draining plug-ins, you will conserve massive amounts of system resources and Digital Signal Processing (DSP) because once an effect is printed, plug-ins can be set offline, freeing up your system to run more tracks or other plug-ins.

Here is an example of how to properly print an effects chain running first through a Digidesign Smack! compressor plug-in and then an Eventide H3000 rack effects processor (a multiuse studio effects processor used by the likes of recording pioneer Brian Eno). In this example, the idea is to take three keyboard parts performed on the venerable Moog synthesizer (RIP, Robert), compress the combined signal, add a complex pitch-shifted delay via the H3000, and finally print the sound to a stereo audio track. In addition to printing the effects, this processing workflow also provides a submix of the three Moog tracks, thus killing two birds with one stone:

1. Set the output on all three Moog tracks to go out an available bus. In this example, Bus 5-6 was chosen.

2. Hit ⌘+Shift+N / Ctrl+Shift+N to make a new stereo Aux Input track. Name the track Moogs sub. Set the new Moogs sub track's input to Bus 5-6.

3. Insert a Smack! (or compressor of your choice; Smack! may be included free in some Pro Tools 7 upgrades) on the Aux insert slot A.

4. Adjust the fader levels of the original tracks to blend them and compress the signal to taste.

5. On insert slot B of the auxiliary Moogs sub track, make an I/O insert on an available output. In this example, output 3-4 was chosen. (This example will work only with a Pro Tools interface that has more than two outputs; sorry, Mbox users).

6. Manually patch cables out of your Digidesign or M-powered hardware interface outputs 3-4 into the external processor (H3000 in this example) and out of the processor (H3000) into inputs 3-4 on your interface.

   Whenever you implement a hardware insert to an external analog processor like the H3000, you are making an additional A/D, D/A conversion. Usually the benefit of the sound you get is worth the extra conversion, but it's good to at least be aware that this is happening.

7. Dial up the sound you like on the external processor (H3000).

8. Set the output of the Moogs sub Aux track to an available Bus. In this example, Bus 7-8 was chosen.

9. Make a new stereo audio track. Name it Moogs print. Set its input to Bus 7-8.

10. Select the entire Moog section in the timeline of your song, making sure to include space at the end for delay/reverb tails. Record-enable the Moogs print audio track, and record away. Figure 4.27 shows the example after printing is completed in the Edit window. Note the input and output assignments in the I/O column of the Edit window.

Note: A good thing to remember while performing complex routing is that busses are exclusively for routing internally in Pro Tools, while I/O hardware routing implies externally connecting devices.

Figure 4.27 After printing the Moog tracks through a Smack! compresser and the H3000

The new effected sound will record (print) into the audio track. But the job isn't over yet; now comes the crucial cleanup part. Now that you have the submixed effected audio you want, it is tempting to delete all the original audio tracks and the Aux track since they are now redundant. Wrong! There is no need to do this; in fact, it would be catastrophic if you decided later to change the effect or the levels of the submix. The right thing to do is make the tracks inactive to remove system resources and hide them.

After the printing, do this:

1. Select only the three Moog tracks and the Moog sub by ⌘+clicking / Ctrl+click-ing each individual track name.

2. Choose Track > Make Inactive.

3. Hide the inactive tracks by deselecting their names in the Track List pop-up col-umn on the left of the Edit or Mix window. Inactive tracks will be italicized in this column.

Note: When you farm out to outside signal processors, you are at the mercy of any latency produced by Pro Tools and the additional internal signal processing of the devices themselves. Refer to the sections "External Processing Latency in Pro Tools TDM" and "Recording through a Plug-In" earlier in this chapter to compensate for any latency while printing FX.

Keep Your Printed FX Discrete: The Crinkler Effect

The example in the preceding section, "The Power of Printing FX," demonstrates how printing FX is used to combine the effect and the original signal together into one new file. Another approach in this workflow is to make the printed effect 100 percent effect and blend this printed track together with the dry original track to create an effect.

As an example, here's how to make the crinkler delay:

1. On a vocal track, make a hardware send on an available output. In this example, output 3 was used.

2. Physically run a cable out of output 3 on your Digidesign or M-powered hardware interface and connect it to the tape recorder's input.

3. Use an old "crinkled" tape in the recorder. If you don't have one, "crinkle" the tape manually. This technique provides the cool lo-fi wow and flutter effect.

4. Connect the output of the tape recorder (or alternately, mic the speaker of the recorder) to input 3 on the hardware interface.

5. Make a new mono audio track called Voice Crinkle and record-enable it. Record-enable the tape recorder too.

6. LE users press Option+K / Alt+K or go to the Track window and click Auto Input Monitoring to toggle into Input Only Monitoring Mode. HD users activate the I (Input Only)Monitoring button in the Voice Crinkle track between the Record Enable button and the Solo button. Play back your session and turn the send level up enough to get a good level going into the tape recorder.

7. Select the entire vocal section in the timeline of your song. Record-enable the Voice Crinkle track and record away.

8. Select the newly recorded Voice Crinkle region and choose Region > Shift. Choose Later and select the delay time in milliseconds of your liking. When you are done, mute the send by ⌘+clicking / Ctrl+clicking on its name in the send assignments area of the Mix window.

9. Mix and pan the Voice Crinkle track fader together with the original vocal track for a unique analog delay effect to get The Crinkler.

Mixing in Pro Tools: Directing Audio Traffic

One way to approach mixing is to imagine all of the audio tracks in your Pro Tools session as lanes of a freeway. When you mix to stereo, all of the lanes have to merge into two—the left and right outputs of your Pro Tools system. This lane merging is quite a challenge, even with a few tracks, and gets increasingly complicated as the track count gets higher. As the mixer of a Pro Tools session, you have the difficult job of conducting all of this traffic. You want to make sure that the lanes merge together seamlessly, without any bottlenecks.

In this chapter, we'll show you how to unlock the full sonic potential of your Pro Tools session with several mixing strategies.

Chapter Contents

Automation Recipes

Panning Techniques

Routing Options

EQ and Compression Ideas

It's in the Mix

Directing the sonic traffic of any mix can be a challenging endeavor. Luckily, Pro Tools's mixer comes equipped with powerful options that you can use while applying the tips and techniques outlined in this chapter. When your mix begins to feel complicated and overwhelming, remember that the right combination of these four essential tools are all it takes to direct that sonic traffic:

Track volume Proper level balance is key to continuous traffic flow.

Track panning Tracks can be panned to create space for themselves in a mix and unclog the roadway.

Processing tools Dynamics processing, such as compressors, help manage level inconsistencies, resulting in a smoother ride. Equalization can assist in those cluttered frequency traffic jams.

Effects Delays and reverbs are tools that create the sonic depth and space around your tracks to shine some light on the roadways.

Don't Lose Your Identity in a Group

For working with more than one track at a time, track groups are powerful tools in the Pro Tools mixing and editing tool belt. Groups let you control massive amounts of information across multiple tracks with a single stroke of a mouse, allowing for a faster workflow and more efficient command over large sessions. You can make a group with as few as two tracks or with as many as every track in your session. You can use groups to control the track view type, automation modes, mute, solo, track height, sample- or tick-based track editing functions, and volume. The following few sections demonstrate key concepts on how you can take masterful control of your session by grouping your tracks.

Creating and Editing a Group

Here's how to make your groups and edit them if you want to add or subtract members of those groups:

1. Select the tracks you wish to group by either Shift+clicking or ⌘+clicking / Ctrl+clicking any track name in the Mix or Edit window you wish to add. Shift selects adjacent tracks, ⌘/Ctrl selects nonadjacent tracks.

2. Press ⌘+G / Ctrl+G to bring up the group window. Name your group; choose one of the 26 possible IDs to assign to the group. There are 26 groups because the groups are labeled alphabetically, from *a* to *z*.

3. Choose either Edit, Mix, or both. This lets you decide whether you want to use the group for editing and selecting regions on the grouped tracks in the Edit window, for grouped mixer functions in the Mix window, or both.

4. To add a track or tracks to an existing group, click the group symbol button next to the group's name. Group names are shown in the groups list in the bottom-left column of the Mix or Edit window. Clicking on this symbol will automatically select all of the tracks in the group. Then ⌘+click / Ctrl+click on your new track(s). Press ⌘+G / Ctrl+G to open the group window. A new group letter will come up in the Group ID box, but reselect the group that you want to add the new track(s) to and click OK. The new tracks are now part of your group.

5. To delete tracks from a group, click the group symbol button for the desired group to select all the tracks in the group and then ⌘+click / Ctrl+click or Shift+click to deselect the tracks you no longer want in the group. Press ⌘+G / Ctrl+G to bring up the group box, select the group in the Group ID menu, and click OK. The tracks are deleted from your group.

Getting the Most out of the Groups List

In a big mix with many tracks, knowing how to efficiently use the groups list can save a lot of time and effort in your mix. The groups list, which is located in the bottom part of the left column of the Mix and Edit windows, gives you visual clues as to the current state of your groups. The group symbols are small icons located just to the left of any group names in the groups list. By clicking in the space to activate the group symbols, you can quickly select all of the tracks in your groups. This is an awesome way to get all the tracks of a group ready for quickly assigning sends or plug-ins or for reassigning their outputs.

Note: After selecting all the tracks in a group, Hold Option+Shift / Alt+Shift while assigning plug-ins, sends, or outputs to make the change to all selected tracks.

The symbols in the Groups List window give you information about which tracks are selected from each group (see Figure 5.1):

- If no group symbols are present, that means no tracks are selected anywhere in the session. In a large session, this is a good place to check before you delete a track; if other tracks are mistakenly selected you might be able to see, depending on what group it is part of, if any. Deleting a track is not undoable and will clear the undo queue.
- A solid circle means that all of the tracks in that group are selected.
- A hollow circle means that some of the tracks in that group are selected but not all.
- A point within a circle means that all tracks are selected in that group, plus other tracks as well.

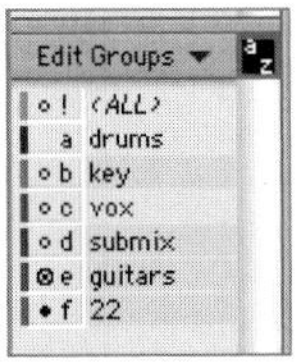

Figure 5.1 The Groups List window with group focus enabled. The different group symbols point to differences in track selection for each group.

Note: Control+click / Start+click any group name in the groups list to show only tracks in this group and hide all other tracks.

More Grouptastic Ways to Employ Groups

While using groups is an incredibly powerful organizational and time-saving tool in mixing, groups are only as good as your skills at making them work. Here's a few more ideas on how to master groups:

- To manually change the order of your groups in the groups list, click and drag up or down on the color-coding strip on the far left of the window and a dashed dividing line will appear beneath the group. Position the group to where you want it.

- To select all of the tracks in a group, click the space between the group letter and the color-coding strip on the far left. This will choose all tracks in that group.

- Option+click / Alt+click any group in the groups list to enable or disable all groups in your session. The All group at the top of the list is not affected by this action.

- Well, this is not a group trick, but it should be, so it belongs here. To apply the same plug-in to all selected tracks, press Option+Shift / Alt+Shift as you apply an insert or send and it will be created on all selected tracks. This also works for assigning multiple inputs and outputs.

- This trick helps when using groups to select different tracks. Option+click / Alt+click any track in the Edit window and you will select or deselect all of your tracks. This is a handy way to clear the board in a hurry or light everything up. Option+click / Alt+click on a track that is selected and all tracks will be deselected. Option+click / Alt+click on a track that is not selected and all of your tracks will be selected.

- Control+click / Start+click on a group in the Groups List window and you will hide all of the other tracks in your session that are not in that group. This is a great technique in a large session for focusing on just the tracks of a specific group. This is not undoable and has a downside; be aware if you have tracks hidden in the Track list Show/Hide column and Control+click / Start+click on the All Group button to turn your tracks back on. This will turn every track in your session on even if they have all been hidden in the Tracks List window. If you have tracks that are not in groups, be aware of them as you use this command. You may have to turn them back on manually. It might help to make a master group that contains all of the tracks you are using in your session. This way, you have an easy way to get back to what you started with.

- You can identify which active group or groups a track belongs to by what kind of letter is shown in the bottom of the Mix window. A lowercase letter indicates that a track is part of only one group. An uppercase letter represents a nested group, meaning a group within a group (see Figure 5.2). When you click and hold on the letter, you will see all of the groups the track is connected to and all of the tracks associated with the group. You can do this only if the group is active.

Figure 5.2 Groups in the Mix window

Exercising the All Group

The All group is part of every session and cannot be removed. Not that you'd want to anyway. The All group is a great way to get every part of your session with a single click. One way to exercise the All group is to lower the gain across every track when you start pushing zero. For better gain structure, don't turn your master fader down; bring your individual tracks down collectively and get more headroom with less chance of distortion. Here's how:

1. Turn on the All group in the groups list (for more information on turning groups on and off, see Chapter 3, "Editing: Slip, Shuffle, and Spot Your Way Home").

2. In the Edit window, choose volume in the track view selector of any audio track. The track view selector is located just below the record, solo, and mute buttons.

3. Choose the Trim tool (F6) and lower the volume of any track. All tracks will be lowered by this amount. This will open up headroom in your mix and is a much better way to address too much level than by turning down the master fader. It will also keep all of the relative volumes of your tracks intact. Turning down the master fader is a western medicine–type approach: treat the symptom, not the problem.

4. Turn off the All group. This is very important to remember or every edit you perform will affect every track.

5. Option+click / Alt+click in the master fader track to return it to zero.

The All group is also great for making cuts using Shuffle mode. For instance, if you have a total session length that is too long for a radio segment, turn on the All group to quickly shuffle-edit every track in the session simultaneously. Here's how:

1. Select the material that needs to be cut. Depending how it was tracked, use either Slip or Grid mode to make your selection.

2. Change to Shuffle mode (F1) and press Delete. Shuffle will snap the material from the right of the edit point back to the front side of the edit. With the All group on, you can edit your entire track with one cut. Switch out of Shuffle unless you need to make more cuts.

Mixing Vocabulary

Pro Tools doesn't try to reinvent the wheel when it comes to mixing terminology. The initial goal of the program was to provide digital tools for professionals (Pro Tools, get it?) working in the field of recording and mixing, which at the time involved analog consoles and signal flow for mixing purposes. One glance at the Pro Tools Mix window should make sense to anybody schooled in audio signal flow, the only difference being that all patching is done virtually. Here is a list of terms commonly used in mixing and what they mean to a Pro Tools session.

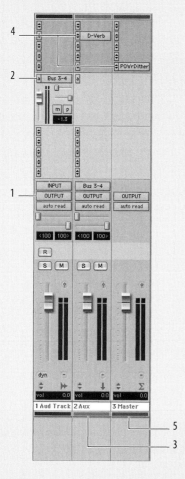

I/O Input and Output. Essential for the routing of a track to take place. If you wish to hear a track at all, its output must be routed somewhere. I/O gets more complicated when there are effects sends and bussing involved. Just remember, on the mixer channel strip, the top bar is input and the bottom bar is output, and the names reflect what you have established in your I/O setup. (1)

Continues

Mixing Vocabulary *(Continued)*

bus An audio pathway used to send an audio signal from one place to another. In Pro Tools, a bus always refers to internal routing. You can even think of a bus as a school bus, driving audio from one place to another inside the Pro Tools mixer. The bus can be used both for the output of audio tracks and to put sends on. A bus can be stereo, as in Bus1-2, or mono, as in Bus 5. A bus also acts like a school bus because it can carry more than one track's signal, so many tracks can be routed through the same bus.

send A send is a way to multiply the output of a track and send its signal to multiple destinations. For instance, the output of a track could be going to the main output 1-2 but could also be multiplied and put on a send for effects purposes or a headphone mix. Sends are cool because they offer their own level control. A send can be designated either pre-fader or post-fader. This means the level set on the send can be independent (pre) or dependent (post) of the levels set in the track fader. To set a send to pre, click the P button in the send view. To see an individual send's view mini-fader in the Mix window, choose View > Sends A-E or F-J and select the send you want to see. To see all at once without the mini-fader, choose View > Sends > Assignments. If the send is going somewhere inside the Pro Tools mixer, it will travel on a bus to get there. If the send is going to the outside world, it must go through an available interface output. In Pro Tools 7, tracks can have as many as 10 sends at once. (2 shows a send on slot a on Bus 3-4.)

Aux *Aux* is short for *auxiliary input*. An Aux track is a mixing tool only; it will never have audio regions in it. Aux tracks are designed to input all the time, so they do not need to be record-enabled to accept a signal. Whatever an Aux's input is set to, it will automatically receive that signal. An Aux track can be designated an effects return track, where a send traveling on a bus goes. An Aux return track will have the effect inserted in its insert slot and will usually provide a 100 percent wet, or effect only, signal. Aux tracks are designated by a down-arrow graphic in the lower-right portion of the channel strip in the Mix window. (3)

insert An insert is where software plug-ins or hardware effects can be "inserted" directly in the audio path. Inserts come before the fader in the Pro Tools mixer (pre-fader). In other words, the audio signal originates from the region in a track. That sound is then routed to inserts, then to the track fader. Because audio is routed in this fashion, it is possible to overload a track's output simply by cranking a plug-in's output too high. There are five inserts per track, and they run in series, from top to bottom. (4)

master fader A master fader represents the last track fader before the signal leaves Pro Tools. The master fader only has an output selector. Any audio or Aux track routed to that output will run through the master just prior to leaving Pro Tools. A master is designated with the Greek sigma symbol in the lower-right portion of its channel strip in the Mix window. In mathematics, the sigma symbol represents the sum, which is exactly what the master fader is outputting, the sum of all tracks. A master track is much more than just a main volume control. In fact, it is best to leave the master volume

Continues

alone, at 0 when mixing. The level meter of the master is especially important because it always shows the summed output post-fader. In other words, the levels you see in your master fader track are exactly what your Pro Tools interface is outputting. For mixing purposes, you can use the master fader as the meter to watch for an idea of your total output levels. If the master output is clipping, it means the sum output of all your tracks is too loud. Leaving the master fader at 0 and mixing all tracks while watching the master meter is a good way to have an unbiased reference as to the final output volume of your mix. Finally, the master offers one last set of inserts before your audio leaves Pro Tools. Because it is last in the chain, any dither plug-ins should be put on the last slot of the master fader. For one-off mixes, many engineers use the master fader inserts for maximizing/limiting their mixes to get more perceptual volume out of their mixes. Keep in mind, however, that all inserts in a master fader are post-fader—an exception to the rule of all other tracks. Therefore, if you are fading out with the master, your mix will hit the compressor/limiter differently as the volume gets lower. For this reason, some engineers run all their tracks through an Aux submix first with compression/limiting and then go to the master. (5)

No Gain, No Pain

How you approach your gain structure in mixing and recording plays a significant roll in determining how your track will sound. Professional-sounding mixes usually sound at least somewhat transparent and undistorted (unless you distort on purpose), and a proper gain structure can help you find your sonic nirvana. Gain structure is about how much level your signal has at every gain point. A gain point is any place you can attenuate or increase volume. If you overload even one spot, then you carry that overloaded signal wherever it goes down the chain. The more complex the routing in a studio is, the more stages you have to induce gain. This concept is as old as recording itself and is certainly not unique to Pro Tools. In the days of analog recording and mixing, every device in the recording chain was a gain point as well as every outboard effect and spot on the board.

You want to get the most out of your dynamic range and get the best signal-to-noise ratio you can as you pass a signal from gain point to gain point. In an analog setup, signal-to-noise ratio was a bigger concern, but it still is a player. One of the tricks to good gain structure is an attention to detail on your session. If you overload a gain point at the beginning of your gain chain, then you will pass a distorted signal all down through your chain. Every point needs to be checked during a mix to see if you are distorting, not just peaking or clipping. Pro Tools now sets fader gain at +12 dB. The older versions of Pro Tools offered +6 of headroom.

To record audio into Pro Tools, there are a number of gain points outside of the box that you need to monitor carefully. If you bring in a sound that is distorted, you can't "fix it in the mix." Once a track is recorded into Pro Tools, there are a number of possible gain spots in the internal mixing chain:

Preamp to input in Pro Tools This is controlled from an outside source in an HD system, most likely by a preamp. In LE systems, you can control the level on the hardware. Bring in a signal that hits red at its peak. It's better to err on the side of caution and get a good clean sound than to try to max out the level, as on tape. You can always get more volume if the signal is clean with a gain change or by normalizing.

Inserts In Pro Tools, inserts are pre-fader (with the exception of the master fader), so the channel fader will not control the level going to the inserts but the inserts will affect the channel volume before the fader level is set. Distortion at any point will pass along the chain. Inserts route signals from the top slot to the bottom. As you instantiate plug-ins, check your levels and adjust accordingly with your input and output controls.

Sends Sending audio out on a bus adds an additional gain stage to watch out for. If you distort your send audio before it gets to the bus, it will arrive distorted at the destinatioin of the bus. If you set the send to post-fader, the channel volume fader will affect the send volume. If you set the send to pre-fader, the channel volume will not changes the send level.

Submix If you are sending individual track outputs directly to an Aux track to submix as you would with multiple drum tracks, then you introduce another gain point. If the Aux track has inserts on it, you bring all of the plug-ins into the equation as well. If you are submixing a lot of tracks down to a stereo Aux track, this is a potential logjam. Don't overload the input into the Aux or the whole deal will sour on you. Digital distortion makes one yearn for the old days of saturated tape.

Master fader Your master fader should be set to unity, but if you add any inserts, especially maximizers, you will have a big gain point to consider. The master fader is by definition the last link in the audio chain. All master fader plug-ins are post-fader and affect the audio after your master fader level. The last gain control you have is the master fader volume level, but don't forget that any plug-ins can add or subtract gain even after the fader is set. One good thing to know is that the Master Volume indicator is also a post-fader/post-plug-in meter and can be used as an accurate idea of where your total output resides after all plug-ins and volume controls.

Panning for Gold (Records)

Proper panning of your instruments in a stereo or multichannel recording can take a song from demo to restaurant quality. Improper panning can ruin a track faster than you can say "Milli Vanilli." Seemingly random or excessive panning can lead to a confused stereo image and defused energy, but a well-panned track will pop with intensity. As music has changed, so have accepted techniques in mixing where panning is involved. Still, there are some common guidelines in mixing pertaining to what and where you pan. If you break up the stereo field into three sections, you can check yourself as you mix. Your main tracks live at 0 on the pan fader. Whatever sounds drive your track should be in the center of the stereo field. From 0 to 50, left or right is where you want from 60 to 70 percent of your panned tracks to be to keep your mix sounding tight and balanced. If you pan too many elements past 50 in the stereo field, you can water down the intensity of your mix. Conversely, if you pan nothing off of center, you will have good old mono, which sounds a little boring in today's world of HD and 5.1. From 50 to 100, either left or right on the pan fader, throw in some spice to your mix. Percussion, incidental elements, and subtle flavors do well on the outside edges of the mix. Panning is a vital part of stereo mixing. With the following techniques, you can create space and a feeling of transparency or create a wall of sound so thick that even light can't penetrate:

1. Center your lower frequencies, kick, bass, and bottom-heavy synths. A lot of chances are taken in mixing modern music as opposed to 30 years ago, but even in this day and age, if you pan lower frequencies off center, it will throw off the balance of your track.

2. Center your main vocals; there are a number of panning techniques for doubles and triples tracks, but start with your main vocal down the middle to give it focus. Adding a small reverb program or a short delay that is panned off center to some degree will add space and depth to your track.

3. Visualize your drums as if someone is playing in front of you. Pan your kit as you would hear it naturally and listen as the stereo image develops to make adjustments. Of course, this is for drums printed on individual tracks and not just a stereo loop. If you write your drum tracks as MIDI, then print them as audio individually so you can treat them and process them. When you pan your cymbals and toms, think of creating a believable image. Percussion can be placed anywhere in the stereo field, depending on how large a part it plays in the main energy of the song. The more important the percussion is to the track, the closer to the center it should start. Spread multiple instruments across the stereo field to give a sense of space and separation.

4. Guitars can be great in the center if they provide an essential rhythm or spread out to the sides if there is more than one similar part—typical for a lot of bands. Another approach to a mono guitar is to duplicate the track, offset it by 10 samples, and then hard-pan both tracks. Big sound! Lead guitars are often in stereo out of a processor, but if you mic a cabinet, you might have a mono lead. Leads tend to be centered or slightly off center in the near field. Active panning is a great way to give motion to your tracks. Add any time-based effect to your guitar track and pan the effect away from the main track to create space and depth. This is a nice technique for most any lead track, including vocals.

5. Background vocals can sound good off to the left or right anywhere from 0 to 100 from center on the pan fader, depending on the effect desired. Hip-hop lives with doubles and triples at varying places in the left and right field, at lower levels and effected. Sometimes doubles can be at 11 o'clock to 1 o'clock and triples panned out from 10 o'clock to 2 o'clock and sometimes even all the way out from 9 o'clock to 3 o'clock.

6. Keyboards can live most anywhere in the mix, depending on the type of tracks and the frequency of the sound. Lead synth parts can sound great hard-panned left and right with a delay or straight up like a guitar lead. Pads can be centered or panned slightly off center. The keyboard in electronic music has no rules in this day and age. The combination of panning and panned effects like delay or reverb is a major part of the electronic feel.

7. Be aware of the "Big Mono" phenomenon. This happens when stereo instruments like keyboards are all panned hard left and right the way a stereo track defaults. The end result of hard-panning all these stereo tracks may be a mix almost as boring as mono. Take your stereo tracks out of hard split panning and pinpoint exactly where they need to sit in the mix, possibly spreading the left and right components out slightly, but not fully.

8. In general, consider balance. If you have one high-frequency sound like a tambourine happening on the far left of your mix, then it is nice to balance that with a similar sound on the right, like a ride cymbal. Pan the low cello sounds away from the upright bass to create room and space for the instruments in the mix.

The Magic of Aux

Aux tracks really play a big role in every part of the recording and mixing chain in Pro Tools. If you are limited by track count as an LE user, or short on voices in the HD world, don't worry; Aux tracks don't count in your total number of tracks, since they don't actually use a voice. They are destinations for buses and submixes and portals for virtual instruments to enter Pro Tools.

Submixing Your Tracks

As described in the sidebar "Mixing Vocabulary," busses can internally route audio from one place to another in the Pro Tools mixer. While busses are often used for sends, they can also be used on a track's output and returned together with other tracks on an Aux track to create a submix. In the mixing arena, submixing is helpful for two reasons:

- You get a "master control" over a group of tracks that have a volume/pan relationship with one another, so you can raise or lower the summed output of all tracks without changing their relationships to one another.

- You can process a large group of tracks with inserts or sends more efficiently. Using one EQ and one compression insert on a submix track is much lighter on your processor or DSP load than having one on every track of your submix group.

Submixes are commonly created for drums; five or six microphones are bussed to one stereo drum submix. Another application would be for a chorus of background vocals, string sections, or synth layers. Remember, Aux Input tracks don't count in your total voice or track count, so be bold with your submixes. Here's how to set one up:

1. Select all of the tracks you want to include in your submix group. Holding Shift while clicking track names extends the selection and everything in between, while holding ⌘/Ctrl while clicking on track names includes only those tracks in the selection.

2. Hold Option+Shift / Alt+Shift while changing any of the selected tracks' outputs to an available bus.

3. Make a new stereo Aux input and assign the input of the Aux to the same bus. Aux inputs in Pro Tools LE always default to -∞. Solo-safe the Aux by ⌘ +clicking / Ctrl+clicking the S button (solo button) on the Aux track.

4. Rename the Aux an appropriate submix name and use the fader as a master control of all the routed tracks. Insert any plug-ins you desire on the submix track for efficient processing.

Figure 5.3 shows a drum submix in action.

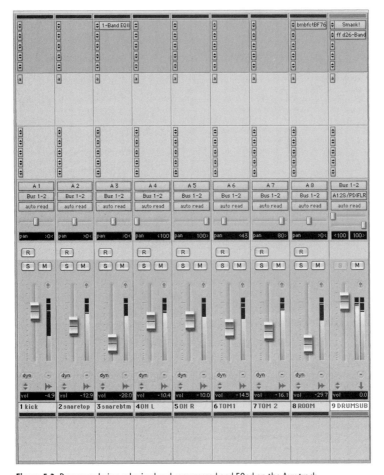

Figure 5.3 Drums are being submixed and compressed and EQed on the Aux track.

Don't Be a CPU Hog, Share the Reverb

Another common use for an Aux track in mixing is to host plug-ins such as reverb or delay to share between bussed audio tracks. This technique reduces the load on your system resources by sending many tracks to one for processing. If you need a number of compressors, most systems can deal with that, but try to instantiate 15 convolution reverbs in a 5.1 mix and watch your computer start to smoke and then blow a gasket.

To create a send on an audio track and bus it to an Aux track, follow these steps:

1. Show Sends View in either the Mix or Edit window.

2. Create a send on your track by choosing an unused bus on any of the 10 available sends (see Figure 5.4). A pop-up send fader automatically appears when a

send is created. Note that it is simply a larger version of the mini-fader in your Mix window Sends View.

3. Create an Aux track and set the track input to the same bus you sent from the track you want to effect (see Figure 5.5).

4. Instantiate up to five inserts per Aux track and send any of your audio-based tracks to the Aux.

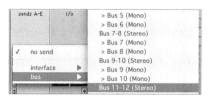

Figure 5.4 Choosing a bus for a send

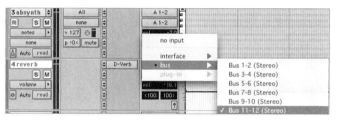

Figure 5.5 Setting your Aux track input to the right bus

Processing the Tracks of Your Mix

Processing is one of the key elements in refining your mix. It would be an unheard-of miracle if a decent mix were finished without the help of equalization or compression. Remember, mixing is all about merging the lanes of your sonic freeway, and you have to make room for everything to fit in there. The following are a few suggestions for where to start with some common musical instruments, as well as some ideas for getting certain timeless sounds. Use these examples as starting points only, and improvise from there. Mixes are like sonic fingerprints—no two are alike. So try these out and then subvert them, try your own techniques, and make your individual mark on the sonic landscape.

Here are a couple of effective techniques for processing electric guitar:

Compression As for processing, it is possible to get a lot of mileage out of some compression on an electric guitar, especially if it is sustain you are looking for. Start with a 4:1 ratio with the threshold low enough to hit most of the peaks and a not-too-drastic attack (20 to 30 ms); you can dial the release time way longer to effectively make each note last longer. Crank the output or makeup gain enough to compensate for lost gain along the way. Try this with a slide and some delay and you'll be approaching David Gilmour land! (See Figure 5.6.)

EQ EQ-wise, pay close attention to the mids, from 300Hz to 2kHz. This is where everything is crucial in the frequencies of an electric guitar. Unlike some of the more natural instruments (voice or acoustic guitar), it is possible to get away with EQing an electric guitar much more drastically without it sounding awkward or fake. (See Figures 5.7 and 5.8.)

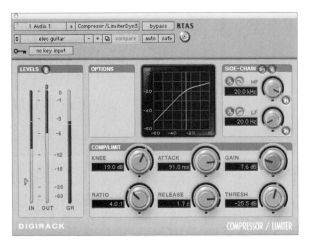

Figure 5.6 Guitar compression to emphasize sustain

Figure 5.7 Guitar EQ emphasizing warmth and fullness

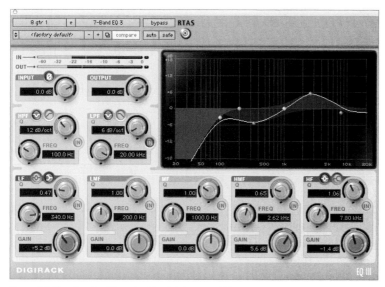

Figure 5.8 Electric guitar EQ emphasizing brittleness and bite

Note: Compression ideas are shown in this chapter with the free DigiRack Dyn3 Compressor Limiter. EQ ideas are shown with the DigiRack EQ 3. If these plug-ins weren't installed with your version of Pro Tools 7, you can download them at www.digidesign.com. Any hardware or plug-in compressor of choice may be substituted.

The lead vocal is usually the most scrutinized element of a mix. Here are some processing approaches to keep it in check:

Compression Because it is virtually impossible for a singer to sing words with exactly the same dynamics the whole song, compression can help make sure that everything floats on top of the mix without being too loud or getting lost. Start with a low ratio, between 1.5:1 and 2:1. Attack can be set moderately, around 1 to 1.5 ms, because you do not want to hear the compressor bite down hard. Release can be around 150 to 175 ms because you don't want to hear any pumping in the compression. Lower the threshold until just the loudest moments are hitting the compressor. You don't want more than 3 or 4 dB of gain reduction. Set the output gain to make up for any lost volume. This is for a mild, controlling compression as in Figure 5.9. For more effect-like drama, increase the ratio, threshold, and attack time.

EQ Equalizing vocals can be tricky. Our ears are very in tune with false boosts or cuts in the frequencies of the human voice, so it is important to be subtle. That said, there are some frequencies you can work with to manipulate a vocal performance. Deep and full aspects can be found in the 120 to 150Hz range, boomy qualities reside at 240 to 320Hz, "nasal-ness" exists in the 1 to 2.5kHz range. Presence and intelligibility can be brought into a vocal sound at 5kHz, but too much will cause sibilance. The sparkle and "air" exist from 10 to 15kHz. Figure 5.10 shows an example vocal EQ addressing a low rumple (the high pass filter is in at 50Hz), a bit of boominess around 240Hz, and adding a bit of sizzle and sparkle to the top end (the high shelf at 3.99kHz).

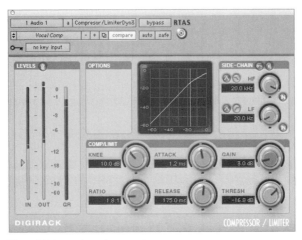

Figure 5.9 A smooth vocal compression

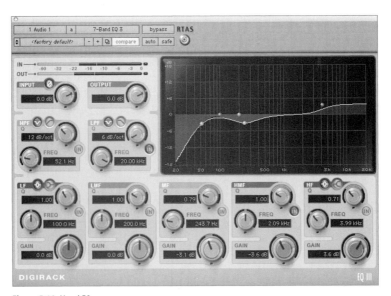

Figure 5.10 Vocal EQ

Here are a couple of effective techniques for processing acoustic guitar:

Compression If you are going for a natural open sound, the acoustic guitar can benefit from some mild compression such as a ratio of 3:1, the threshold set low enough to hit the peaks, a relatively fast attack time of 1 to 2 milliseconds, and a medium release time of 150 to 200 milliseconds. Use the makeup gain just enough to match the input with the output after the compression. (See Figure 5.11.)

If you want that heavily compressed Buffalo Springfield sound, try a vintage-type compressor insert like the Bomb Factory BF76 at a ratio of 12:1 with the input set at about 12 o'clock and the output a bit higher than that. (See Figures 5.11 and 5.12.)

EQ The acoustic guitar fills up a lot of the frequency spectrum, so it is possible to emphasize or de-emphasize the sound dramatically with EQ. Be frugal with your choices, however; because this instrument is of an acoustic nature, you should be very sensitive to wide EQ changes.

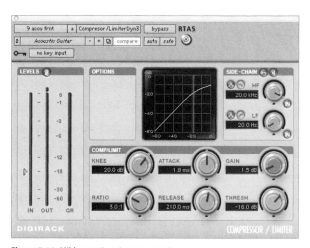

Figure 5.11 Mild acoustic guitar compression

Figure 5.12 Heavier vintage acoustic guitar compression

Around 300Hz, you will find the lower body of the sound. If it is too boomy, try to carve out a little bit in this range with a wide Q and make up for it in the upper mids by adding a little boost around 5kHz. Be careful in this range that you aren't bringing out too much fret and string noise. You may add some silky top end if necessary by using a high shelf, about 10kHz. (See Figure 5.13.)

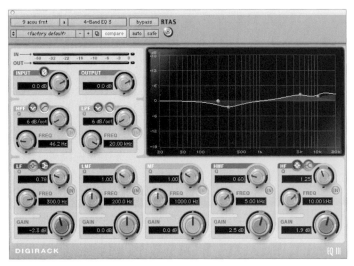

Figure 5.13 Carving away a bit of the boxiness and adding a little presence of the acoustic guitar with EQ

Here are some effective techniques for the bass guitar:

Compression The bass guitar usually benefits from a bit of compression. Depending on the musician, bass can have a lot of difference in dynamics from note to note and up the fretboard. Once the flagrant notes are tucked into place with a little dynamics control and the quiet notes are brought out, the bass sound falls right into place when it is time to mix. Start with an attack time of 7 to 10 ms so the faster transients get by the compressor. The release may be lengthened here to create some beefier sustain. Set the ratio from to 2.5:1 to 3:1, and bring the threshold down enough so that most of the louder notes are hitting the compressor. It may be helpful to put a second limiter in place after the initial compressor to catch any wild notes that poke through the compression. (See Figure 5.14.)

EQ By adding around 80Hz, you can get more out of the lowest bass frequencies, but the real important stuff often exists in the lower mids. Check out EQ in the 120 to 350Hz range as this is where the main character of the sound is defined and also the frequencies that will translate on most home stereos. Don't forget about the frequencies that exist in the higher mids, around 2 to 4kHz, because these are where the punchy aspects reside. You may want to suppress these or bring them to forefront depending on your taste. (See Figure 5.15.)

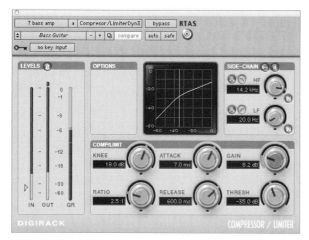

Figure 5.14 A common bass compression

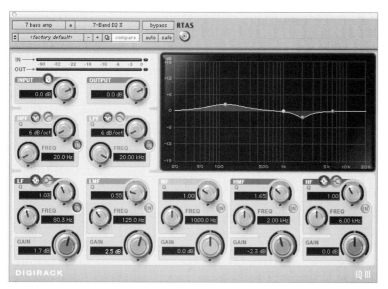

Figure 5.15 This EQ removes some of the punch and emphasizes a bit of the low mid.

Remember that room microphone you put up for the drums? Here's how to turn that mic into the Zeppelin-esque Bonham crunch: It's all about a fast attack and fast release here with a very high ratio and high threshold to emphasize the decay of the drums almost as much as the attack. By grabbing hold and reducing the gain of the initial transient and then releasing the compression quickly, you will allow the decay to flourish and bring out the resonance and room of each drum hit. Try a ratio of at least 20:1 if not higher, and set the attack and release as fast as they will go. Output gain is going to have to be cranked here, maybe as much as 10 or 20 dB. The threshold should be set low to grab almost all of the sound. Try this compression on the room microphone and mix it in with the other microphone for optimum Bonham crunch. Is that a type of ice cream? (See Figure 5.16.)

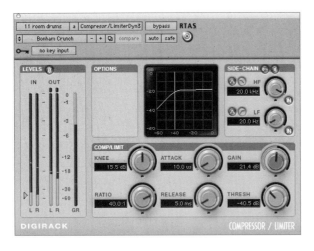

Figure 5.16 Example settings to push a compressor hard on the room mics for that Led Zeppelin big-room sound

Automation Modes

As important as automation is in the modern studio, production house, and even home studio, an intimate knowledge of the different automation modes in Pro Tools can reap big benefits. To change between modes, click on the automation mode selector, located just underneath the solo, mute, and record buttons in the Edit window and below the output selector. Use the right tool for the right job and get things done faster. The different modes control how automation is written, edited, and played back.

An HD system offers the ability to use a Trim tool in conjunction with the other modes, which allows a trim control over whatever particular mode you are in. The automation modes are accessible in either the Edit or Mix windows. Here are the five basic modes.

Continues

Automation Modes *(Continued)*

Read Playback mode, green for safe. Read mode follows any automation that is written in your track.

Touch Touch mode will follow any existing automation until you click on, or touch, the fader or parameter and then will write your movements until you unclick, or let go of, the fader. Touch can be used to overdub automation. If you have a passage of automation that needs to be redone, go to Touch mode and play the track. After you nail the overdub, just let go of the mouse or fader and the original automation will take back over. You can set the amount of time it takes for the original automation to kick back in using the Touch Timeout setting (Preferences > Automation > Touch Timeout).

Latch This mode will follow the existing automation until you touch the fader and then will write your movements. When you let go of the fader, Latch mode will continue to write automation until you stop playback. Latch is useful to set a constant level in a track or in a group of tracks.

Write Write mode is the usual suspect for the first pass of automation. You can refine the automation later with either Touch or Latch mode. This mode is a destructive mode that will plow over any existing automation data. To switch to either Touch or Latch mode automatically after you write a pass of automation, select Settings > Preferences > Automation > After Write Pass, Switch To and take your pick.

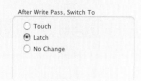

Off Automation mute is a good way to do an A/B comparison with your current automation and the original track.

Control+Option+click / Start+Alt+click on any automation parameter in the track view selector to disable only that specific parameter.

Automating Your Mix

There comes a time in every Pro Tools session's life when the sounds within are ready to emerge as a fully realized mix. Traditionally in audio production, mixing and automation comes last, after all the tracking is done. In digital audio, this kind of linearity isn't always necessary; you can be setting initial mix levels at the same time you are tracking and overdubbing new parts. Automation, the automatic movement of mix parameters, can also be done at any stage in the life of a Pro Tools session. Because it can be easily cleared and redone, written in real time, and controlled via a control surface, automation can practically be used like an instrument in a Pro Tools mix. But the best part about automating in Pro Tools is the ability to recall any mix at any time. Automation playlists are saved right into the Pro Tools session file, allowing for instant and total recall of an entire mix and all of the automation moves. Like a fully automated SSL console stuffed inside your computer, Pro Tools automation is a powerful feature for creating those mixes that pop.

Writing Automation in Real Time

Here's an automation workflow technique for mixing a song in Pro Tools. The order in which the steps are performed is not the only way to do an automated mix, but the concepts within are useful ideas for any automation workflow:

1. Choose Windows > Automation Enable (⌘+Keypad3 / Ctrl+Keypad3). The Automation Enable window contains global automation controls that are useful when you automate your mix.

2. Choose the All group from the groups list. The All group is designated with a exclamation point (!) and makes all of the tracks in your session one large group.

3. Open the track volume playlist on any track by clicking on the track view selector just under the record, solo, and mute buttons in the Edit window. All tracks now show volume automation.

4. Click into the longest track of the session in the Edit window and press ⌘+A / Ctrl+A to select all. Press Delete to erase any volume breakpoints that have been previously written.

   Assuming you have no valuable automation yet written for your mix, erasing all breakpoints in an automation playlist initializes your tracks and provides a clean slate for automation. This means that even in Read automation mode, you can set the knobs and faders to any value you want and the controls will stay there when you play through your session. It is helpful to have all tracks initialized for setting basic levels prior to any automation moves.

5. Apply step 4 to the pan playlist as well, and any other playlist (like plug-ins or mutes) for which you wish to rewrite automation. Deselect the All group.

6. Set all of your initial level balances, pans, and processing for the mix.. This is probably the most time-consuming part of the mix; it could take one to two whole days, depending on the complexity of the mix.

7. For Pro Tools LE users, select the All group, and with the Grabber tool, click before the start of the song on the volume playlist line. Pro Tools HD users can choose Edit > Automation > Write to All Enabled.

This creates a single breakpoint across all tracks that will lock in the mix starting points you have set in your initial mix—in essence, an "automation snapshot" of the current parameters. Now in Read mode, the faders will always snap back to this position because there is a single breakpoint established in the automation playlist.

8. LE users, repeat step 7 to set a snapshot for all other playlists (pan, plug-ins).

9. On the first track to be automated, click on the automation mode selector (below the output selector in the Mix window), and choose Touch.

10. Ride the automation, one parameter at a time. If you have a tactile control surface, you may be able to automate more than one parameter in a pass. You can audition a move without recording by choosing either the global Automation suspend button on the Automation Enable window or by turning the individual track's automation mode to Off.

Note: Don't forget that automation parameters follow groups, so you can automate more than one parameter at a time and preserve relative values by grouping tracks together. See the section "Don't Lose Your Identity in a Group" for more on groups.

11. Repeat step 10 for all tracks that require automation in the mix.

Not sure what to automate? Here are some common automation mix moves:

• Riding vocal levels, emphasizing phrases and ends of words

• Turning up instruments that take a solo or important riffs

• Bringing up drum toms during a drum fill

• Panning left to right for a moving effect

• Ducking organs, strings, or synths during singing to make way for the voice

• Turning up crucial elements during a chorus section

The idea is to always have a solid point of focus in the mix's spotlight. While a mix without automation may play fine and sound okay, it will seem flat in comparison to the mix that always has subtle movement of its most interesting elements going on. Automation is the key to a fluid, stirring, and dynamic mix that really grabs the listener as opposed to a dull and passive mix with no expressive automation.

Editing Automation

When you edit automation playlists, many of the editing tools look and act differently than they do for waveform editing:

Grabber tool Instead of the familiar hand, the Grabber tool turns into a finger. On an automation playlist, a single click with the Grabber creates a breakpoint. The tool can be used to move breakpoints up or down and left and right in between any bordering breakpoints. Option+clicking / Alt+clicking with the Grabber tool deletes breakpoints.

Selector tool Looks and acts the same as it does in waveform view.

Trim tool The Trim tool is turned sideways and performs the valuable function of adjusting any selected breakpoints up or down. The tool is useful because it will preserve relative changes between breakpoints and pull a whole section up or down. It can also be used to just pull up or down on automation for a single selected region.

Pencil tool The Pencil tool can draw automation. Opening the Pencil tool pull-down window reveals some different pencil tool modes. The default Free Hand mode offers freehand drawing, while the Line tool constricts the Pencil tool to a straight line, useful for exact fade-outs or pans. The Triangle and Square tools are useful for creating cool automation effects. The duration of their shapes is dependent on what nudge value you have set. For example, if you wanted a track to pan on every quarter note, set the nudge value to quarter notes first and then draw in pan automation with the Pencil tool.

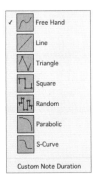

Hold Option/Alt to turn the pencil upside down to so its eraser can delete breakpoints when you click on them.

Cut, Copy, and Paste work as you might imagine. It is possible to copy automation from one place on a track and paste it elsewhere on that track or another track as long as it is the same automation type. To cut and paste from one automation type to a different automation type, use the new Edit > Copy Special and Paste > Special menu options. These options allow you to choose what type of automation you are copying with the additional choice of All Automation (see Figure 5.17). This way, you could copy pan automation from a track and paste it into the automation for a send level, for example. Holding Control/Start as you do a traditional paste works the same way, though this way you can't choose what type of automation to copy or paste.

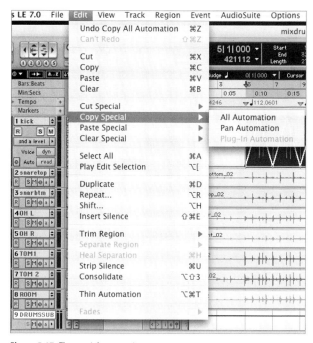

Figure 5.17 The special copy option

Note: When editing regions after automation is written, you have the option to make automation move with your edits or stay in the timeline regardless of what happens to the regions. Choose Option > Automation Follows Edit. If this option is checked, automation will move with regions; if it's unchecked, the automation will be independent from any region editing.

Thinning Automation

When you write automation in real time, you have a choice about how many breakpoints are going to be created. The more breakpoints there are, the more accurate the automation is, but a lot of breakpoints can make editing of the automation later difficult and time-consuming. This degree of thinning can be set by choosing Setup > Preferences and clicking the Automation tab, shown in Figure 5.18. To thin automation after writing automation in real time, you must check Smooth and Thin Data After Pass. Next, you can choose a Degree of Thinning option in the range of None to Most. When Most is chosen, you will be left with the fewest amount of breakpoints after an automation pass.

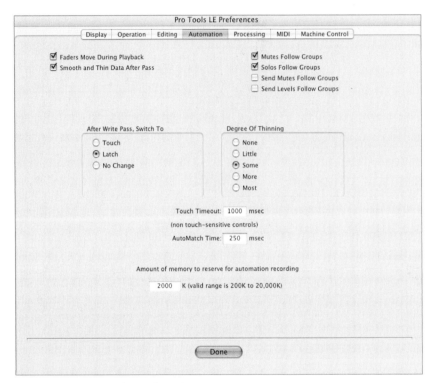

Figure 5.18 Automation preferences for an LE system

Automation drawn freehand with the Pencil tool is not automatically thinned and always creates a lot of automation breakpoints. To thin these, select the area you want thinned, and then choose Edit > Thin Automation or type Option+⌘+T / Alt+Ctrl+T. The automation data will be thinned by the amount set in the Degree of Thinning section of the Automation tab of Pro Tools > Preferences.

Undo That Last Action

How many times have you wished that you had an undo in life? Well, at least you have that option on a computer. In the days before undo (analog), you had to choose right up front, make a decision, and stick to it. The Undo command gives you the ability to try many different ideas before you decide on an edit, take, or automation. This can be a very creative way to work. Pro Tools has 32 levels of undo and a brand-new Undo History window that gives you a visual reference of your last moves by name (see Figure 5.19). This feature is a big improvement over just clicking Undo over and over until you get back to where you need to go. To open the Undo History window, choose Window > Undo History. You can see as many actions as levels of undos you have selected.

Back in the day, undo cost you big in the RAM department, but with RAM now measured in the gigs, that might not be much of an issue. People still don't always turn it up to 32 levels, though, because some engineers don't want to undo the last 31 actions to get to the 32nd action unless it's a big mistake. You lose all of your other work to get to the one mistake. If, for example, you go 12 moves forward from an edit and then think better of it and want to put it back to its original state so you can make a different edit, all of the other undos in the history window and in the queue get flushed. Think through what will be wiped out before you start undoing. You choose the number of undos you like to work with by choosing Setup > Preferences and clicking the Editing tab. The Levels of Undo setting is shown in Figure 5.20.

Another possible pitfall with this undo system is the nasty beast of clearing the undo queue with an undoable action and not knowing it.

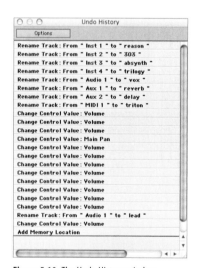

Figure 5.19 The Undo History window

Figure 5.20 The Undo preference

These are the dangerous moves to make if you want to keep your actions undoable:

- Delete a track from your session or a region from the regions list.
- Import session data.
- Choose Select > Unused or Select > Unused Audio Except Whole Files from the regions list.

No matter what you have in your undo history list, any of these actions will wipe the queue and clear your undos, and that's not undoable!

Note: To redo an undo, press Shift+⌘+Z / Shift+Ctrl+Z. By using the two commands, you can scroll forward and backward through time to see different states of your session. You can move by the number of undos set in your preferences.

Save Yourself with Alternate Mix Versions

No matter how hard you try to avoid working on a mix late into the night, sometimes the hours fly right by and the next thing you know, it's 4 o'clock in the morning. The chances are good that you will be mentally and physically fried by this time. Working long hours on a mix may be required to get it sounding just right, but there are a few dangers in working this way. Ear fatigue is a real phenomenon. Even when mixing at conservative levels below 85 dB SPL, (Sound Pressure Level, or SPL is a way to measure audio volume on the decibel scale), it is easy to lose perspective on the key elements of your mix. If at all possible, you should try to leave a mix up overnight, make a rough CD copy, wake up with fresh ears, and come back the next morning to finish up. This is a proven technique that works wonders.

Even when you employ the next-morning technique, alternate mixes are indispensable when it comes time to master the record. Alternate mixes are simply a few different versions of a mix that are methodically printed or bounced after the initial mix is done. They have saved many mix engineers' reputations and many records. When it comes time to master a record, it becomes apparent that what sounded good by itself needs a little more bass or a slightly louder vocal next to other songs on the record. How a single mix will stand up in comparison to other mixes is impossible to tell when mixing one song at a time. Here are a few guidelines to making alternate mixes:

The lead vocal The vocal level is typically the hardest thing to nail perfectly in a mix. Print separate mixes that include a vocal up .5 to 1 dB and vocal down .5 to 1 dB mix for safety. Also consider making a vocal mix with and without effects.

The bass The other hardest level to get right in a mix. Sometimes just the dimensions of your mix environment will mask or emphasize the elusive low end. Try a bass up .5 to 1 dB, bass down .5 to 1 dB mix. Also consider printing different compression mixes for the bass, one compressing with a lower threshold/higher ratio and one with a higher threshold/lower ratio.

Note: Important: Make sure to alter only one element per alternate mix. If the vocal up version ends up being the perfect choice mix, you don't want any other elements to differ in that version.

A cappella and instrumental Always print a version with and without vocals. These mixes come in handy if you miss the vocal level altogether, even with your vocal up and down mixes. It is always possible to rejoin the two mixes in the mastering stage. Soundtracks, radio edits, and remixes are a few other places where these come in handy.

Use your judgment Not every mix is the same. Sometimes you know you've nailed the perfect vocal level and bass but there's another element of the mix you aren't sure about. Whenever there is any doubt, print an alternate mix—it takes a few more minutes but ultimately can save a record.

Label correctly None of these alternate mixes will do you any good if they are not labeled correctly. In addition to filenames, make a key that describes exactly what makes each mix different.

Bounce That Track

Well, your masterpiece is ready to see the light of day outside of Pro Tools. Baby's all grown up and wants to move in with a low-resolution MP3 to file-share, but that's another story. There are two ways to mix in Pro Tools: internal bouncing or routing your tracks out to a console and mixing analog. Some people don't want to use math to mix their tracks and prefer to have analog circuitry sum their audio. Check out mixing outside of Pro Tools for more info on that method. To read more about the 48-bit mix engine that Pro Tools uses, check out http://digidesign.com/ and read the white paper on how Pro Tools sums audio. A very interesting read indeed. Internal bouncing is a real-time endeavor in Pro Tools, but you can export regions of audio in non–real time if you don't need any inserts or automation. Real-time bouncing does allow you to listen back to your track and make sure that everything sounds right. Many a mistake has been caught and corrected listening to the bounce. Bouncing is selection-based and will play any track that is not muted, including hidden tracks. The tighter the selection you make, the tighter the bounce will be. To make an exact selection, follow these steps:

1. Press F7 to get the selection tool and make your basic rough selection on any track in your session. You do not have to select all of the tracks you want to be in the mix. Your selection is for the length of the bounce, not which tracks will be included.

2. To return your selection to the beginning of your session, press Shift+Return / Shift+Enter.

3. To extend your selection out in time to the end of the last region, press Option+Shift+Return / Alt+Shift+Enter. To make exact selections or selections off of the grid, switch to Slip mode (F2). For more on making selections, see the section "Loop Selection Techniques" in Chapter 3.

4. If you have any reverb or delay after the last audio event, remember to select enough time past the end of the last region to allow the track to decay. Putting an automated fade out on the Master track is useful here because you can extend your selection to where the volume is all the way down to ensure that all reverb tails and delay are out.

Time-Stamp Your Tracks for Easier Reimporting

One of the cool things Pro Tools does as it bounces is label your mix with a time stamp so you can reimport your track into a session at an exact location. This is a great feature for LE users needing to bounce as a submix to free up tracks. Pro Tools submix bounces are 100 percent digital first-generation files with no added artifacts from bouncing. This method is far superior to the old days of bouncing noisy tape tracks to open up more tracks!

Here's how to bounce:

1. Select File > Bounce To > Disk to open the bounce window and select your bounce destination.

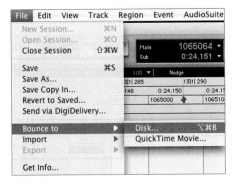

2. Choose your bounce-to file type in the Bounce window. The WAV file is the safe bet for most duties, but choose whatever file fits your needs (see Figure 5.21).

3. Choose the channel format. If you are going to make a stereo mix to take to CD or iPod or such, choose Stereo Interleaved. If you are bouncing down tracks and want to bring them back in to Pro Tools, choose Multiple Mono.

4. Choose Convert After Bounce if you need to convert your sample rate and have a lot of automation. Choose Convert During Bounce if you have to convert a basic session with little automation or few inserts. Some people always choose Convert After Bounce to be safe. As for the conversion quality, with any kind of a modern computer, select perhaps the best preset name in the history of presets, Tweak Head (slowest but best).

5. Listen to your track as you bounce. If you hear anything that needs correcting, press ⌘+. / Ctrl+. to stop the bounce and start over.

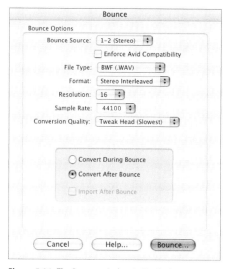

Figure 5.21 The Bounce window in Pro Tools

How Loud Is Loud?

Loudness, intensity, and decibels are sometimes misunderstood in music. All things being relative, you have the physics of sound and the variables of human hearing working hand in hand. We all hear a little differently from each other for a myriad of reasons.

No matter what your audio endeavor, knowledge of these concepts and ideas can help you find your way in the confusing maze of audio jargon:

Sound Pressure Level (SPL) is measured in decibels. The range humans deal with can be measured from 0 dB at the threshold of hearing to 130 dB at the threshold of pain and then to 160 db when the eardrum will rupture. Sound levels over 160 db exist, but it's best to run if they're coming your way. In the studio, an 85 dB max is the rule of thumb for long-term exposure to audio. If you start mixing above that level, your ears will get fatigued more quickly, leading to improper mix decisions and hearing damage. That said, people get to their mixing zone in different ways. However you get the best out of your abilities, remember one thing: your hearing is invaluable! SPL is also a rating on microphones. The level rating tells you what you can get away with on the microphone before the diaphragm will break up.

Decibel is the scale used to measure intensity in sound. It is a logarithmic scale based on 10. If a sound is 10 db louder than another sound, it has 10 times the intensity. If a sound is 20 db louder than another sound, it has 100 times the intensity. If a sound is 50 db more than another sound, it has 10 to the 5th or 100,000 times more intensity. It's like measuring earthquakes. An 8.0 quake is 10,000 times more powerful than a 4.0 quake.

Intensity can be measured. Intensity and loudness are two different things. The ear exaggerates the 1k to 5k bands of the frequency spectrum and gives the illusion of more loudness than other frequencies at the same intensity. If a sound at 400Hz has the same intensity as a sound at 3kHz, you will hear the sound at 3kHz with much more perceived loudness than the tone at 400Hz.

Loudness is where the individual comes into play. Intensity can be measured scientifically, but loudness is a personal experience. The differences between people are based on a number of variables, such as age, gender, health, environment, and other elements. Generally speaking, the more intensity a sound has, the louder it's perceived, but exactly how loud will be a little different to everyone who hears it.

Here is a list of some real sound levels in the modern world, in SPL:

Threshold of hearing (TOH)	0 dB.
Whisper	20 dB.
Normal conversation	60 dB.
City noise average	70–80 dB.
Factories/construction	85–110 dB. 85 dB is the threshold at which hearing damage can start after eight hours exposure. As the levels go up, the time you can safely spend around factory/construction noise goes down.
Close to the stage at rock concert, very loud clubs	110–120 dB. Hearing damage starts after about 10 minutes if you are not protected. Wear ear protection!

Jet takeoff or gun firing	130 dB. This is considered the threshold of pain (TOP). All ears should be protected at all times at these levels.
Explosions	160 dB. Eardrum perforation. Never safe. Stay away!

Your good hearing is critical in creating and producing audio. You are not Beethoven, and his life didn't end that well, anyway.

Mixing outside the Box

Some call it voodoo; others call it flavor. Some mixers say it's absolutely necessary, while others aren't advocates at all. Say what they will, "mixing outside the box" is a widely used mixing practice among today's Pro Tools mix engineers. It means taking your Pro Tools tracks and running them through outboard gear before they get summed into the final stereo mix. There are several ways this is done and several reasons why some Pro Tools users prefer this kind of treatment:

Summing When multiple tracks are combined through a stereo output, the audio travels through what is called a summing mixer. Although Digidesign goes on the record with scientific proof that the Digidesign summing mixer in Pro Tools operates at the highest capacity possible with no degradation to the audio signal, some audio engineers choose to bypass the Pro Tools summing mixer altogether and opt for their own devices. Why? Some feel that a little coloration by summing mixers is a good thing. The analog summing circuits in classic consoles such as Neve, API, Trident, and SSL are responsible for some of the most exceptional and memorable-sounding recordings of our time. Many engineers who endlessly chase the myths of the mixing signal chains that were used on these recordings find part of the magic in the summing mixer.

Outboard processing options There is a plug-in modeled after just about every classic analog compressor, EQ, limiter, and effect unit in the history of recording. The manufacturers of these plug-ins claim that they are flawless emulations modeled after the real hardware-based units. But which units were they modeled after? Not the ones in *your* studio! One of the best things about analog gear is that no two units are exactly alike. When there are vacuum tubes, capacitors, and resisters involved, there are infinite options as to why a specific unit sounds just the way it does. For this reason, many engineers still swear by routing out of their Pro Tools systems through their own coveted analog processing chains.

Analog flavor If you were to scientifically investigate why audio engineers and listeners love the sound of analog, you would probably find it due to a combination of distortion, noise, overmodulation, and psychology (many people's first musical experiences came off of vinyl). Whatever the reasons may be, some engineers wish to get back a little of that analog flavor to their mix simply by outputting their tracks through some analog circuitry before the final mix-down.

There are several ways in which mixing outside the box can occur. Here are a few examples of how you can take advantage of the process:

- Set the output of each track to a different output and connect all of the outputs of your interface to the inputs of an analog console. Full use of an external mixing console requires as many outputs of your Pro Tools interface as there are tracks in your session, give or take a few. It is possible to sum outputs to the same output in Pro Tools so they can share a mixing channel, but then you are back into the idea of Pro Tools summing.

- Create stems in your Pro Tools session, such as drums, vocals, and guitars, and run them out of your Pro Tools interface with a few stereo pairs of Auxiliary tracks. Although those stereo pairs are technically summed in Pro Tools, you can still run them through an analog summing mixer. This would be a cheaper option for smaller systems than the preceding method.

- Use hardware inserts and sends to farm out to external analog processors and then come back into Pro Tools.

- Mix down to tape. Even though you are summing in Pro Tools, you can breathe some analog air into your recording this way. Nothing sounds as good as a two-track ½-inch tape deck running at 30 IPS.

After the Bounce, or Life outside of Pro Tools

There are far more applications for music and audio today than there have ever been: TV, film, video, radio, the Web, podcasting, cell phones, video games, computers, iPods, and even a good old-fashioned CD. The final destination for your track heavily influences the production and mastering techniques you'll want to perform. For the most part, this is life in the digital era, and since Pro Tools creates a digital file when you bounce, you're set.

Chapter Contents

Know Your Audio Formats

If you remember when your choice was either LP or cassette, it could be a little overwhelming out there right now in audio land. There are so many different formats you can choose from that the list might rival the number of people using them. Audio formats have changed many times over the past 120 years, so the evolution of audio is to be expected. What might not have been expected was the rate of development over the past few years. You could add together all of the other audio mediums developed before 1995 and you would get fewer than what has been developed since then. From the tin cylinder to the wax disc, from analog tape to the silicon chip, we've come a long way. With the onslaught of the Internet, file sharing, fast computers, and the demise of analog tape, digital audio has exploded over the past decade. There is less debate over which format you should work with while you are tracking, mixing, and mastering music. Professional studios and most everyone else use high-bit-rate, full-sample-rate, uncompressed WAVs or AIFFs. 24-bit files with a sample rate of 48kHz, 96kHz, or higher are common in the creation of music, but unfortunately the general public seldom hears the music that way (yet).

In 2006, the debate over what will replace Red Book audio (CD-DA) is raging on as strongly as ever. There is no clear-cut winner, with every company touting its own proprietary format and not working with the others on a generally supported specification. MIDI would never have been developed in this day and age. We are in the middle of a change in technology right now and are caught between the quality of sound we create and the quality of sound that most people use in everyday situations. Listening to low-quality MP3s on computer speakers is very common. So if you have a high-resolution track mixed for DVD audio or an SACD (Super Audio CD), not only do you have to sample and bit-rate-convert it down to a 16-bit 44.1kHz file for CD production, as soon as someone takes it to the Internet, iTunes, or an iPod, you most likely now have an MP3 to reproduce your masterpiece. File compression in the hands of someone listening to your track with computer speakers can be the final nail in the coffin of fidelity.

To make the best of this situation, you need knowledge of some of the more successful current audio formats; it can help you keep at least a little sonic dignity as your music passes down the chain. Tests done by many companies and individuals have shown that different formats excel with different bit rates and different styles of music or audio. With a little experimentation, you can find the right codec for the right need and keep your sound quality as high as possible. One thing to be aware of as you convert your files is general compatibility—what plays with what software on what platform and on what portable devices. This list of different formats is but a sampling of the ever-changing world of audio formats, but it can serve as a basic guide to see some of what's out there and what's best for each situation:

MPEG-1 Audio Layer 3 (MP3) is the most common and well-known compressed audio format. It is hard for one acronym to elicit such varying opinions and attitudes from people, but theMP3 does that. To some it brought about the 10,000-song iTunes library and portable playlists, but to others it brought about both the demise of audio quality and the contraction of the music industry. Talk about two ends of the spectrum. To read more about MP3s, see the next section, "Making an MP3 to Write Home About."

MPEG-4 AAC (Advanced Audio Coding) is a codec used by iTunes, the iPod, and XM radio to name but a few in an ever-growing list. With a sample rate to 96k, it was designed it to be an upgrade to the MP3, but views differ on that depending on how much you compress the file. In listening tests of the two files compressed down to the same size, people have found the AAC to have better sound. Even with the AAC compressed down smaller than an MP3, listeners found the AAC to sound as good or better. This is still subjective, so test and listen and decide for yourself. AAC is commonly used to code musical podcasts and is compatible with all Apple products, Sony PSP (PlayStation Portable), and many cell phones.

Ogg Vorbis was created in direct retaliation to a licensing-fee boost from the holders of the MP3 format. This is a hot codec for a number of reasons, not the least of which is the fact that it's free and it sounds very good. Its specs are better than the original MP3 at the same bit rates. This compression will encode true CD specs at 160Kbps, while the MP3 needs 192Kbps to achieve the same. This format is growing in popularity and now enjoys a huge fan base through support from hundreds of applications and an ever-increasing list of hardware.

Windows Media Audio (WMA) is Microsoft's system of encoding and decoding media native to Windows Media Player. It can be used by numerous hardware devices and is a big player in the Internet audio game.

RealAudio is the native audio for RealPlayer found on many websites. Thanks to RealPlayer, RealAudio is a widely supported format.

Apple Lossless encoder (ALAC) is a lossless compression format that realizes about a 60-percent file reduction with no loss in quality. The ALAC codec works only in iTunes and Quicktime for now but there are rumors about a broader future. The file size reduction is much less than an MP3 or AAC, but you get the sound of the original. There are other lossless compression formats out, and with the release of ALAC there could be more in the future.

Making an MP3 to Write Home About

All MP3s are not the same! You can make MP3s that sound like anything from AM radio to CD quality, depending on the bit-rate setting. MP3s have their good sides and bad sides. The good: file compression. The bad: what file compression can do to your audio at a low bit rate. The MP3 codec was developed in the late '80s, but it was almost a decade before computers and the Internet could encode and send the data fast enough to make it useful. The ability to compress audio files to send over the '90s version of the Internet spawned the file-sharing revolution and put a hit on the music industry. The low bandwidth of the time needed a smaller file than a WAV, so the MP3 was a winner. Still there was a large trade-off, and quantity won out over quality. The conversion of the original MP3s at 64Kbps, 32Kbps, or even lower was one of the main reasons that MP3s sounded like they were recorded in a shoe. By compressing a file too much (or at all), you can cause your audio to lose much of its high-frequency content and low-frequency energy. The original MP3 codec has been greatly improved upon, and today's MP3 is not your father's MP3. While there are numerous codecs available to encode audio, the MP3 format has hundreds of supporting playback devices and boatloads of software using it to keep it afloat. Even with faster upload speeds, sending WAV files can take time, so making MP3s to get tracks to people over the Internet still makes sense. If you build an iTunes library or equivalent with good-quality MP3s, you can store 10 times more music than if you rip your tracks in as WAVs. As the encoding gets better, the MP3 sound is almost indistinguishable from the original CD—not that CDs are the bar to aim for; as an industry, we can do better than that.

Encoding MP3s Using iTunes

There are a number of variables when you encode your MP3s, but if you use iTunes, it's pretty easy to set things up:

1. Launch iTunes.

2. Open Preferences (⌘+, / Ctrl+,).

3. Choose Advanced and select the Importing tab.

4. Choose Import Using MP3 Encoder for the file type. The import window contains the different file types available in iTunes, the quality settings, and other import preferences.

5. Click and hold the Settings menu to see the different bit rates. If you want to achieve the best sound quality possible using an MP3, then choose Custom in the Settings menu and crank up the bit rate. The higher the bit rate, the better the sound but also the bigger and slower the file.

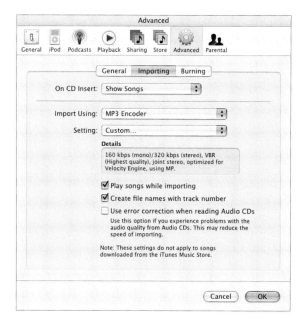

6. For the best MP3 conversion you can theoretically get in iTunes, set the stereo bit rate to 320. The math says one thing with this setting, but sometimes your ears say another (see Figure 6.1).

7. Scale back from these settings if the files are too big and listen to the sound quality as you change settings until you find the right mix between compression and quality. If compressing audio were an exact science, there would be no guessing here. But it's not. To make it a bit more ambiguous, different tracks and different kinds of music sound different with the same settings and format, so you really need to rip, convert, and listen to find your favorite. Everyone's ears are different, so experiment with the settings and types until it sounds right to you.

These settings will apply to any CD ripped into iTunes or any file that you convert from the library using Advanced > Convert MP3.

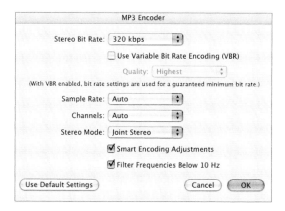

Figure 6.1 The Custom MP3 Encoder window

All CDs Are Not the Same

So you've spent a lot of time and money recording your masterpiece and you were going to burn it to a blank CD that you bought at the corner liquor store. And you wonder why it will play back only during a full moon? Contrary to popular urban legend, it's not true that one factory makes all of the CDs for the entire planet (and all the batteries and all the bottled water), so you need to pay attention to what you buy. There is a lot of repackaging so certain retailers can sell "their" brand, and even the best CDs are fairly inexpensive these days, so there is no excuse for skimping. The quality of your audio CDs, the burner you use, and the software you burn from will greatly affect the disc compatibility and to a lesser degree the sound quality itself. As soon as CD burning got cheap, quality control in CD manufacturing dropped significantly in favor of quantity control. There are good CDs out there; you just need to know what to look for.

Format The different CD formats are known by color code. The specification for an audio CD is called Red Book. CD-ROMs are known as Yellow Book, while CD-Rs and CD-RWs are both Orange Book. The formats contain information about the contents and the physical properties of the disc. Released by Sony and Phillips in 1980, the Red Book standard determined that audio CDs would be 16 bit and 44.1kHz. Now you know whom to blame.

CD-R (Orange Book) The home of the one-off. You get one burn and you're done, but it's also the cheapest of the formats. Used for both music and data. Written CD-Rs are fully compatible with the Red Book and Yellow Book standard for audio CDs and CD-ROMs. CD-Rs have become a landfill disaster.

CD-RW (Orange Book) CD-RWs are better for the environment than CD-Rs, but they're much slower and more expensive. CD-RWs allow you to use a CD as you would a floppy or hard drive by rewriting the files over and over again. Used mostly for data. Written CD-RWs are fully compatible with the Red Book and Yellow Book standard for audio CDs and CD-ROMs.

DVD-+R This is a single-burn format like a CD-R. The DVD format has many times the disc space that a CD has, so is great for data backups as well as authoring video. Audio in this format can be out of the Red Book standard and be up to 24-bit 96k.

DVD-+RW The rewritable version of the DVD format. DVD-RW discs are ideal for backing up big chunks of data or for video use. The DVD format war is in full swing, so who knows what will happen.

Size Okay, so size matters this time. Red Book audio has a 74-minute maximum, so if you use 80-minute CDs for your one-offs, you might have problems with compatibility. If you are just burning discs for everyday purposes, you can get away with more than if you are sending a disc to the duplicator to make 10,000. Going to CD duplication, you have to meet Red Book standards.

Color Looks like a box of crayons got loose in the CD spindle. The different colors in CDs are due to the use of different materials by different companies during manufacturing. Color has to do with the way the disc will record information. There are different attributes associated with the different colors, but that leads to compatibility issues as well. Silver discs are the most compatible, while gold discs are the most durable, rated at well over 100 years of life. By the way, how do we really know that, and also, please let the future have better sound than a 16-bit CD!

Burn Speed CD burners have reached some impressive speeds. From 52x and beyond, burning has come a long way from the days of 1x real time! Your burn speed does not usually affect a data disc as much as it does an audio disc, but be aware. There are many schools of thought on the matter, but it seems to be the consensus that the slower burn speeds sound better and are more compatible with different players. Even though you can burn at 300x, it does not mean you should if it's a music disc.

Brand Yes, this really matters. As to what brand to use, sometimes you shouldn't point or name names, but some common sense helps. Don't ever buy CDs just because they are cheap or buy them from a place that has no connection to music or computers. If something is important enough to burn or back up, then do it right, and if it's really important, make two copies. A quick Goggle search for a consumer rating of blank CDs will show you what you need to know brandwise.

Bounce and Burn

After you bounce your tracks out of Pro Tools, you need another application to burn your audio to CD. iTunes can be a quick and easy solution for this if you just want a one-off.

Burning a CD

Before you import your track or tracks into iTunes, set up your Import preference file type (Preferences > Advanced > Import > Import Using) to reflect what you want to do with your tracks.

- If you are going to burn a Red Book audio CD, import your tracks as WAVs.
- If you are going to burn an MP3 CD, import your tracks as MP3s and import as you will export. The less file conversion the better. If you want to make an MP3 CD, you need to change the Disc Format preference in iTunes to an MP3 CD (Preferences > Advanced > Burning > MP3 CD).

After you have chosen the file type for importing, bring in your tracks using any method:

- Chose File > Import or Shift+⌘+O / Shift+Ctrl+O. Choose your file and iTunes adds it to your library.

- Drag your file directly into the library from the OS.

- Drag your file directly into an existing playlist from the OS.

If you used the first or second method, create and label a new playlist (⌘+N / Ctrl+N) and drag the file into it from the library. iTunes will burn a CD only from a playlist.

Load a blank CD and click the burn disc icon. When it comes time to burn, the speed you select has a role in influencing quality and compatibility; slower is better for audio.

If you want to copy from one disc to another or have more elaborate plans than a basic one-off audio burn, then use a program like Toast Titanium or Jam from Roxio. Toast Titanium is a robust application capable of creating all sorts of different CD and DVD types. Toast does it all. Jam is even better if you want be 100-percent Red Book–compatible for CD duplication. (See the section "Mastering Your Tracks in Pro Tools" later in this chapter for more Jam information.)

Note: With iTunes, you can burn data CDs or DVDs and even MP3 discs by changing the burning preference in Preferences > Advanced > Burning. Burning data DVDs allow you to put a lot of tracks on a single disc as long as you play it back on a computer drive.

Cast No Pod before Its Time

Blogs, IM, file sharing—all move over because podcasts are changing the digital landscape. Podcasts have infused some life back into the digital "airwaves" with a pirate radio–type energy and diversity. This is because podcasts are uncensored and not subject to the bylaws of the FCC (yet). Using the RSS 2.0 technology, podcasts are server-based media files usually containing audio or video content. In plain English, podcasts are just digitally formatted shows of any kind that you can subscribe to, download, and play back on a digital device. While podcasts can be created and played back on most any system, Apple has put podcasting on the mainstream map by including podcasts in iTunes 4.9 and above and by drawing from its enormous iPod branding as part of the de facto name. This technology may go the way of the 8-track, but it may also be a harbinger of things to come in terms of production and content delivery. *Wayne's World* was a podcast hit waiting to happen! So what does it take to create and produce a podcast? Depending on the how deep you want go, a computer, some music software and hardware, a camera, an Internet connection, and an idea will get you going. Anyone can be a podstar, so lights camera, action!

For an audio podcast, follow these steps:

1. Create your show. Okay, that's like saying move that piano over here. It's easier said than done, but for argument's sake, let's say you just made the best show since *Fernwood Tonight*. If you are making an audio show, then it's a little easier technically. You can use most any current audio software to create an audio-only podcast. Video is a bit more complicated, but with the right gear and a little skill, you don't need to be NBC. This is like the first days of radio and TV.

2. In Pro Tools, bounce your files out as either a WAV (.wav) or AIFF (.aif). This is one of the times to actually use a maximizing plug-in on your master fader. You need to get your track loud and compressed considering that most people will listen back to your cast on less-than-stellar gear. (See "Mastering Your Tracks in Pro Tools" later in this chapter.)

3. In the iTunes preferences, set your import method to whatever format you want to use (Preferences > Advanced > Importing > Import Using). Even with the large bandwidth available these days, you need to compress your files to podcast them. The question is, how much? To compress your files, choose either the AAC or MP3 format. Either format will work well for podcasting. Reports vary on what has the best quality at the lowest settings, so you will need to try both formats and do a critical listening to see what works best.

   Even when it's compressed, the file size of a long podcast will be quite large, so just to throw it out there, a mono podcast containing only spoken word will sound pretty good, and in a pinch, even music podcasts have been mono in the past to create a smaller file size instead of using a lower bit rate. You can choose mono as an option under Preferences > Advanced > Importing > Setting > Custom > Channels.

4. Import your tracks into iTunes using whatever method you like. If you already have your bounce on a CD, then as you import to iTunes, the file will be converted automatically to your current Import Using setting. If you drag the file in from the Finder, the file will not automatically convert, so you need to select the file in the iTunes library and go to Advanced > Convert Selection to MP3 or AAC to convert your files (see Figure 6.2).

5.   After the file is converted, you need to make an RSS feed to start the pod ball rolling. An RSS feed is not as intimidating as it sounds. Not if you use Feeder on the Mac or something like it on the PC and let it do the work for you. Feeder is available from Reinvented Software for a small fee and is well worth it. The Reinvented Software website has lots of great material on it to help you though the entire process. An RSS feed is an XML file that holds your audio file.

6.   After you create the feed, you need to upload it to your server. You need your own web space to hold your show. iTunes is a portal and a delivery system but not a storage space. After you have uploaded the RSS feed to your server, you need to go to iTunes or whatever portal you are using and submit your podcast. This is done by entering the URL of the site that holds your show. You can test your podcast by selecting Advanced > Subscribe To Podcast in iTunes. You just enter in your URL and see if it works (see Figure 6.3).

7.   Sit back and wait for your Poddie nomination!

Figure 6.2 Converting files in iTunes

Figure 6.3 iTunes podcast URL subscription window

Setting Up Your Tracks to Be Mastered

The final stage of the audio production process is mastering. Before the session, you need to set yourself up right to get the best possible shot at sonic nirvana. Mastering can be done in dramatically different systems, but no matter how your tracks get mastered, a few things always help get the job done in an efficient (cheaper) manner.

Where your tracks will be going plays a big part in deciding how to master and format them after you have mixed them:

1. Eliminate any EQs, compressors, or maximizers on your master fader. If you leave these types of plug-ins on your master fader you can kill all of the headroom the mastering engineer would have to work with. You can do a version with the FX inserted to reference the sound for the mastering engineer, but make sure you have an unaltered version labeled as such.

2. Put your bounced-out files on a data CD instead of an audio CD if possible. Don't let iTunes or any consumer audio application manipulate your data until it's mastered and you just want to play it back. Leave your tracks at 24 bit if they started at 24 bit, and at full resolution.

3. Make sure your tracks are organized and labeled on the data CD—not just the numbers, but also label different versions of your tracks, such as "full mix, soft vocals."

4. Have a good idea of your track ordering. You may want to change it after you are at the mastering facility, but have a plan beforehand. Many musicians and producers are of the mind that an album's song order plays a large part in how it is received by the public.

5. Have a CD or two handy that are representative of the sound you are looking for to play for the mastering engineer. Be realistic, though. As big of a difference as mastering can make, if your record sounds thin to begin with, no engineer on the planet can make it sound like a million-dollar production, just better.

6. Bounce stems or alternate mixes if you are not sure about a mix. Try bouncing these four versions if there is any doubt:

   - Full mix
   - A cappella
   - Instrumental
   - Music bed with only chorus

   With all of these versions, you can adjust levels in the mastering studio if you need to. Mastering rooms will probably sound much different than the room or rooms you made your record in, so be ready to listen carefully.

7. Know your budget before you book the time. If you know what you have to work with before you start, you'll budget your time per track accordingly.

8. As you start looking for a mastering engineer and facility, listen to some tracks mastered by the engineers you are interested in working with. See if the style and sound is what you're after. Ask about gear and experience, but not necessarily in that order.

9. Don't settle!

Mastering Your Tracks in Pro Tools

After the bounce, where do you go? While there are many different styles and methods of mastering, Pro Tools offers an extremely flexible and powerful system to master audio. From a one-off for the club to a large-scale production, Pro Tools lets you scale the level at which you want to work. You can choose your hardware and plug-ins to fit your needs. If you are mastering a major-label record, you need a different setup than if you are mastering an underground-style podcast. There are different schools of thought about mastering your own music; some musicians and engineers think it's best to have other ears do it, and some like the control of doing it themselves. Engineers or producers working in project studios have a tendency to see a track through all the stages of development, so tracking, mixing, and mastering a song is an everyday occurrence for them.

You can improve the sound of your audio with the default plug-ins, but an investment in additional plug-ins is part of the deal if you are serious about mastering in Pro Tools. Here is a list of the usual mastering suspects in the insert chain:

> **Multiband Compression/Limiter/Gate plug-ins** Multiband plug-ins allow you to apply different settings to different frequencies. Multiband plug-ins give you much more flexibility than single-band plug-in in mastering. (See Figure 6.4.)
>
> **EQ** Give a similar overall tone to all of your songs when mastering an album or when working on individual tracks you use EQ to fix mistakes made during mixing. EQ is one of the most common effects used during the mastering process (see Figure 6.5).

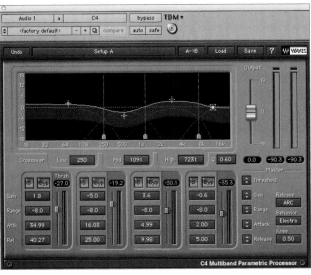

Figure 6.4 The Waves C4 Multiband Parametric Processor

Stereo Imaging Check and adjust the width and depth of your stereo field (see Figure 6.6).

Exciter An exciter can put a little presence and sizzle into your track.

Reverb Apply a global reverb to add overall consistency to a track on which different reverbs might have been used while mixing, or to give depth and sheen to an entire mix that might be a little thin (see Figure 6.7).

Figure 6.5 McDSP 6 Band EQ

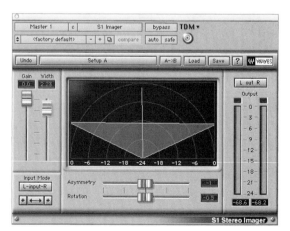

Figure 6.6 The Waves S1 Stereo Imager

Figure 6.7 The Trillium Lanes TL Space Reverb

Maximizer Bring your track up to commercial volume levels and add fullness. The Waves L1, 2, L3, and Digidesign's Maxim are great examples of track slammers (see Figure 6.8).

Dithering A dithering plug-in smooths out the process of converting down the bit rate. If your session is 24-bit and you need to make a CD, then you will have to convert to 16-bit during or after the bounce to conform to Red Book audio (see Figure 6.9).

Here are some suggestions for the gear outside of Pro Tools:

Monitors The best Pro Tools rig and mastering engineer in the world will not get you great sound if you can't monitor your audio correctly. If your speakers color the sound in a misleading way, your tracks will probably sound different and confused everywhere else. Good speakers and a room you can trust are worth their weight in gold or convolution reverbs—you choose. Genelecs are industry standards and sound sweet, but have your checkbook ready because these Swedish beauties are not cheap. Monitors have changed greatly in the past decade. Most studio monitors are now self-powered. Forget about that 50-pound amp and the extra cables. Even though the prices have come down, it can still be a large investment, so before you part with a considerable amount of money, listen before you leap.

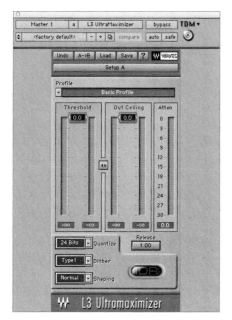

Figure 6.8 The Waves L3 Ultramaximizer

Figure 6.9 The POW-r dither plug-in

Room acoustics Your room should be as acoustically true as possible to get anywhere close to the sound you really want. You can master at home to some degree, but you have to take into account the sound of a room that is not tuned. If you have to work this way, you should listen to some CDs that you are familiar with to reference your work. This is where Auralex foam comes into play—not for soundproofing, but for acoustical treatment to get rid of standing waves.

Ears You must rest these amazing devices and treat them well. Working around 85 dB helps your ears from overloading and closing down. Crank it every so often to listen with a little more detail and to see what the higher volume does to the track, but then bring it back down to the same level you started with. Ear fatigue will bring down the accuracy and quality of your work faster than a government-awarded contract.

Decibel meter Cheap and invaluable. Find 85 dB and mark your monitor level so you know where it is. This will give you a chance to visit the boys at your local RadioShack.

Now that you're armed with the pertinent information on the tools you need inside and outside of Pro Tools, here are the steps for mastering an audio CD:

1. Check your track for dynamic range. Before you touch an insert, make sure your mix still has some dynamic range in it. If your track is bumpin' zero all of the time, then rebounce it with no maximizing or limiting on the master fader or remove the master fader altogether. Some still think the math for the master fader handling all of the audio is too confusing for the computer, so bounce without it and do an A/B comparison. Without any headroom in your track, you really limit your capabilities in mastering.

2. If you are mastering more than one track, such as for an album, then you can load all of the mixes into one Pro Tools session sequentially on different tracks to easily check levels between songs as well as overall tone.

3. Check your track in mono at every stage of mastering. This can reveal phase issues and give you perspective on how some people might hear the track.

4. Shape and tone your EQ. When you EQ in mastering, it's mostly for achieving an overall tonal balance instead of trying to get in to an individual sound. Individual track EQing should be done during mixing. EQ is the main tool for creating tonal balance across all of your tracks if you are mastering an album.

5. Create more space for your track with reverb. Reverb can do a number of good things to a mix in mastering, but it's not always used by any means. If your mix has a number of different reverbs, a little overall reverb will paint over the differences and add some cohesiveness. Using short reverb programs at a low level, you can add fullness or depth to a track. Watch the amount of reverb and keep it transparent.

6. Excite your listeners. If your track needs a little something extra in the top end, then an exciter might do the trick. Exciters work differently from EQs. EQs boost or cut what is already in your track, but an exciter creates additional harmonics. Adding these new harmonics to your track can bring out presence or brightness. Too much excitement can make your track sound harsh or fuzzy, but the right amount can really put some life back into a dead track.

7. Imagine your track in stereo. Using a stereo imager allows you to rebalance the stereo field of a mix. You can adjust the left, right, and center components of a mix independently of each other. This can be used transparently to clarify the stereo field of a mix, or you can use it as an effect to exaggerate the width of the left or right channels or both. If you have a multiband version of an imager, you can apply different width and depth to different frequencies. This allows you to tighten up your kick and bass by moving the low frequencies toward the center

while spreading your higher frequencies wider. The S1 from Waves is a good example of a typical stereo image processor. The S1 works with the information contained in the track and does not add anything. Check your track in mono as you work with an imager.

8. Don't stress, compress. Multiband compression is a vital part of the mastering chain and a place to add some fullness and thickness to your track. These plug-ins can really bring out the character of your track and are a key in getting that great bass sound. By compressing the lower frequencies, you can not only bring out the bass without adding extra EQ, but you can balance out the dynamics of your kick and bass to get a more consistent and polished sound. Dial in specific spots to bring up presence on vocals or warm up the low-end bass or cut a muddy low mid for clarity.

9. Maximize your potential. The common solution to low volume is to just raise your output to maximum and lower your threshold to a point where most of your mix is being treated. This will boost your output level, but at the expense of some of your dynamic range. That is a big trade-off, no doubt. While you certainly want to get your tracks as saturated and loud as other commercial music, there is a current fascination with crushing the life out of tracks by overmaximizing. For more-acoustic styles of music, back off on the L2 a bit and let your track breathe a little. Some styles of electronic music can sustain L3 crushing and sound better for it. When you master, are you looking for some room in your track for some volume peaks and valleys or for pure unadulterated intensity? It's your call. Experiment and listen to your results on as many different systems as possible. In the wrong hands, these plug-ins can be the most misused and abused plug-ins out there.

10. To dither or not to dither? Converting the bit rate down as you bounce your track artifacts the audio regardless of the quality of gear you use. When you apply dithering to your track, you are actually adding noise to the artifacts created by reducing the word length. The added noise rounds off the edges caused by the number crunching and smooths out the transition. Use dithering as the last insert in your chain when you are going from a higher to a lower bit depth.

11. Bounce your tracks, burn a CD, and listen everywhere you can. Be careful about listening to your mastered mixes on an iPod or similar device unless you leave your tracks as full-resolution WAV files. Never trust an MP3 to do a critical listening. Try bouncing all of your mastered tracks without a master fader. You can use all of the necessary plug-ins per song on the individual track, so no need to induce any possible artifacting when you don't need to.

If you are going to have your disc duplicated by a manufacturer, you need to set it up as Red Book audio. The Red Book audio spec puts audio at 16-bit and 44.1kHz, sets the number of tracks at 99 and the minimum track length at 4 seconds, and dictates the physical construction of the disc. Depending on what your needs are, you may need to edit the CD PQ codes. PQ codes contain information about start and stop IDs, ISRC codes (dates, label information, copy protection), and other bits of pertinent data. Jam from Roxio can generate 100-percent Redbook premasters and edit PQ codes, while programs such as iTunes burn the Red Book standard but can't edit PQ codes. Do your ordering, crossfading, indexing, and PQ editing in to Jam. Digidesign's Masterlist Pro was the favored software back in the day, but Digidesign never upgraded it into OS X. When it's all right, burn a copy and take it out of the room you are working in and listen to it on as many different systems as you can. Don't forget to listen in mono to see how it holds up. When you are sure it flows, the EQ is right, the levels are balanced, and the fades are good, then send it to the duplicators.

Postproduction and the World of Surround

Just like audio, video has undergone a revolution in the recent past. Digital video formats, cameras, and workstations have made it possible to produce a fully professional DVD without the employment of a full-fledged postproduction facility. Systems like Avid and Apple's Final Cut Pro have made all aspects of picture editing possible inside a computer. For Pro Tools engineers, this is a blessing in disguise: these picture editing programs are limited in their sound-editing capabilities and that means more job opportunities. Additionally, measures have been put into place that allow for seamless transfer of media and synchronization between video and audio systems. This chapter delineates some working methods and techniques for post-producing with Pro Tools.

Chapter Contents

What to Tell the Video Editor

The Open Media Framework Interchange (OMFI) format was created by Avid and Digidesign to make useful and efficient transfers of data between video- and audio-editing systems. For the most part, OMFI transfers are simple and effective; however, it is necessary to properly prepare a project in Final Cut Pro or Avid before the transfer is made. As the Pro Tools engineer, it is you who suffers when an OMFI file is not properly put together, so it is in your best interest to communicate clearly to the video editor what is needed.

Note: Prepare a comprehensive dummy-proof list to give to the video editor or producer outlining exactly what you need to do your job. This is called a list of deliverables. Most video editors appreciate this since they are more concerned with the picture edit and have little time to spend on thinking about the paltry sound mix. As audio engineers, we politely refrain from reminding them that no matter how good their picture edit is, we can make or break the show with our sound mix!

Which Audio Deliverables to Ask For

Here's what to ask for in your list of audio deliverables for Avid and Final Cut Pro OMFI transfers:

- An OMFI file generated from the Avid or Final Cut Pro system. This can be provided on a FireWire hard drive or a recordable DVD. If the show is longer than 25 minutes, it's best to break it down into 25-minute reels. Each reel's OMFI file should be provided separately on DVD-Rs or as separate files on a hard drive. Breaking down a show into reels will help your Pro Tools system deal with very large video files if you plan to sync to QuickTime video. OMFI files should be created without the video embedded. The video will come in separately as a QuickTime file.

- All audio should be included in the OMFI file(s). This means dialog from any sources used in production, like boom and lavaliere microphone sources, temp or final music, sound effects, and room tone/ambience that was recorded. This audio should come on separate and discrete tracks, even if it wasn't used in the making of the video editor's rough cut.

- When the video editor is making the OMFI file, there is an option to choose how much of a handle to include on all of the audio cuts. This refers to the amount of audio that exists outside each region boundary. A minimum of 5 seconds is recommended so you will have enough media to make appropriate crossfades between regions in Pro Tools.

- Any music used in the video should be included on a CD, separate from the OMFI files. Often, Pro Tools editors have to resample or reedit music cues and having the source material helps in this regard.

- All digital audio files should be 16-bit/48kHz AIFF files because this is currently the standard video sample rate/bit depth/audio file type. Remember to abide by these settings as you create your Pro Tools session, as well.

- The first frame of action should begin exactly at time code hour 1, which is 01:00:00:00 in time code.

Note: A *sync pop* is one frame of -20 dB tone at 1kHz. It sounds like a quick pop or blip and is used in conjunction with exactly one designated frame of picture to align and sync up audio and video. Avid and FCP have methods for generating audio sync pops.

- Both head and tail sync pops should be included on all tracks. Head pop should appear exactly 2 seconds before the first frame of action (FFOA), at time code 00:59:58:00, and tail pop exactly 2 seconds after last frame of action (LFOA). The head pops are also referred to as 2 pops, occurring 2 seconds before the picture starts. The pops allow instant verification at the beginning and end of a reel to ensure that sync was maintained. Subsequent reels should start before the hour on the time code timeline for the corresponding reel number (i.e., reel 3 of a program should begin at time code 02:58:30:00, with the sync pop occurring at 02:59:58:00 and the first frame of the picture at 03:00:00:00).

- Any other materials used in production, such as sound logs and original DAT tapes, should be provided in case it is necessary to go back to the source material.

Which Video Deliverables to Ask For

Probably the most important thing about delivering video to the Pro Tools editor is that the picture is *locked*, meaning that all editing is completed and there are no changes to be made. In the postproduction process, audio editing and mixing always come after the picture edit is completed. Because the audio and video are physically separated during the sound mix, major complications and problems arise if the picture is edited because it is difficult to conform the audio to match.

Here's a list of video deliverables to ask for if you are syncing to a QuickTime movie in Pro Tools:

- A full-resolution, self-contained DV-NTSC QuickTime Movie. This format makes it possible to choose Options > QuickTime DV Out Fire Wire in Pro Tools so you can connect a FireWire cable to a transcoder box or camera and view the video on an NTSC video monitor outside your computer monitor (see the next section, "Working with Video in Pro Tools"). The movie should begin 1 minute, 30 seconds before first frame of action (00:58:30:00) and include a 10-second countdown/academy leader or other suitable visual sync reference exactly 2 seconds before hour 1, or the first frame of action.

- Each reel should also include a time code window burn that matches exactly the timeline of the audio OMFI file. The window burn should be placed strategically in the frame so as not to obscure dialog sync. A time code window burn is a graphic visual reference of time code numbers usually overlaid at the bottom of the screen.

- A stereo audio reference track (16-bit/48kHz) should be included with the QuickTime export. The reference track is the sound mix from the picture edit. This can be used as you are editing and mixing the picture to reference any sync problems or intentions the producer or video editor had in the rough cut. It is usually brought into Pro Tools as a stereo track and then muted until needed.

Working with Video in Pro Tools

Every type of Pro Tools system supports the import of any QuickTime movie as long as you have a Digidesign-qualified version of Apple's QuickTime extension. Any video codec that QuickTime will play, Pro Tools will play. The movie comes into Pro Tools as a floating window of the size at which it was originally saved. It is not possible to resize the video window from Pro Tools. For the best performance, you should try to stream the QuickTime movie off of its own dedicated hard drive going into a separate FireWire or SCSI bus from the one being used by the drive with your audio files. Getting QuickTime video into Pro Tools is relatively simple; just choose File > Import > QuickTime Movie. The movie will come into Pro Tools as a floating video window and a video region on a movie track. Movie tracks have the following options:

- You can insert a sync point and move it in the timeline with the Nudge or Grabber tool, but you cannot edit the movie region with the Selector or Trimmer tool.

- The movie track can be seen in either Blocks view or Frames view. Frames view provides you with still thumbnail images for reference, as shown in Figure 7.1. Frames view takes more system resources to run than Blocks view and isn't necessarily that useful, so it's usually better to minimize the video track's size and stick with Blocks view. This will additionally save screen real estate and CPU performance.

- An imported movie comes with an FPS indicator telling you the frames per second of the imported video.

- There is a circular button next to the FPS indicator in the Movie track. When activated, this button takes the movie offline, preventing real-time playback. This can also be done by typing Shift+⌘+J / Shift+Ctrl+J.

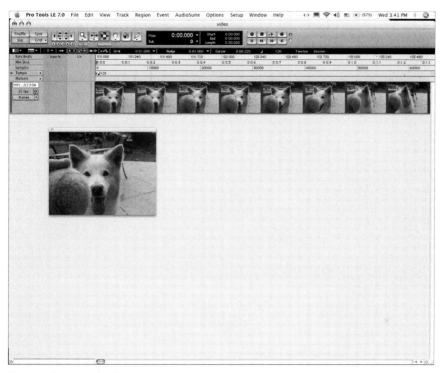

Figure 7.1 A movie track in Frames view

Going out NTSC

Although it is possible to edit with a floating video window, it is even better to view the video on an NTSC monitor. (NTSC stands for National Television System Committee, but even a consumer television will work if you're on a budget.) This is possible if the QuickTime movie is encoded as a full-resolution, self-contained DV-NTSC Quick-Time Movie. Avid and Final Cut Pro can export QuickTime movies in this format. When an imported movie in this format is brought into Pro Tools, you can choose Options > QuickTime DV Out Firewire. You can then take a FireWire cable out of a FireWire port on your computer and plug it into a transcoder box or DV camera and view the video on an NTSC video monitor outside your computer monitor. The transcoder box/camera is used to convert a DV FireWire signal into a composite RCA video cable that can be hooked up to an NTSC or TV monitor for viewing. When you do this, however, you have to watch out for any time delay the transcoder/camera is causing. You can usually find out this delay amount from the manufacturer or from an Internet search. To adjust for the time delay, choose Setups > QuickTime Movie Offset (see Figure 7.2).

A popular transcoder is the Canopus ADVC100, which splits a FireWire DV connection into composite video. The frame offset for this particular device is 22 quarter frames.

Figure 7.2 Use the QuickTime Movie Offset setting to adjust for any time delay when sending video out the FireWire port.

OMFI: The Standard for Video/Audio Transfer

OMFI is an acronym for Open Media Framework Interchange. It was developed in part by Digidesign and Avid to provide an industry standard for transfer of information between video and audio systems. OMFI transfers are also called OMF transfers, referring to the .omf file extension of OMFI files. OMF transfers are the best way to get the audio tracks out of Avid, Final Cut Pro, or other video editing applications and into Pro Tools. The OMFI option is found in the export options of video applications and usually results in the creation of a single large OMFI file embedded with all of the audio media, track information, region names, and lengths. If Avid is used to make the OMFI, volume automation can be included. Currently, Final Cut Pro–created OMFI files don't include volume automation. The most current version of OMFI is 2.0. This version should be used if a video application supports it. In short, OMFI export offers these benefits:

• The original audio material is digitized only once (by the video editor) and the same files go directly to the audio session. This means that the video editor is responsible for correctly setting input levels and calibrating the system to get an optimum transfer.

• The audio tracks are transferred digitally from hard disk to hard disk; they don't have to be recorded into Pro Tools in real time.

• All of the edits, region names, and media remain the same. Basically, the audio editor can start up right where the video editor left off. Because handles can be included outside each region boundary, additional crossfade flexibility is possible. If the session is prepared correctly before OMFI file creation, minimal, if any, reloading of original material is needed.

• All the media maintains its sync relationship to the picture.

Continues

Translating OMFI Files with DigiTranslator

Pro Tools must use a tool called DigiTranslator to decipher OMFI files. Originally, DigiTranslator version 1 was a stand-alone application that simply opened OMFI files and saved their contents into new Pro Tools sessions. In Pro Tools 6.*x* and beyond, DigiTranslator version 2 is rolled into the software, allowing direct importing of OMFI contents into an existing Pro Tools session. However, DigiTranslator is an add-on and must be unlocked in the software via the iLok USB hardware key. Once DigiTranslator is activated, OMFI files are read from the Import Session Data dialog box, accessed by choosing File > Import > Session Data. In the initial import data dialog, you can choose OMFI files as well as session files when you have DigiTranslator. Once you choose an OMFI file, you will see the Import Session Data dialog where Pro Tools allows you to import elements just as you would import data from any Pro Tools session. DigiTranslator 2 can also support Advanced Authoring Format (AAF) and Media Exchange Format (MXF). Figure 7.3 shows the Import Session Data dialog box while data is being imported from an OMFI file.

In the Import Session Data dialog, the following options should be checked for proper importing:

•   Set Audio Media Options to Copy From Source Media. This will create a typical Pro Tools audio files folder with the transferred files in it.

•   The Video Media Options setting is insignificant. You will import the QuickTime movie separately.

- In the lower-left portion of the dialog, there are options about clip-based gain. Usually, you want to uncheck these boxes because you are going to do any volume automation yourself. It is possible here to check Convert Clip-Based Gain To Automation if you want the Avid volume levels to come across.

- Uncheck Pan Odd Tracks Left/Even Tracks Right. Usually, the panning from the video session is not correct anyway.

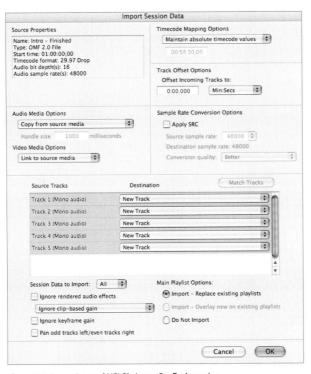

Figure 7.3 Importing an OMFI file into a Pro Tools session

DV Toolkit in LE Systems

You can postproduce audio for video on both LE and HD Pro Tools systems. The main difference is that the basic LE system does not come with Timecode or Feet/Frames as Main Time Scale rulers. Although it is still possible to use LE systems for audio post without time code, it helps to have a frame-accurate reference. To give the LE user complete postproduction support, Digidesign offers the DV Toolkit package, which is an add-on software package including DigiTranslator, noise reduction plug-ins, voice-over alignment plug-ins, and the Timecode and Feet/Frames options as Main Time Scale rulers. The DV Toolkit is authorized through a USB iLok hardware key. More info about DV Toolkit can be found at www.digidesign.com.

Working with Stems

In audio postproduction, the three different elements of a sound track are broken in to smaller groups called *stems*. The three typical stems are dialog, effects, and music. In your track naming, all tracks containing dialog should start with *DX* (for dialog tracks), all effects tracks start with *FX*, and all music tracks begin with *MX*. Ideally, every distinct sound will have its own track. So it may be possible that a character in a film has four separate tracks, one for the lavaliere microphone, one for the boom microphone, and two more for a different-sounding lavaliere and boom in a different scene. The end edit will resemble a checkerboard, with regions segmented across multiple tracks. The idea is that when it comes time to mix, every different character or microphone source should have its own track for discretely processing options in the mix.

Breaking Out the Tracks

Usually, when the OMFI file is transferred in to a Pro Tools session, the video editor has not split out the tracks the way you want them. So the first step is to lock and deactivate the original OMFI contents and then *break out* the tracks into their proper stems. Here's how:

1. Select every track by clicking on the first track's name and Shift+clicking the last track's name in the Edit or Mix window.

2. Choose Track > Duplicate and duplicate all track data when the Duplicate Tracks window appears.

3. Select every region in the duplicated tracks by dragging the Selector tool diagonally from the first duplicated track region across the entire length of the session. Press ⌘+L / Ctrl+L to lock all regions.

4. Select all of the duplicated tracks and choose Track > Make Inactive. Hide all duplicated tracks by deselecting them in the Show/Hide Tracks column on the left side of the Edit window. You now have an inactive, locked copy of the original OMFI file contents to refer back to in case of any errors you make while breaking out the tracks.

5. Make as many new audio tracks as you think will be necessary. Name tracks with the appropriate stem prefix; for example, DX Samantha for a character named Samantha, or FX amb and FX foley for effects tracks containing ambience and Foley, respectively.

6. Carefully edit the regions, cutting where different characters speak or different mic sources are heard. ⌘+E / Ctrl+E will be an important key command here since you will be doing a lot of splicing. (To separate regions, you can also use the B key with the Keyboard Focus function activated in the Edit window; see the sidebar "Keyboard Focus" in Chapter 3.)

7. As you edit, move your newly created regions onto the appropriate tracks. Remember to hold the Control/Start key as you move regions vertically from track to track with the Grabber tool. This will ensure that you don't slip the regions left or right out of position while moving them vertically from track to track.

8. Use the Trimmer tool to pull out the handles of regions when necessary and crossfade between edited regions. The idea is to not have any blank spots or pops and clicks between edits. With Keyboard Focus in the Edit window, the D key is great for quick fading in to the edit cursor, the G key will create a quick fade-out from the edit cursor, and the F key will crossfade a selection. All of these one-button fades create fade slopes according to the Default Fade settings on the Editing tab (Setup > Preferences). Figure 7.4 shows an example of a fully broken-out session.

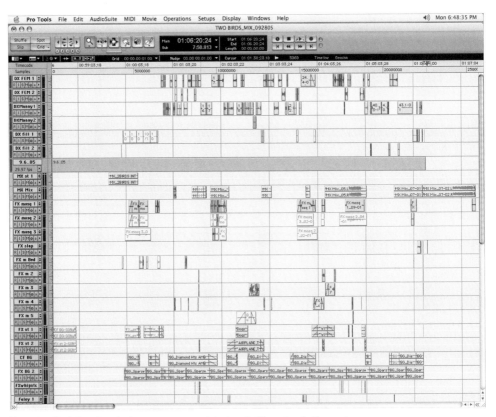

Figure 7.4 Tracks have been broken out onto appropriate stems in this postproduction session.

Routing the Stems

Once the audio regions are broken out into their proper stem tracks and finely edited, you'll want to route the tracks' outputs appropriately for the mix. Using Pro Tools's internal busses, you will set up different auxiliary submixes for each stem and route the corresponding tracks to those stems. First, make a custom I/O setup for stem mixes:

1. Choose Setup > I/O and click the Bus tab and label three stereo busses DX bus, MX bus, and FX bus. Then, label the next three busses DX stem, MX stem, and FX stem. Label the next bus MIX. Finally, you may name other busses for sending reverb and effects if you want. When you are done, the I/O Bus tab should look like Figure 7.5.

2. Create three Aux input tracks and label them DX BUS MASTER, MX BUS MASTER, and FX BUS MASTER. Set the input of each Aux to the corresponding bus. Figure 7.6 shows the mix window with the three Aux tracks assigned properly. Solo-safe the tracks by ⌘+clicking / Ctrl+clicking on the tracks' Solo button.

3. Route the output of the tracks to the corresponding stem bus. For example, DX Bus Master will be routed to the DX stem bus.

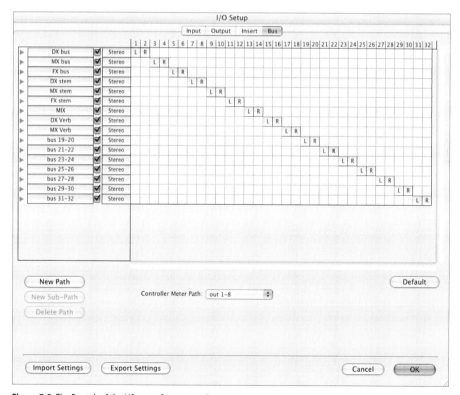

Figure 7.5 The Bus tab of the I/O setup for a stem mix

Figure 7.6 The Aux submixes are routed here to accept input from the DX, MX, and FX busses and are outputting to the DX, MX, and FX stems. Note the + symbol on the output, indicating that the outputs are also multed to the MIX bus.

4. Route the Aux track's output to two locations simultaneously by holding Control/Start as you choose MIX from the Output Path Selector for each Aux track. This technique is called *multing* the output. When you are done, the routing will look like Figure 7.6.

Note: Pro Tools supports multiple outputs for tracks. This means that you can send the output of any track to two or more places at once. In audio engineering terminology, this is called *multing*. To get this to work, press the Control/Start key as you select the additional output or bus you want the track to be routed to. When you are done, you will know your track has been routed by the + symbol preceding the track's Output Path Selector in the Mix or Edit window. Anytime you see a + in the Output Path Selector, it means the track's output has been multed to one or more places.

5. Route all of your dialog track outputs to the DX bus, all of your FX track outputs to the FX bus, and all music track outputs to the MX bus.

Printing the Stems

When your mix is complete, you'll want to print all of the stems separately and as a stereo mix by routing each auxiliary submix back onto stereo Pro Tools audio tracks. Why? This way, in case of a foreign-language version, music adjustment, or remix, for example, each stem will be its own separate file. Because you set up your I/O for the stems and multiple outputs, getting this to happen all in one pass is simple. Here's how:

1. Create four stereo audio tracks. Name them DX STEM, MX STEM, FX STEM, and Stereo Mix.

2. Set the inputs of each audio track to its corresponding stem bus. For example, DX stem will have an input assignment of the bus named DX stem. It is easy to do this complex routing since you labeled everything in the I/O setup before routing the tracks.

3. If your studio allows you to monitor separate outputs, you may want to give each audio stem track a separate output so you can independently listen to them on an external mixer. In Figure 7.7, the stereo mix goes out 1-2 output, the DX stem goes out 3-4, the FX stem goes out 7-8, and the MX stem goes out 5-6. This way, it is possible to route all of Pro Tools's eight outputs to separate stereo channels on an external mixer and isolate each stem for monitoring purposes.

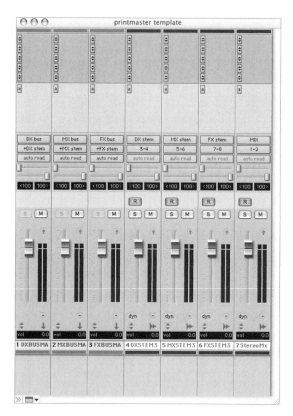

Figure 7.7 The Mix window with all four stems routed and record-enabled

Calibrating Your Postproduction Mix

Mixing for video and film is different than mixing for music, where the only general guideline is to make it as loud as possible. When you are mixing a video or film session, it is a given that your mix will need to translate properly to playback venues other than your studio. Whether the mix will be played in a movie theater, played on a home entertainment system, or nationally broadcast on television, what you hear coming through the monitors on your Pro Tools system must play correctly elsewhere. To achieve this goal, you need to calibrate your system's output with the outside world. Have you ever noticed that there are no numbers on Pro Tools's track level displays? This is by design. Pro Tools output level can be relative to whatever system it is calibrated to. But numbers and meter calibration make up only half the picture. When you are mixing for postproduction, you also have to think about how loud your monitors are in the room you are working in. You can use Pro Tools's internal signal generator to make sure you are listening at the proper volume and that your mixes arrive at the appropriate levels when they leave your studio. Additional tools required include an external device with a VU or digital meter and an SPL loudness meter.

Here are some guidelines to calibrate your studio:

1. On an available stereo audio track, make a selection for about a minute in an empty part of the track. Make sure the track volume is at 0.

2. Open the Signal Generator plug-in by choosing AudioSuite > Other. Set the Signal Generator to produce a 1000Hz (1kHz), -20 dB sine signal and click Process to make a calibration tone for the length of the selection. This method is preferable to running the TDM or RTAS version of Signal Generator since it requires file playback off of a hard drive.

3. Play the tone region in Loop Playback.

4. If you have access to an external VU meter, the signal coming out of Pro Tools should be calibrated by some kind of attenuator (such as a mixer or input volume of a deck) to read at 0 on the VU meter. The VU meter may be also be on board on an analog record deck, a video deck, and so on.

5. If there is a digital meter such as on a DAT recorder, DA88, or Digital Betacam deck, then the digital scale should read -20 dB.

6. Open the Signal Generator plug-in again (AudioSuite > Other). Set the Signal Generator to produce a -20 dB Pink Noise signal and click Process to make a

calibration tone for the length of a 1-minute selection. Do this on a separate stereo track so you can cross-reference with the tone.

7. Play the pink noise. Start with your monitor volume control very low.

8. Hold up an SPL loudness meter that is set to C weighted with response time set to slow. An affordable solution is the RadioShack Digital Sound Pressure Level (SPL, for short) Meter. It is about $60 and is available at any RadioShack. The device should be held at ear level exactly at the distance your ears are from the monitors when you are mixing. Use a tripod if you have one.

There are some discrepancies between listening levels depending on what you are mixing for and the size of your room:

- For broadcast listening levels, slowly turn up the monitor volume on each channel until the meter reads 78 dB.

- For film mixes, play the pink noise through each channel and turn up the monitor until it the SPL meter reads 85 dB. However, this level may be much too loud and fatiguing to the ear for near-field monitoring in a small room.

- For film mixing in a small, near-field studio, or editing suite, Chris Forrest of Studio Guapo recommends setting the SPL meter to 85 dB while playing the pink noise out in stereo from both speakers simultaneously (more on this technique in the sidebar "Audio Engineer Chris Forrest's Tips for Calibrating a Studio").

- The Sony spec for mixing for surround DVDs for home theater use states that each speaker should be monitored at 82 dB while the mix is also checked on a stereo television at 78 dB.

Audio Engineer Chris Forrest's Tips for Calibrating a Studio

Chris Forrest, owner and head audio engineer at Studio Guapo, a postproduction studio in San Francisco, shares some of his experience with calibrating his studio to a proper mixing volume.

"Working at an 85 dB monitoring level in a near-field monitoring situation can be pretty taxing on your ears over long periods of time. If you're monitoring in surround, I would suggest sticking with the Sony (or similar) spec. But if you're primarily listening in stereo and working on anything that's going to be screened in a theatrical monitoring environment (cutting dialog, FX editing, sound design), I've had good results at my studio using the following method. Whether the final mix comes out of my Pro Tools rig to the studio TV or I'm taking the tracks to Skywalker Sound for a final mix, the levels translate to multiple environments.

"Calibrate your mix/bus master(s) output(s) using a −20 dB 1k sine wave using the above method so that your external or console VU meters read 0 VU. Next, set up your pink noise track as explained

Continues

Working in Surround Sound (HD Only)

Before you can mix audio in surround, you have to be properly set up in your studio. For the Pro Tools user, a surround setup is a gear-intensive endeavor. Not only must you have a surround monitoring system, including multiple speakers, you must also have a Pro Tools HD system. Once your studio is equipped with the proper gear, you have to consider a few options about how Pro Tools is going to talk to your speakers. This involves both routing internally through Pro Tools's I/O setup and physically wiring the speakers from the Pro Tools interface through your monitor control system. Finally, you have to be sure that your mixes will easily translate to the outside world so you can properly lay off your mixes for DVD creation, theatrical exhibition, or broadcast. The following are some guidelines for setting up your Pro Tools system for surround mixing in the most popular of surround formats, the 5.1 system.

The 5.1 system uses six discrete audio channels and therefore requires six output channels on the Pro Tools hardware interface. The listening environment is set up around the audio engineer as follows:

- Three speakers at the front, left (L) and right (R) at 22 to 30 degrees and center (C).

- Two surround speakers at 90 to 110 degrees to the side or rear, surround left (Ls) and surround right (Rs).

- A low-frequency effects (LFE) channel carries supporting deep bass sound effects, ranging from 10Hz to 80Hz, which can, for example, be used by a subwoofer. The LFE is the .1 in the 5.1 name, referring to its limited bandwidth.

Setting Up the Pro Tools I/O for Surround

The first order of business for surround mixing in Pro Tools is to configure your I/O setup. This can be done automatically when opening a new session by choosing one of the three default 5.1 setups in the I/O Setting pull-down menu of the session parameters. There are three types of output configurations you can use to determine which output of Pro Tools is going to which channel of the surround speakers. Choosing your output layout is extremely crucial because it will later dictate how your mix translates to the outside world. The three Pro Tools default output configurations are shown in Table 7.1.

▶ **Table 7.1** Default Output Configurations

Type	Parameters	Notes
Film Mix	1 is L, 2 is C, 3 is R, 4 is Ls, 5 is Rs, and 6 is Lf.	This configuration is less stereo-compatible because your first two outputs, which are usually left and right, have been changed to left and center.
SMPTE/ITU Mix	1 is L, 2 is R, 3 is Center, 4 is Lf, 5 is Ls, and 6 is Rs.	This order is the default if you are monitoring through a Digidesign Control 24 control surface. Since the 1 and 2 channels are still stereo left and right, it is easier to get in and out of this layout if you are moving back and forth between surround and stereo mixes.
DTS Mix (Pro Control Monitoring)	1 is L, 2 is R, 3 is Center, 4 is Lf, 5 is Ls, and 6 is Rs.	Digidesign's Pro Control surface monitoring section is designed to work with this configuration in its surround-monitoring mode.

Figures 7.8 through 7.10 show the Output tab of these three surround setups. Note that the sub-paths are revealed in these shots, which show that there can be smaller subdivided sections of a surround output. These will show up as different options in a track's output paths from the Pro Tools Mix window, allowing you to output a track strictly into LCR or L/R Stereo from within the larger surround matrix.

Once your I/O setup is complete, any audio track, mono or stereo, can be output in surround. Simply choose the 5.1 path from the Audio Output Path Selector. Once a surround output is chosen, then the typical two-dimensional fader turns into a surround fader with a green dot in the middle. To show the full-size surround fade options, click on the track pop-up slider below the pan display in the Edit window track I/O view or under the Mute button in the Mix window track fader. Figure 7.11 shows a mono track with the pop-up surround fader in action. The figure also shows a 5.1 master fader with all six channels outputting a signal.

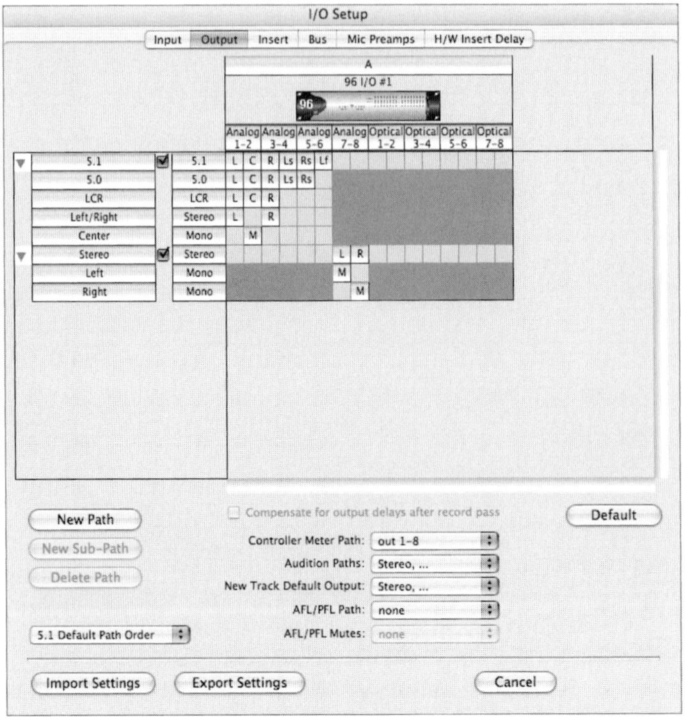

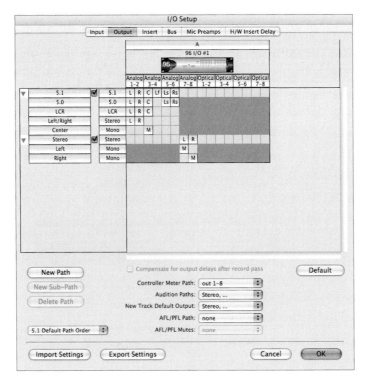

Figure 7.8 The Film Mix I/O setup output configuration showing sub-paths

Figure 7.9 The SMPTE/ITU Mix I/O setup output configuration showing sub-paths

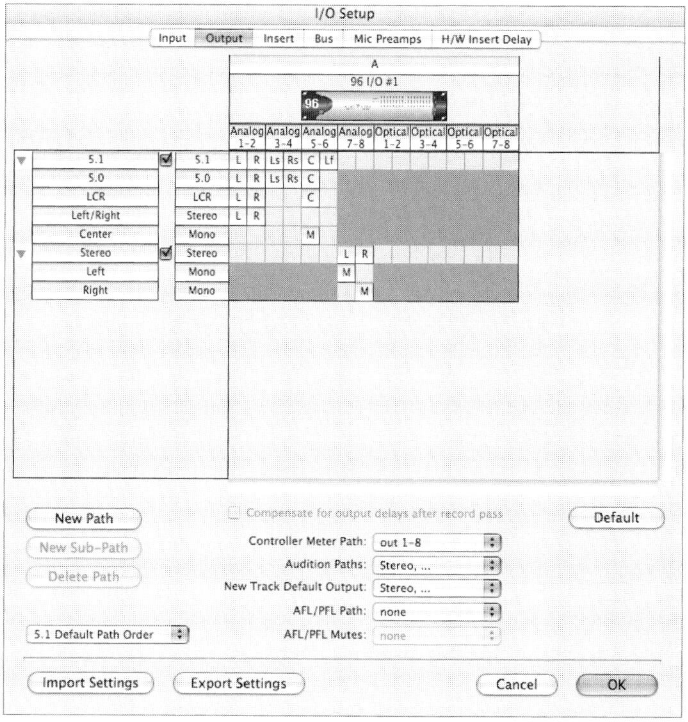

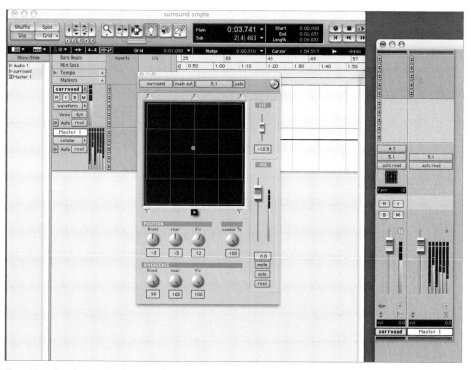

Figure 7.10 The DTS Mix I/O setup output configuration showing sub-paths

Figure 7.11 A track outputting in surround

Working in Surround

Working in surround can be compared to working in the early days of stereo audio. The format and experience are so new that there is a lot of variance in styles and techniques. As the mixer, you get to decide what elements of your mix come out the different channels. For film and video postproduction, the multichannel setup is most often used to establish a spatial dynamic. For example, the viewer is sonically placed in a jungle environment with effects tracks in the surround speakers. Movement between speakers is reserved for motion effects like a plane flying overhead and behind the viewer. The center channel is specifically reserved for on-camera dialog and voice-over.

According to Dolby Labs,

Traditionally, dialogue is placed only in the Center speaker to tie the on-screen sounds to the picture. When a Center speaker is used, all center-panned dialog appears to come from the screen regardless of the listener's position. If the dialogue comes from the Left or Right speakers, the stereo image differs depending on the listener's position. This is highly undesirable. It does not bar voices from the other channels, but generally only effects or incidental voices should be in any channel other than center.

—From the *Dolby Surround Mixing Manual*

Music mixing in surround offers some different options. There is still the traditional viewpoint that spatial dynamics can be upheld. For example, the listener is positioned in the sweet spot of an orchestral hall, where the orchestra playing Tchaikovsky's Fourth Symphony is spread across the front speakers and the rear surround speakers have more reverb and room sound. Or the listener is in the center of the barn where Neil Young's *Harvest* album was recorded, with instruments all around. Or the listener is at Dylan's infamous 1966 rock performance at Royal Albert Hall—a live spatial dynamic. But is the audience in front of or behind the listener? Is the listener on stage with the band or sitting in the audience? These are all things to consider. Electronic music opens up even more doors for mixing in surround. Because acoustic instruments, which inherently suggest space, are no longer generating sounds, any digital sound could conceivably come from any channel. The possibilities are endless.

Working around the Surround Limitations of Pro Tools LE

Although Pro Tools LE systems have the DV Toolkit package available for postproducing, this package falls short of offering an "in the box" solution for surround mixing. Audio tracks are strictly limited to mono or stereo outputs in Pro Tools LE, so the google.com setup relies on multiple outputs, so a Digi 002 or a Digi 002 Rack is a perfect interface candidate for the job. The Mbox and Mbox2 will not work because they have only two analog outputs. Here is how to "trick" your LE system into a surround-capable mixer:

1. Choose Setup > I/O and click the output tab.

2. Click in the name fields of each output assignment and change Analog 1-2 to L & R for your left and right front outputs, and use L and R for the mono sub-paths. Analog 3-4 should be renamed CTR & LFE for your center and low-frequency effect channels, with CTR and LFE for the mono sub-paths. Finally, Analog 5-6 should be renamed LS & RS for the left and right surround channels, with LS and RS for the mono subchannels.

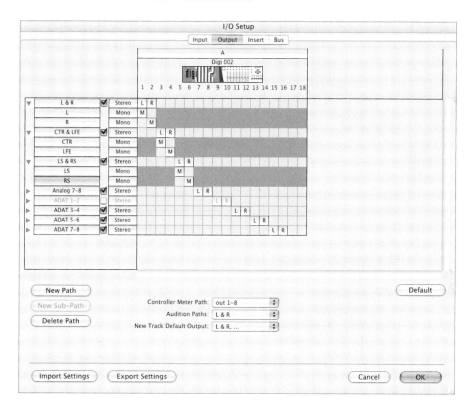

3. Physically hook up the outputs of your audio interface to your surround speakers in the order you labeled them in the I/O setup.

4. Press Shift+⌘+N / Shift+Ctrl+N and make three Stereo Master Fader tracks. Their outputs should automatically be set to the three outputs you assigned in the I/O setup. Name the tracks according to the three outputs.

5. With all three tracks selected, press ⌘+G / Ctrl+G to make a group of all three tracks. Name the group Surround. These three grouped tracks are now your master volume control for your entire surround output.

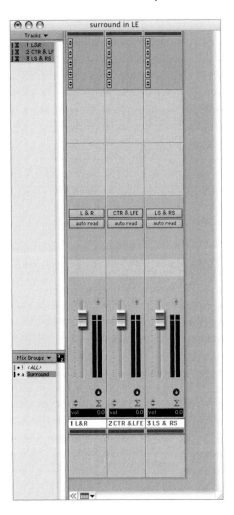

Now when you wish to assign any given track to a certain output, you can just choose the corresponding output for the track. To blend more than one track into multiple outputs, you can use sends. For example, if you wanted dialog coming from the center speaker and some room reverb coming out of the left and right speakers, you could route the output of the track to center and then use a send going to the L&R to blend a little in to the left and right speakers.

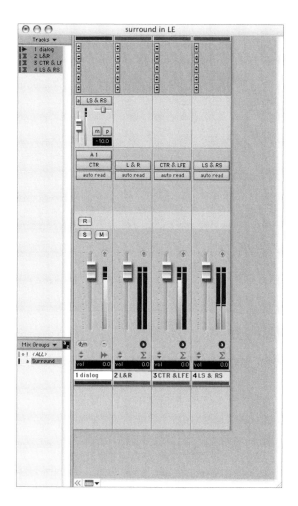

Of course, surround panning for this type of setup would require some pretty smart automation send moves, but it can be done. Surround delays and reverbs can be faked too, by using different types of stereo reverbs in the different output channels.

Slaving and Syncing with SMPTE, Not Scrimpty

Many postproduction audio sessions require slaving a Pro Tools HD system to various video formats. When Pro Tools is slaving, session playback is controlled and consequently moves in sync with an external machine, usually a video deck in a postproduction scenario. Digidesign makes a hardware unit called the Sync I/O, which allows for this kind of communication to occur between your Pro Tools system and external recording and playback decks.

LTC and VITC

Pro Tools HD systems employ SMPTE time code in order to sync to video and film much more accurately than MIDI time code, which is discussed in Chapter 2. SMPTE stands for Society of Motion Picture and Television Engineers, so you know that SMPTE time code is going to be vital for post-production synchronization. The two ways SMPTE time code can be sent to the Pro Tools Sync hardware are LTC, or Linear Time Code, and VITC, or Vertically Integrated Time Code.

LTC is encoded as audio pulses on video or audio tape. It can be written on a special audio track of digital or analog videotape or even a single track of a 2-inch 24-track analog audiotape. When you listen to LTC time code, it sounds like a very fast series of beeps and blips, like a laser ray gun from a science fiction movie. LTC works best for synchronization when the tape is moving. Pro Tools cannot use LTC to sync if the tape is not at full playback speed.

VITC is SMPTE time code that is encoded into lines of video outside the normal viewing area of a video frame. You can see VITC as white dots and dashes if your video monitor supports an H/V delay button, which allows you to view outside the frame. Pro Tools can sync to VITC even when the tape is paused.

Common video SMPTE frame rates (in FPS, or frames per second) that you will encounter in audio postproduction are as follows:

- 29.97 FPS (the NTSC standard for North America)

- 29.97 Drop FPS (same as above, but with a frame dropped every 10 minutes to compensate for actual time used in broadcast)

- 25 FPS (Phase-Alternating Line, or PAL video standard frame rate used in Europe and much of Asia)

- 24 FPS (frame rate for film)

Pro Tools can be set to run at all of these frame rates in the Session Setup window, located via Setup > Session.

Here is a step-by-step recipe to set up a Pro Tools HD system with Sync I/O hardware to slave to a video deck. Although this example represents only one conventional postproduction workflow, the concepts and choices involved are common to many other typical postproduction workflows. (Figure 7.12 shows the back panel of the Sync I/O.)

Figure 7.12 Digidesign's Sync I/O hardware interface

Here are the steps:

1. Connect the Sync interface's Video Ref input to a common video sync reference. Most postproduction facilities have a common "house sync" or "black burst generator" that can be tapped into by all video and audio decks and workstations in the facility.

2. Connect the Sync I/O's Video input to a composite output of the video deck (usually output 2, or monitor output) if you plan to sync to VITC time code.

3. Connect the deck's LTC out to the LTC in on the Sync I/O to sync to LTC time code.

4. Connect the Word Clock Out on the Sync I/O to the Word Clock In on the Pro Tools hardware interface, such as a 96 I/O or 192 I/O.

5. Connect the Digi Serial port of the Sync I/O to the HD core card in your computer's PCI slot.

6. In your Pro Tools session, choose Setup > Peripherals and click the Synchronization tab. In the Device pull-down menu, choose SYNC. You may also choose SYNC Setup if you need to update Sync I/O firmware or would like Pro Tools to spit out a time code window on any video monitoring routed from the Sync I/O.

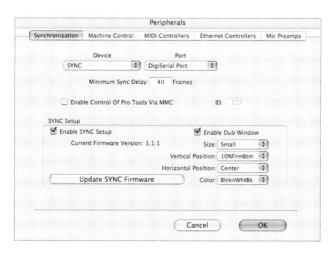

7. In Pro Tools, press ⌘+Keypad2 / Ctrl+Keypad2 to open the Session Setup window. Open the Sync Setup and Time Code Offsets disclosure triangle.

8. In Sync Setup, choose Video Reference to make the Sync I/O clock to house sync. For Positional Reference, LTC, VITC, or Auto LTC/VITC can be chosen, depending on which type of SMPTE time code you wish to sync to. On Auto LTC/VITC, Pro Tools will sync to whatever signal is more convenient: LTC when tape is running and VITC when tape is paused. When the Locked and Speed Cal lights are solid, it means that sync between Pro Tools and the outside world has been established.

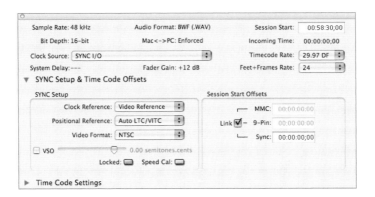

9. Click the online button in the transport window of Pro Tools (the blue clock button), or press ⌘+J / Ctrl+J. Now Pro Tools is in "slave mode" and is waiting for the attached video deck to play.

10. If all connections are correct, Pro Tools will listen for incoming time code, and when the attached deck plays, Pro Tools plays. It is now possible to edit, mix, and lay off audio to this video deck. Everything is held in sync between the two systems thanks to SMPTE time code.

Postproduction Editing Tricks

Postproduction Pro Tools editors have their own secret arsenal of quick editing shortcuts specifically suited to their needs. Here are a few handy ones, and in the next section, "Spotting Your Foley With Beeps," a recipe to use one to set up cue beeps for a foley recording.

Control+click / Start+click any region with the Grabber tool and its start point will jump directly to where your edit cursor is. This shortcut can be used like a quick Spot-mode-style edit. It can be used to sync up a sound effect region in the Regions list. Just hold Control/Start as you drag the sound effect region from the Regions list and it will snap to the edit cursor that you've prespotted in the timeline against the video.

Control+Shift / Start+Shift any region with the Grabber tool and it will move the region's sync point to the edit cursor. This is the same as above, only if the region has a sync point (⌘+, / Ctrl+, to add a sync point), it will align the sync point to your edit cursor. This technique is great for quickly spotting sound effects that have a middle sync point, such as a car door closing.

⌘+Control / Ctrl+Start any region with the Grabber tool and its end point will align with your edit cursor. Again, this is the same as the above two shortcuts, but it can be used to end-align regions. You can use this shortcut in the next example to end-align cue beeps for a foley or Automated Dialog Replacement (ADR) session.

Spotting Your Foley with Beeps

Here's another pro technique for Pro Tools post. Foley, named after sound effects pioneer Jack Foley (1891–1967), is the process of artificially recording sound effects to match action in a movie, such as footsteps and environmental sounds. Before foley can be recorded, the sound effects editor has to find all of the places where foley is needed and "spot" those areas as places to record. Some editors use markers to do so, but this cool technique uses a blank region, which has additional organizational benefits. Here's the technique:

1. Make a few mono audio tracks and name them Foley 1, Foley 2, and so on.

2. On these tracks, find the first place where foley needs to be recorded. Make a selection for about 30 seconds.

3. Record silence for the length of the region. Once the recording is done, trim the region to approximately how long the first foley recording should be.

4. Double-click the region with the Grabber tool and rename it with a specific idea of what the region should contain. For example, Foley_cup_dwn would be an appropriate name for the sound of a character putting a cup down on the table. Once you name the region, you can optionally erase the media for this recording by going into your audio files folder and trashing the audio file. If you do this, this Pro Tools session will open with a Missing Files dialog, but the region pointer will still remain in the session italicized. Once this happens, you can choose Region List > Clear on the selected whole file region and remove it from the session.

5. Copy and paste the region to other spots where foley is needed. Rename and resize each region accordingly. When you are done, your foley tracks should look something like Figure 7.13. Note the abbreviation *FS* is used for footsteps and a description is added after of the sound to be recorded.

Figure 7.13 Blank regions have been made here in order to spot foley recordings.

Now that the regions are spotted, it's time to record. While the convention in postproduction studios is to use an expensive hardware device called a streamer to provide video cues for your foley artist, here's a way to employ beeps using one of the postproduction editing tricks to cue the artist:

1. Make a mono audio track called Beeps.

2. Select exactly 500 milliseconds in the region with the Selector tool. You can use Grid mode to help make an exact selection.

3. Open the Signal Generator AudioSuite plug-in (AudioSuite > Other). Chose a 1000Hz, -20 dB sine wave and process a 1-second beep.

4. Copy and paste this beep two times, 1 second apart.

5. Select all three beeps, including 1 second after the last beep. Choose Edit > Consolidate. This is your beeps region. With the region still selected, type ⌘+Shift+K / Ctrl+Shift+K to export the region. Keep the beeps region somewhere special on your computer so you can always import it later into other sessions.

6. Go back to Slip mode. Place the edit cursor exactly at the first foley place-marker region in the time line. Tab (with Tab To Transient off) can be used to snap the cursor right to the start of the region.

7. With the Grabber tool, hold ⌘+Control / Ctrl+Start as you click on the beeps. Voila, the beeps are end-aligned with the foley region.

8. Press Tab once more to move the cursor to the end of the beeps region.

9. On the transport window, enter a pre-roll amount of 4 seconds.

10. Double-click the blank foley region. Highlight the name of the region and press ⌘+C / Crtl +C to copy the name. Double-click the track name and press ⌘+V / Ctrl+V to paste the name. Now the recording you are about to make will have the descriptive region name.

11. Record-enable the foley track. When you hit record, the three beeps will play in pre-roll to cue the foley artist to give warning as to exactly when the action occurs. For safety, you should go into QuickPunch mode here to record any early movements since QuickPunch is secretly recording during Pre-Roll.

12. Repeat for all spotted foley regions. This technique can also be used to help in Automated Dialog Replacement, or ADR.

Figure 7.14 shows recording in action.

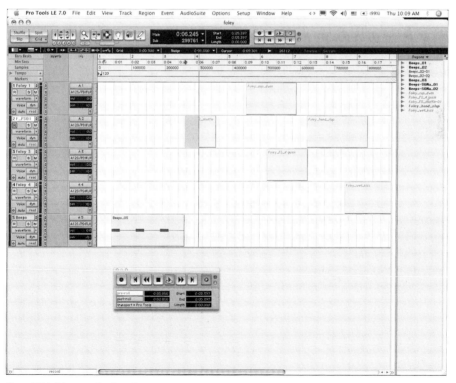

Figure 7.14 Foley recording in action

Setting Up Pro Tools

Every user has different audio needs, so we've gathered some information for you in one place to answer your questions about setting up a system that suits you best. Keep in mind that this is just starting point for your research and that specs change rapidly in this area.

Appendix Contents

Pro Tools Hardware Considerations

There are three types of Pro Tools hardware: HD, LE, and M-Powered / M-Audio. How much Pro Tools power you need and how much buying power you have will determine what works best for you.

HD Hardware

Pro Tools HD is the crème de la crème in the recording industry, but the gold standard doesn't come cheap. The price of the entry-level system is almost five figures, and depending on how you configure your system, it could run much, much more. Pro Tools HD is flexible and expandable, allowing the user to configure a system to individual needs and taste.

An HD system comprises a core system PCI card, an HD audio interface, and, depending on your needs, additional Accel PCI expansion cards for more horsepower. The chip-laden core card hosts all of the Digital Signal Processing (DSP) used to run your session and is the heart of any Pro Tools HD rig. Pro Tools HD, like TDM before it, processes audio in its own hardware and doesn't use your computer. An LE or host-based system is the opposite and gets all of its resources from your computer. The core cards install into your computer in either PCI or PCIe slots, so you must have a tower to run HD. You must have both the core card and an audio interface to run an HD setup; the Accel expansion cards are not necessary to run HD. The Accel cards add track count, amount of I/O, and processing power to your system. They are included with HD 2 and 3 systems, and more can be added at any point in time to expand your system. The kind of work you are doing usually reflects how many extra cards, if any, you might need. The higher your track count, plug-in use, and automation use is, the more resources you need. Each card is its own separate piece of gear and its own purchase. There are three levels of HD you can purchase off the shelf, but remember that you can add up to seven total cards to your rig.

HD 1 comes with a core system card and the ability to handle 92 tracks of audio with 32 channels of I/O. HD 1 has no Accel card.

HD 2 comes with a single core card and a single Accel card. The Accel card provides 192 tracks of playback, an additional 32 channels of I/O, and extra processing.

HD 3 comes with a single core card and 2 Accel cards for 192 tracks of playback with 96 channels of I/O and additional processing power.

HD Interfaces

After you have chosen a core system that best suits your needs, you need to add an interface for Pro Tools to communicate with the rest of the world. All HD systems support multichannel outputs and at least a 96kHz sample rate.

The 192 I/O is the flagship Digidesign interface with 16 simultaneous channels of inputs, with 8 analog and 16 digital and a sample rate up to 192kHz. There is an expansion slot for an additional 192 I/O with 8 channels of either analog or digital I/O.

The 192 Digital I/O offers up to 16 channels of 96k or 8 channels of 192kHz input over a variety of formats if your needs are digital. There are no analog channels on this interface,

The 96 I/O interface has 16 channels of inputs with 8 analog and 8 digital with a sample rate to 96kHz. This is the least expensive way into an HD rig. For a more keyboard-friendly version of this interface, the 96i I/O has 16 channels of analog ¼-inch inputs for keyboards, effects, turntables, and what have you along with a stereo digital SPDIF input option, and only two outputs. The 96i I/O is also ideal for tracking bands that require a lot of inputs and only a stereo output.

LE Interfaces

Digidesign LE interfaces support only LE software and have a maximum sample rate of 96k with no surround-sound support. They are connected with either a FireWire or USB cable.

As this book is being written, the USB Mbox 2 is the most recent venture into entry-level Digidesign hardware and software. The USB model has different preamps and the ability to track four channels at once, two analog and two digital. The overall sound quality has been improved and a MIDI port was added. This box comes with Pro Tools LE software as part of the deal. M-Powered software is not included with Pro Tools–compatible hardware. It's a handy and easy way to run Pro Tools—one USB cable and you're in. The FireWire 002 is the entry-level Digidesign control surface and audio interface. As an interface, the 002 offers up to 18 channels of simultaneous 96kHz I/O made up of 8 analog, 8 ADAT, and 2 SPDIF. The 002 offers 4 channels of mic preamps and can act as an 8-by-4-by-2 stand-alone digital mixer. As a control surface, the 002 is like a little slice off of a control 24. The 002 uses a FireWire cable to communicate with your computer. This is an easy way to run Pro Tools for not much setup. It offers good features in a small package.

The FireWire 002 Rack Mount is the same interface as the 002 minus the control surface and stand-alone mixer function. The rack version is less than half the price of the 002, so if you don't need the control surface but want a 96kHz sample rate and lots of inputs, this is a good choice.

M-Powered Interfaces

M-Audio is now under the Digidesign/Avid umbrella, so there is a slew of Pro Tools-compatible interfaces on the market. All interfaces run only M-Powered LE software, at a maximum sample rate of 96k. M-Powered interfaces are either USB or FireWire and work fine on either the Mac or PC.

Currently there are almost 20 M-Powered audio interfaces capable of running Pro Tools, from the portable and pocket-sized stereo mini-input Transit to the 18-input FireWire 1814. The Transit lists for under $100 and the 1814 for $599, so all models are on the low end of the price curve for Digidesign-compatible hardware. The different interfaces cover various types of recording needs and get very specific, so check through the entire catalog before you decide.

The Ozone and the Ozonic keyboards both serve as interfaces for M-Powered Pro Tools. This combination of a keyboard and audio interface reduces the amount of gear needed for a mobile setup. They also function as MIDI controllers with a robust set of faders and knobs.

The ProjectMix I/O is a 8-input interface/control surface similar to the 002 but with a smaller price tag. The ProjectMix I/O works as a control surface with most applications, not just Pro Tools.

 Note: M-Powered Pro Tools is not compatible with the standard Pro Tools LE software. In fact, they don't even like living in the same place. When you install LE, it will tell you to uninstall M-Powered Pro Tools, and vice versa.

Pro Tools Software Considerations

There are currently three types of Pro Tools software. Here is a quick breakdown of the systems.

HD Software

HD software comes with and runs through HD hardware. HD is the top of the Pro Tools pyramid. HD software can be adapted to run in almost every conceivable audio environment. From radio to theater and from film to the recording studio, HD can do it all with the right plug-ins and enough resources. TDM has changed to HD, so TDM refers only to plug-in types and to the way HD works. HD can run on either a PC or a Mac. A few key HD features are listed here:

- Surround-sound capabilities
- TDM plug-ins
- Expandable system resources
- Professional features for film and post
- High sample rate
- High track counts

HD systems come with a steep price tag but still far less than they were in the '90s with far more features than an analog setup from the bygone era.

LE software

Pro Tools LE is an extremely solid, well-built, full-featured application. For many music applications, LE software is capable enough to get the job done. LE has most of the abilities of big brother HD with a few exceptions:

*   No surround sound support.

*   The maximum sample rate is 96kHz. (If you need a 192kHz sample rate, you should go with HD.)

*   Postproduction functions are limited in the basic LE package. If you need these abilities, purchase the DV Toolkit 2 or go with HD.

*   LE plug-ins are RTAS and AudioSuite only, unless you use a VST wrapper to attempt to port in VST plug-ins. No TDM plug-in in LE, and your computer does the processing.

*   The basic voice count is 32 with 64 internal busses and a maximum sample rate of 96k. There is an expansion option to take your voice count to 48 with the Music Production Toolkit. Beat Detective and other functions that were once solely in the TDM domain have trickled down to LE and the music world is better for it.

M-Powered LE Software

Basically, this is the same version of LE you would get with a Digidesign piece of hardware but at a small fee, and as a bonus the logo is red. All of the normal LE rules apply, except that M-Powered can not support DV Toolkit or the Music Production Toolkit. All Pro Tools session formats are 100 percent interchangeable, so you can start a piece in LE and take it into a bigger HD studio to track vocals, and back to an M-Powered studio to add keyboard parts to it. Just remember that Pro Tools 7 sessions are not backwards compatible with Pro Tools 6 unless they are saved as such.

Configurations

The following sections describe three possible setups and their applications. This is a staring point for you to see what might be in each type of configuration.

Mobile Setup

The heart of a mobile rig is your computer. It's been only a few years that you could really run much of an audio-based session on a laptop, much less try to rewire something. With faster CPUs, bigger hard drives, and the advent of FireWire and USB interfaces, Pro Tools got loose in the real world. Your choice of computer and components is key in this endeavor, so do get the fastest laptop you can afford.

Mac laptop A new day has dawned and brought forth a sure sign of the apocalypse. The Mactel chip. Hell has officially frozen over. An Intel chip in a Mac—a real Mac— not something you see in the back of *Popular Hackers*. The MacBook Pro laptops are faster and cheaper than their older Mac counterparts, and most of the current generation of music software is porting its way to compatibility. As of this writing, Pro Tools is *not* compatible with the Mactel machines but will be very soon. If you are going to buy a Mac laptop to run Pro Tools, be sure to check www.digidesign.com for compatibility information. The MacBook Pro laptops outpace the G4 Ti-Books by quite a margin, but remember that these new machines will never run Mac OS 9. The old G4 laptop iBooks are a good deal but will be outdated sooner than later. You need to think about your requirements musically before you buy. Will you rewire programs or just run one application? Will you ever run video? Buy for the future as much as the present if you can afford to.

Windows laptop Compatibility is the main concern on this platform. With so many different manufacturers and different standards, problems abound. The best resource for PC compatibility is the compatibility chart on the Digidesign site. All PCs are not compatible with Pro Tools, so you need to look at www.digidesign.com to find out. If you are buying a preconfigured system, the chart has a list of models that will work. If you are going to build your own PC, which is a fine idea, you should look at the chip-set info and the motherboard info first. You need to be more technically savvy to keep a PC laptop with Pro Tools and soft synths running smoothly. As with the Mac, install as much RAM as your machine can take and get the best machine you can. The old rule of thumb is to spend up to your budget and then add a little more to get something that will last.

Audio interface In a mobile rig, you want a portable and rugged system small enough to move around but capable enough to get the job done. An Mbox 2 is certainly small enough to be portable, but it's perhaps a bit awkward in its shape. The M-Powered series of interfaces offers truly mobile solutions. An HD system is possible for mobile use, but you need special gear to get an HD rig to a laptop and that would mean rack-mounting an interface. This could be done if the risk-to-reward ratio were good enough. The film industry does use HD from a laptop to record wild sound. The days of the Nagra are numbered, and that's being polite.

Keyboard A portable keyboard like the M-Audio Oxygen 8 is small enough to take most anywhere, including on airplanes. Most of the small controllers are powered by your computer instead of needing their own AC. M-Audio now makes both the Ozone and Ozonic, which double as Pro Tools–compatible audio interfaces. These are pretty compact little packages with a preamp, 4-in 4-out I/O, and 24-bit 96k resolution.

Headphones The mobile version of your studio monitors. Individual headphone taste can vary greatly, so the best strategy is to listen to as many headphones as you can before you buy. One person's headphone heaven is another person's headphone hell.

Additional software Ableton Live, Reason, Logic Atmosphere Trilogy, and Ivory Stlyus RMX are some you might consider.

LE Setup

Mac G5 iMac, MacBook Pro laptop, or an entry-level tower dual-core Mactel machine. Buying into older technology is very dangerous unless you have a well-thought-out reason, such as plug-ins from an old system that you can't upgrade. Just because something is cheaper doesn't mean it's worth it. A newer-generation Mactel is the choice for the future. Speed and value are a deadly combination.

Windows In the ever-changing world of PC hardware, there is a short shelf life for compatibility. No printed material would last long enough to be completely up-to-date. With this in mind, www.digidesign.com has a list of the currently compatible PCs, PC hardware, and system requirements. The website is an incredibly comprehensive resource, so check it first before you buy or build. The rule of thumb for a PC is the same as for a Mac: get as much computer as you can afford, and then a little more. For a mid-range setup, a minimum 2GHz Pro Tools–compatible PC will get you running.

Video monitors Get two flat screens if at all possible, but one screen will work. CRT monitors are still usable but certainly not recommended. LCDs use less energy and space and are better for your eyes. The price of flat screens has dropped like Enron stock.

RAM 1G minimum. RAM powers your system, so the more the merrier. Add as much RAM past the minimum as you can afford and you will be the better for it. Everything you do on your computer will be faster.

External FireWire or USB 2 hard drive 120G minimum. You never want to record audio to your internal system drive. Drive space is unbelievably cheap for anyone who remembers the $1,000, 200MB drive. You will always fill up a drive no matter how big it is.

Hardware Mbox 2/002/002 rack. If you want to go with a Digidesign system, you have three choices. If you need more than four inputs total or more than two analog inputs, then you need the 002 of either flavor.

M-Powered interface If you want to use M-Powered hardware and software, you have many options. Choose an interface based on your application and budget and then to be safe get one that is just a little better. There are almost 20 M-Powered systems, so check www.m-audio.com to see what is current and compatible.

ProjectMix I/O, 002 or Command8 control surface If you want affordable external control over Pro Tools, all of these surfaces provide a very usable and user-friendly set of features, knobs, and faders.

MIDI controller A MIDI keyboard like the M-Audio Radium or Keystation is a key ingredient in a modern studio. Most new controllers come with the ability to map to different applications and control the different parameters. Anything that generates MIDI will work, but the newer keyboards usually get their power from your computer and weigh next to nothing. On the downside, they do not play like real weighted-key keyboards and have limited key range.

Audio monitors Monitors are a vital part of your setup on any level. There are a number of price points to consider when you think about monitors in a mid-range setup. You might not need Genelecs, but you still need something that has a good sound. There are quite a few quality speakers on the market for under $1,000. Monitors are like shoes. You can't just be told how they fit; you have to try them yourself. Don't underestimate the positive effect of quality speakers.

Additional software Ableton Live, Reason, Logic Atmosphere Trilogy, Ivory Stlyus RMX.

HD Setup

HD core system Choose one of the three different systems available. Think about the workload you will be carrying and the system resources you will require. You can start with just a core card and go from there. See "HD Hardware" earlier in this appendix.

HD interface Choose an interface that matches the work you will be doing and the core system you have. What sample rate do you need and what type of inputs serve you best? See "HD Interfaces" earlier in this appendix.

G5 dual core or Mactel dual core Two processors at the least. The quad processor is not a bad thought. Even in an HD system, using RTAS plug-ins to share the load gives you more overall resources, and the faster the computer you have, the more resources and RTAS soft synths you get.

Windows PC The same guidelines apply here as for the PC in the LE setup as far as looking to the Digidesign site for all of your info about current compatibility. That said, for a PC-based HD rig, get the biggest, baddest system you can. No one ever says, "Hey, my computer is too fast today; I should have bought a slower model." Max out everything you can, just as you would a Mac!

Video monitors Dual-monitor setup. Seventeen-inch flat screens are down to under $200, but two 19-inch screens are better. The second monitor may need an additional video card to run it. Check your system info to see what type of card you have and if it supports a second monitor.

RAM 2G minimum. The new-generation machines can handle 16 gigs of RAM, so get out your credit card and have more memory than NASA when Apollo 11 landed on the moon. A lot more….

External drive space 250G minimum. If possible, have at least two drives of this size. The bigger, the better. Drives still crash, so a DVD burner to back up these monsters is a necessity as well.

Control 24, Pro Control, or Command8 control surface All of these surfaces offer big-time capabilities and take the experience to another level. It is not necessary to have a control surface to run an HD system, but it definitely makes a good thing better.

A MIDI keyboard An M-Audio Oxygen 8 v2, Radium, or Ozonic. Most new controllers come with the ability to map to different applications and control the different parameters. If you want to play a synth like Reason or Hybrid, you need a controller like these or a full-featured MIDI keyboard like the M-Audio workstation 88 weighted-key controller. Anything that generates MIDI will work, but the newer keyboards usually get their power from your computer and weigh next to nothing. On the downside, they do not play like real weighted-key keyboards and have limited key range.

Audio monitors With an investment like you have in an HD system, you need to honor that with some quality monitors. Good speakers are a little less expensive than in the past, but they still aren't giving them away. One of the most important things to consider and remember when you are buying monitors is to match the speakers to the room. They may sound great in the Dulcimers R Us, but when you get them in your studio, they don't quite do the trick. Don't buy more speaker than the room can handle.

Additional software Ableton Live, Reason, Logic Atmosphere Trilogy, Ivory Stlyus RMX.

Using Control Surfaces with Pro Tools

Freeing yourself from the binding restraints of your computer mouse can enhance recording, mixing, and editing in Pro Tools like nothing else. After all, you are recording audio here. Shouldn't you have a big console with lots of buttons and knobs? True, the advent of the digital audio workstation has ended the need for a traditional console-style mixing desk, but the necessity for tactile control of the Pro Tools system while in the heat of a session still remains. The solution is the control surface. Control surfaces are a new generation of consoles that provide tactile control of your Pro Tools system without the heft, girth, and cost of a traditional audio mixing console. This appendix will provide an in-depth look at all of the control surface options.

B

Why Use a Control Surface?

A positive aspect of using Pro Tools in a digital audio workstation is that now most of the recording setup is consolidated inside the computer. With a flexible virtual mixer inside the Pro Tools software, there is no longer a need for big clunky mixing consoles in your workspace. The trade-off is that when working exclusively inside the computer, Pro Tools users no longer have tactile access to the traditional recording and mixing controls such as faders, knobs, playback controls, scrub wheels, and LED displays. Control surfaces such as Digidesign's Command|8, Control|24, Pro Control, and the new ICON fill this void by offering tactile control reminiscent of the controls in a traditional recording studio but without the large footprint and cost of a traditional console such as an SSL, Neve, or Trident. In essence, the Digidesign control surfaces for Pro Tools act like a physical extension of the software–almost like a very complex mouse. This tactile control is transferred via an Ethernet connection between the surface and the main computer.

The benefits to using control surfaces with Pro Tools:

- Touch-sensitive faders. Great for mixing, offering a way to control more than one track at a time.
- Knobs that can be mapped to various controls–such as pan or send values–on some surfaces and are dedicated on others.
- Large level output meters on most surfaces.
- Scroll wheel for shuttling and scrubbing through your Pro Tools Timeline.
- Dedicated control room monitoring section. All control surfaces offer a dedicated control room monitoring section, which gives you control of phones and monitor levels right from the surface. Some control surfaces offer a built-in talk-back microphone, giving you valuable studio communication controls.
- Navigation controls for moving around your Pro Tools session.
- Dedicated buttons for editing and processing controls. For example, a single button on the surface will "cut" while another will "paste."
- A dedicated color-coded keyboard, track ball, and track pad on some control surfaces.

  A control surface is *not*:
- A control surface is not like a traditional audio console. There is no actual signal running through each channel in a control surface as in a traditional mixer. Control surfaces do, however, have audio inputs and outputs in order to route outputs of your Pro Tools interface.

- A control surface does not replace the computer or Pro Tools interface. The surfaces are strictly peripheral add-ons to existing Pro Tools systems. A few exceptions to this are the Digi 002 surface and the M-Powered Project Mix I/O, which are both interfaces and control surfaces combined into one unit.

Different Types of Control Surfaces

Control surfaces fall into two groups: (1) those made by Digidesign and M-Audio for specific use with Pro Tools LE, HD, and M-Powered Pro Tool systems and (2) those made by other companies but are compatible with Pro Tools systems. The levels of sophistication and price vary greatly from the simplest, most basic surfaces to the large-scale high-end control surfaces for the serious, big-time recording studios. If you are a freelance Pro Tools engineer, it is important to be familiar with all of the options you could have in a studio you may find yourself operating.

Digidesign Control Surfaces

The following sections describe Digidesign control surfaces and their functions and features, followed by descriptions of third-party control surfaces and their features.

Command|8

The Command|8 control surface is one of the smallest and most affordable control surfaces available for Pro Tools systems. It is a great entry-level option into the world of control surfaces, no matter what platform Pro Tools system you are running, because it is compatible with all Pro Tools LE, HD, and M-Powered systems. It is connected via a USB cable to your PC or Mac. One possible downside to the Command|8 is that it only has eight faders and is not expandable, although those eight faders can be mapped to any group of eight tracks in your session.

Command|8 features:

- Small footprint; easily fits into small workstation environments
- LCD that automatically updates to track information in your session
- Built-in, one-input, two-output MIDI interface
- Onboard Focusrite control room monitoring section with headphone mix knob
- Not expandable, but will work in conjunction with the Control|24, Digi 002, and Pro Control surfaces
- Eight motorized touch-sensitive faders
- Eight automatable rotary encoders with LED rings

Digi 002

The Digi 002 surface is almost identical to the Command|8 in terms of features; however, it also works simultaneously as a Pro Tools LE interface. It has eight analog inputs and outputs, including four onboard microphone preamps, and connects to your computer via a FireWire cable. One additional feature is that the 002 can work in "stand-alone mode," where it acts just like an 8×4×2 digital mixer with EQ, dynamics, and effects.

Features of the Digi 002:

- LCD that automatically updates to track information in your session
- Built-in, one-input, two-output MIDI interface
- Onboard control-room monitoring section with headphone mix knob

- Not expandable, but will work in conjunction with the Control|24, Digi 002, and Pro Control surfaces
- Eight motorized touch-sensitive faders
- Eight automatable rotary encoders with LED rings
- Four mic pres with individual gain and high-pass filter; 48V phantom power enabled on channel pairs
- Eight channels of ADAT optical I/O, two channels of S/PDIF I/O
- Outputs 1 and 2 mirrored on 1/4-inch TRS monitor output (with dedicated volume control) and RCA-based -10 dBV fixed output

Project Mix I/O

The Project Mix I/O is an M-Audio-manufactured control surface that is similar in design and function to the Digi 002. With the acquisition of M-Audio by Digidesign and the integration of M-Powered Pro Tools systems, the Project Mix I/O is now compatible as an interface and control surface to Pro Tools M-Powered systems.

Features of the Project Mix I/O:

- Eight touch-sensitive motorized channel faders
- One touch-sensitive motorized master fader
- Eight assignable rotary encoders and a large LCD for channel or plug-in functions
- Record-enable, select, solo, and mute buttons on each channel
- Dedicated keys for in/out points, locate, region nudge, loop, and so on
- Two separate switchable headphone mixes with level controls
- Eight analog mic/line inputs (1/4-inch TRS and XLR balanced), each with signal/peak indicators and mic/line switch
- Four analog outputs (1/4-inch TRS balanced)
- ADAT lightpipe I/O
- Two-channel S/PDIF digital I/O
- Built-in 1×1 MIDI input and output

Control|24

The Control|24 is the first step toward a bigger, more substantial control surface. The board includes 24 channels of touch-sensitive motorized faders. This is not expandable or modular like some of the other high-end control surfaces, but the Control|24 occupies a unique role in Digidesign's product line. It has 16 channels of Class A Focusrite mic preamps built into it, even though it is not a stand-alone hardware interface. This functionality makes it the perfect control surface for the up-and-coming studio owner who needs both a control surface and a lot of mic pres to record bands, for example.

The Control|24 is compatible with Pro Tools HD and LE systems. In addition to having 16 channels of preamps, the Control|24 connects to your Pro Tools system via an Ethernet cable.

Features of the Control|24:

- Twenty-four touch-sensitive, motorized faders
- Sixteen Focusrite Class A mic/line preamps
- Flexible control room monitoring section capable of up to 5.1 surround monitoring
- Illuminated switches for Mute, Solo, Record Arm, Channel Selects, and Automation Mode on every channel
- Dedicated EQ and dynamics switches on every channel
- High-resolution LED display for transport location at a glance
- Ability to "flip" sends and plug-ins to touch-sensitive faders
- Heavy-duty shuttle/scrub wheel
- Dedicated number pad for easy timeline navigation and memory access

Pro Control

The Pro Control is Digidesign's first modular control surface. Modular control surfaces are made up of a main unit and optional expandable fader sections. For the Pro Control, this means a main unit with eight attached fader channel strips and expandable fader packs of eight channels at a time. This flexibility accommodates studios of any size, although the Pro Control is primarily aimed at higher-end Pro Tools users since it is an HD-only control surface. Unlike the Control|24, the Pro Control is strictly a controller; it had no mic preamps of any kind. It does, however, include a complex surround-capable monitoring section with a built-in talkback mic.

Features of the Pro Control:

- Main unit comes with 8 touch-sensitive motorized faders. Expandable fader packs of 8 channels at a time can be added for a total of 48 faders (including the main unit).
- Dedicated DSP control section makes it easy to use plug-in controls.
- Channel matrix section allows for multiple tasks such as soloing, muting, record-arming, and selecting tracks.
- Heavy-duty scrub/shuttle wheel

- Surround-capable monitoring section with talkback microphone and separate auxiliary mix options
- Numeric keypad
- Track pad
- LED level displays for each track and main output

Edit Pack

The Edit pack is an optional modular add-on to the Pro Control. It offers even more flexibility to the Pro Control package, including, most significantly, two linkable surround panning joysticks and a dedicated color-coded keyboard and track ball.

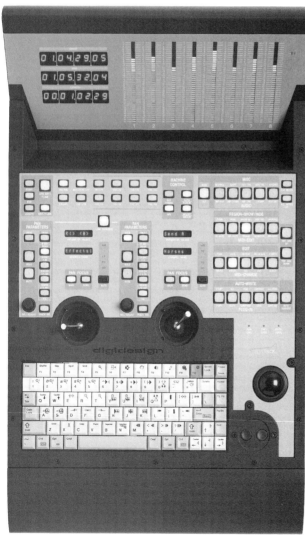

Edit Pack features:

- Touch-sensitive motorized surround panners
- Color-coded keyboard for command-focus-mode-style keyboard commands
- Track ball
- High-resolution (one step per dB) output display
- More one-button edit commands, such as New Track and Capture Region

ICON D-Command

ICON, or Integrated Console Environment, is Digidesign's newest attempt at high-end control surfaces. The D-Command picks up where the Pro Control left off, providing a modular solution to Pro Tools HD studios of any size. Like the Pro Control, the D-Command core unit includes a main unit with 8 attached faders. This can be expanded upon with a modular 16-fader expansion for a total of 24 tracks. The D-Command goes beyond the capabilities of the Pro Control by offering more dedicated controls and more touch sensitivity where it is needed, like in the rotary encoders. The D-Command is shown here with the expansion fader pack.

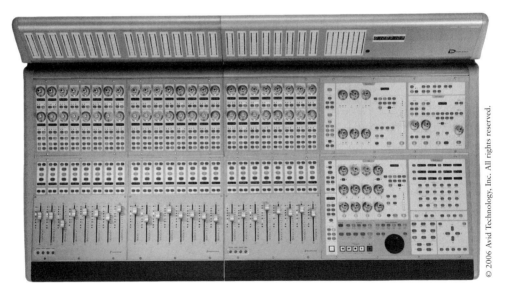

Features of the D-Command:

- Touch-sensitive motorized faders
- Two touch-sensitive, multipurpose rotary encoders per channel strip with single-color LED rings displays encoder position or metering. Each rotary encoder includes a six-character alphanumeric LCD display for function parameters in addition to one display for the channel scribble strip

- Comprehensive monitor/communications control section
- Dedicated, center-section control panels for EQ and dynamics plug-in editing
- Includes XMON remote, rack-mounted analog I/O audio monitor, and communications system capable of monitoring up to 5.1 surround.
- Two rows of touch-sensitive rotary encoders
- Dedicated EQ and dynamics control sections
- Custom fader grouping/viewing
- Dedicated buttons for editing, operations, and session management

ICON D-Control

The D-Control is the big daddy of the ICON family. It is Digidesign's "flagship" control surface and as this book is being written, it is only found in a handful of the most up-to-date studios around the world. The D-Control is similar in functionality and look to the D-Command, but the integration of the system components differs. The D-Control comes with a minimum of 16 faders with expandable options of 32, 48, 64, or 80 faders. There is a dedicated keyboard and separate rack-mounted monitoring routing, and the entire frame of the console is included.

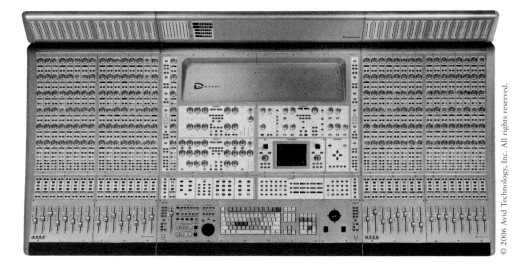

Features of the D-Control:
- Touch-sensitive motorized faders
- Six touch-sensitive, multipurpose rotary encoders per channel strip with multicolor LED rings that display encoder position and metering. Each rotary encoder includes a six-character alphanumeric, multicolor LCD display for function parameters in addition to one display for the channel scribble strip.

- Twenty-nine illuminated push buttons per channel strip facilitate fast selection of channel modes and attributes.
- Inline console monitor mode enables control of input and monitor levels from a single channel strip.
- A centrally located focus channel strip
- Comprehensive monitor/communications control section
- Dedicated center section control panels for EQ and dynamics plug-in editing
- XMON remote, rack-mounted analog I/O audio monitor, and communications system is capable of monitoring in up to 7.1 surround with complete, nondestructive solo.
- Advanced surround panner mixing option with integrated touch screen and touch-sensitive joysticks
- Ergonomic console frame
- Mounting arm for flat-panel display (display not included)

Third-Party Compatible Control Surfaces

Control surfaces that are not manufactured by Digidesign can be set up easily for use with Pro Tools. Obviously, the complete integration with Pro Tools will be a bit lacking, but the benefit of having these types of control surfaces is that you can use them with other software, such as Apple's Logic, MOTU Digital Performer, or Steinberg Cubase. Pro Tools actually comes with drivers for some of these devices. The Mackie Control Universal, or Mackie MCU, and the Tascam FW-1884 are two examples of popular universal control surfaces.

Mackie MCU

The Mackie MCU is well known for offering control surface support to many applications, even video-editing programs. Pro Tools 7 is supported. The MCU has removable overlays that can be placed on the surface, depending on what program you are using.

Features of the Mackie MCU:

- Complete integration with Logic Pro 7, Logic Express 7, Final Cut Pro 5, Soundtrack Pro, Nuendo, and more
- Integrated HUI mode for control of Digidesign Pro Tools, MOTU Digital Performer, and others
- 100 mm Penny + Giles motorized touch-faders
- Multi-function V-Pots for fast control of panning and effects
- Comprehensive automation controls

- Full meter display with track names and parameters
- Seven-segment time code display

Tascam FW-1884

The Tascam FW-1884 is similar to the 002 and Project Mix I/0 because it is a FireWire interface as well as a controller. Unlike those two devices, however, the FW-1884's audio cannot work directly with Pro Tools, but it can be routed via a digital lightpipe or S/PDIF connection to a Digidesign-supported interface. The control surface section of the FW-1884 can communicate directly with Pro Tools as well as many other digital audio software platforms.

FW-1884 features:

- Comprehensive mixing, automation, editing, and navigation tools
- Eight motorized touch-sensitive channel faders, one motorized touch-sensitive master fader
- Dedicated controls for pan, solo, mute, and select functions on each channel; tactile control for four bands of parametric EQ
- Shortcut keys for various popular audio software applications
- Eight balanced XLR analog mic/line inputs with high-quality mic preamps
- Phantom power and inserts on every channel
- A/D and D/A (24-bit/96kHz) converters; full 96kHz operation on all analog I/O channels with compatible software
- Eight channels of ADAT lightpipe, stereo S/PDIF inputs and outputs
- Eight analog outputs, allowing connection of L/R and 5.1 surround matrices
- Dedicated headphone output
- Four MIDI inputs, four MIDI outputs

Setting Up and Integrating Control Surfaces

Setup of control surfaces is a simple process. The most important thing is that the connection is made between the surface and your computer; from there, Pro Tools takes charge and integration is straightforward. For all Digidesign control surfaces with the exception of the 002, Project Mix I/O, and Command|8, an Ethernet connection is required, and this usually means a standard 10BaseT Ethernet hub or an Ethernet switch (preferred) is necessary since you most likely want to connect to the control surfaces and the Internet as well.

Here's how to set up Ethernet control surfaces:

1. Choose Setup > Peripherals, and click Ethernet Controllers. This opens the Ethernet controllers panel (see Figure B.1).

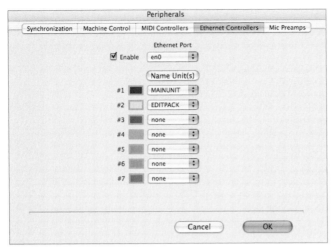

Figure B.1 The Ethernet controller peripherals panel set up for a Pro Control

2. Choose the Ethernet port that is connected to your control surface if you have multiple Ethernet ports on your computer.

3. Click the box next to Enable and wait while Pro Tools scans your Ethernet network for all attached control surfaces.

4. Depending on how many units you are connecting, you will now open the pop-up windows to assign the units.

   • For Control|24, just open pop-up #1 and assign it to CNTRL|24.

   • For Pro Control, it is necessary to start with the leftmost unit. The leftmost unit will be pop-up window #1, titled FADER if you have a fader pack. Then MAINUNIT will be #2, and #3 will be EDIT if you have an Edit pack, for example.

   • For D-Command, it is also necessary to start with the leftmost unit as pop-up #1. It will be called D-CMD-F if you have the 16-channel fader pack. Then the #2 pop-up will be D-CMD-M.

5. Your control surface units should now appear online and ready to go. If not, there is probably a connection problem

   To configure non-Ethernet controllers such as the Command|8, follow these steps:

1. Choose Setup > Peripherals and click MIDI Controllers

2. As shown in figure B.2, Command|8 was chosen to connect to a Command|8 surface. The Receive From and Send To columns refer to MIDI going from and to the Command|8 surface and may be configured to whatever MIDI devices you want the surface to talk to.

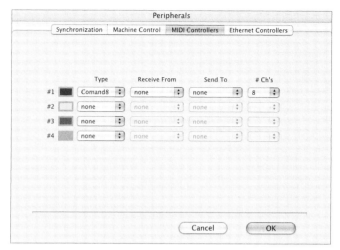

Figure B.2 The non-Ethernet controller peripherals panel

The other non-Ethernet controllers, such as the Digi 002 and the Project Mix I/O, will be configured this way as well.

Protecting Your Ears *and* Your Equipment

When you are routing audio through your control surface monitoring sections, you must be very careful of the order in which you power up and down the components of your digital audio workstation. Since your audio monitors are most likely going to be connected directly to your control surface, turning the surface on or off with the monitors powered up will cause a very loud pop to come through the monitors. This is potentially very dangerous to your ears and the gear, so do things in this order to be safe:

1. Make sure all equipment, especially monitors and amplifiers, are turned off.

2. For systems with an expansion chassis, turn on the chassis.

3. Turn on any external hard drives and wait for them to spin up.

4. Turn on all control surfaces and modules.

5. Turn on any MIDI interfaces, devices, and synchronization peripherals.

6. Turn on Pro Tools hardware.

7. Start your computer.

8. Turn on your audio monitors or amplifiers.

When powering down, do so in the opposite order.

Index

Note to the Reader: Throughout this index **boldfaced** page numbers indicate primary discussions of a topic. *Italicized* page numbers indicate illustrations.